Lennox Browne, Emil Behnke

Voice, song, and speech:

A practical guide for singers and speakers; from the combined view of vocal

surgeon and voice trainer

Lennox Browne, Emil Behnke

Voice, song, and speech:
A practical guide for singers and speakers; from the combined view of vocal surgeon and voice trainer

ISBN/EAN: 9783337815189

Printed in Europe, USA, Canada, Australia, Japan

Cover: Foto ©ninafisch / pixelio.de

More available books at **www.hansebooks.com**

VOICE, SONG, AND SPEECH:

A

PRACTICAL GUIDE FOR SINGERS
AND SPEAKERS;

FROM THE COMBINED VIEW OF

VOCAL SURGEON AND VOICE TRAINER.

BY

LENNOX BROWNE, F.R.C.S. Ed.,

SENIOR SURGEON TO THE CENTRAL THROAT AND EAR HOSPITAL,
SURGEON AND AURAL SURGEON TO THE ROYAL SOCIETY OF MUSICIANS;
AUTHOR OF 'THE THROAT AND ITS DISEASES,' 'MEDICAL HINTS ON THE
SINGING VOICE,' ETC.

AND

EMIL BEHNKE,

LECTURER ON VOCAL PHYSIOLOGY AND TEACHER OF VOICE PRODUCTION;
AUTHOR OF 'THE MECHANISM OF THE HUMAN VOICE,' ETC.

WITH NUMEROUS ILLUSTRATIONS BY WOOD-ENGRAVING AND PHOTOGRAPHY

CONTENTS.

	PAGE
LIST OF ILLUSTRATIONS	xi
PREFACE	xiii
A PLEA FOR VOCAL PHYSIOLOGY	
THE LAWS OF SOUND BEARING UPON THE VOICE	18—34

Definition of musical sound—Vibrations can be seen and felt—Require a medium to be perceived as sound by the ear—Reflection of sound—Echoes, 20—Vibrations may be either simple or compound, 21—Simple or pendular vibrations—Compound vibrations—Simple tones—Compound tones—Force or loudness, 22—Pitch, 23—Partial tones, 24—Quality of tone, 26—Stringed instruments, 29—Flute or flue-pipes—Reed instruments—Stiff reeds—Flexible reeds, 30—Clarionet, 31—Hautboy—Bassoon—Horn—Trumpet—The human voice—Resonance—Sympathetic resonance, 32—Tuning-forks.

SPEAKING AND SINGING .. .. 35—37

Distinguishing points between the speaking and the singing voice.

THE ANATOMY AND PHYSIOLOGY OF THE VOCAL ORGAN .. 38—83

The chest or thorax—The ribs—The midriff or diaphragm, 40—The muscles of the chest, 41—The lungs—The pleuræ, 43—The windpipe or trachea, 44—The bronchial passages or bronchi—The mucous membrane, 45—Respiration, 45—Different methods of, 49—Its great importance in relation to voice, song, and speech, 50.

The voice-box or larynx, 51—The framework, 53—The ring cartilage—The shield cartilage—The lid cartilage, 55—The pyramids, 57—The vocal ligaments, 58—The muscles of the larynx, 61—The glottis, 65—The vocal chink—Tabulation of muscles governing (1) the vocal chink, (2) the pitch of the voice, 68—The pocket ligaments, 69—The pockets of the larynx, 71—The cartilages of Santorini, 72—Folds of the larynx—The vestibule of the larynx, 73—Closure of the larynx and closure of the glottis two different things, 75—The prop cartilages.

The resonator, 77—The pockets—The upper part of the throat, or pharynx, 78—The cavities of the nose, 79—The mouth—The hard palate, 80—The soft palate—The tonsils—The uvula, 81—Importance of soft palate in vocalisation, 82.	38—82
DIFFERENCES OF THE LARYNX IN CHILDREN, WOMEN, AND MEN	83—86
Growth from infancy to puberty—Varying dimensions in the sexes—Female larynx not simply reproduction of male.	
MOVEMENTS OF THE LARYNX WHICH CAN BE SEEN OR FELT—in *In*spiration, *Ex*piration, and in various vowel sounds.	86—87
THE HUMAN VOICE AS A MUSICAL INSTRUMENT	88—94
The string theory—The flute-pipe theory—The reed theory—Influence of windpipe below, and of resonating portion above, on pitch of the voice, 91.	
PHYSICAL CAUSES OF THE DIVISION OF VOICES	94—98
Differences between soprano, contralto, tenor, and bass—Speculations on the subject.	
THE HYGIENIC ASPECT OF THE VOCAL APPARATUS	99—135
Importance of knowledge of general laws of health to all voice-users—Division of subject.	

I. *Hygienic aspect of management of the motor portion—Respiration*, 102—Respiration chemically considered—Importance of fresh air in dwelling-houses and in buildings in which voice is publicly used, 104—Nose-breathing—Influence on voice, 105—Hygienic aspect of respirators, 106—Lungs must be filled primarily at the base, 107, then laterally—and never in health by upward elevation of collar-bone—Detrimental influence on chest expansion from stays—Mr. Bernard Roth on the subject—Description of hygienic stays, 115—Influence of stays on obesity, 118—Experiments with spirometer, 120—Other influences of costume, 122—Constricting collars, tight belts, and heavy clothing—Influence of posture, 124—Beneficial effect of respiratory exercises on general health of persons with weak chests, 125—Influence of digestion on respiration—Table of vital statistics according to sex and height, 123.

II. *The hygienic aspect of the vibrating element—The larynx and the vocal ligaments*, 126—Most troubles in larynx may be attributed to wrong respiration—Vocal ligaments but rarely affected organically except under specific diseases of general health—Directions for avoiding laryngeal fatigue, 127.

III. *The hygienic aspect of management of the resonating portion of the voice*, 129—Troubles in this region principally affected by disorders of secretion and digestion, but mainly attributable to faulty respiration—Importance of physiological knowledge of formation of letters with regard to perfection in articulation, 129.	99—135

Concluding remarks, 130—*Fatigue* in whatever division of vocal apparatus almost always to be attributed to defective breathing—Cases illustrative of benefit of lung gymnastics on the voice, 132.

THE RELATIONS OF THE THROAT AND EAR IN REGARD TO VOICE 135—139

Physical causes from local disorder of direct relation between throat and ear which may disturb power of judging one's own voice—Indirect relation due to failure of control over laryngeal muscles to govern pitch, 137—Or auditory nerve is at fault—Comparison with sight—Distinction between the musical and non-musical ear—How to train the musical ear, 138.

EXPERIMENTS BEFORE THE INVENTION OF THE LARYNGOSCOPE 140—145

Ferrein (1741), Kempelen (1791), Dutrochet (1806), Liskovius (1814), Savart (1825), Malgaigne (1831), Lehfeldt (1835), Magendie (1838), Joh. Mueller (1839)—Experiments on exsected larynges from the dead subject, 144—Are of value only if confirmed by investigation on the living.

THE INVENTION OF THE LARYNGOSCOPE .. .. 145—149

Bozzini (1807), Senn (1827), Babington (1827), Beaumês (1838), Liston (1840), Avery (1840), Warden (1844), Manuel Garcia (1855), Merkel on Garcia, Czermak and Türck.

THE LARYNGOSCOPE AND HOW TO USE IT .. .. 149—155

Description of mirrors—Illumination, 149—Directions, 151—Objections to its facility refuted, 152—The "Laryngo-phantom," 154—Auto-laryngoscopy—The process—A lamp for the purpose.

THE TEACHINGS OF THE LARYNGOSCOPE .. .. 156—172

Description of various portions seen in the mirror—The way in which the object is reversed, 158—not laterally but from before backwards—The laryngeal image in gentle breathing, 160—in deep breathing, 160—and in tone production—Consideration of the movements of the vocal ligaments in tone production—The registers—Definition of a register, 163.

—Divisions into "lower thick," 163—"upper thick," 164
—"lower thin," 167—"upper thin," 168—"small," 169—
Explanation of the causes for differences in laryngoscopic
observations in the various registers, 170.

LARYNGEAL PHOTOGRAPHS AND THEIR LESSONS .. .. 173—178

Differences between them and the customary engraved view
—Causes thereof—Refutation of many objections and fallacies
held by non-laryngoscopic observers, 173—Differences in
appearance of glottic chink in "thick" register and "falsetto."

ON VOICE CULTIVATION .. .. 179—242

1. *Breathing.*—Reconsideration of the best methods of filling
the lungs, and the evil effects of wrong methods—Explanation
of diagrams illustrative thereof, 183—Artificial hindrances to
breathing, 184—Breathing exercises, 1, 186—How to fill the
lungs slowly, 2—How to hold the breath in the lungs, 3—
How to empty the lungs slowly, 4—To control both inspiration and expiration—Caution not to overfill the lungs by too
deep or frequent inbreathing, 192—Also not to exhaust them
before taking fresh breath, 193—Nostril-breathing habitually
enjoined, 193—Mouth-breathing only occasionally necessary,
194.

2. *Attack,* 195—Definition—Exercises for firm and clear attack
of tone, 196—Cautions against overcrowding of lungs, 197—
Refutation of false theory of attack by "Shock of Upper
Glottis"—Evidence that Dr. Wyllie's support of this theory
rests on garbled quotations, 199.

3. *Resonance,* 201—Examples of power to reinforce feeble
sounds by resonators.—Resonance of vocal tone modified
in five different directions : 1. by the pockets in the larynx ;
2. in the vestibule of the larnyx ; 3. the upper throat
(pharynx) ; 4. the mouth ; and 5. the nose—Opinions as to
fixed or moveable position of the larnyx, 203—Consideration
of the mouth as a resonant cavity, 204—Defective articulation
the common fault of English singers and speakers, 205—
Exercises for regulating free movements of its muscles, 206
—Control of the tongue, 207—Objections to artificial aids to
its depression, 208—Exercises for control of tongue, 209—
Throaty tone—Device for cure of, 210—Movements of soft
palate, 211—Nasal quality, 212—Exercises for control of
soft palate and avoidance of nasal tone, 214—Vowel sounds,
218—their relative pitch—Exercise on all vowels, not on one
only, 220—Causes for varied "reach" of the voice—Directions
so as to obtain it—Hints as to accurate articulation, 222.

Flexibility, 223—Definition and explanation of the term— 179—242
Exercises for its attainment.

The Registers, 225—Should be equalised, not differentiated—Illustration of the registers of various voices by comparison with stringed instruments—Differences of registers considered in detail—Importance of understanding nature and causes of physical sensations experienced by singers in use of the various registers—Exercises for developing and strengthening the registers, 234—Dangers of forcing registers up—The mixed voice, definition and mode of production—Falsetto, its varieties—All remarks on voice cultivation as applicable to speakers as to singers, 239.

Position, 240—Examples of what it should *not* be, and what it should be.

THE DAILY LIFE OF THE VOICE-USER .. .. 243—267

Controlled by 1. *Residence*—2. *Ablutions*, 244—How to bathe—Turkish baths—Washing teeth—Cold water in the mouth *versus* gargling—Warnings against excessive use of face powders and cosmetics, 247—3. *Clothing*, 248—Necessity for care of, to all professional voice-users—Hints as to—Description of sensible dress for ladies—4. *Diet*, 252—Explanation of various kinds of food and of its relation in quantity and quality to the amount of physical work of each individual—Time for meals when using the voice—Dietary aids to voice exercise—Suppers, 255—General dietary directions—The question of drinking Tea, 258—reasons of its injurious effects on some voices—Coffee—Cocoa—Effervescing drinks—Aërated waters—Alcohol, 260—not to be taken before or during work, only at conclusion—Varieties of wine to be taken—Malt liquors—Spirits—5. *Exercise*, 261—Distaste of singers for—To be always moderate—6. *Amusements*, 262—What may be allowed, and which avoided—Lastly: *Habits*, 263—Smoking—Snuff-taking.

THE AILMENTS OF THE VOICE-USER .. .. 268—287

Special colour given by vocation to all general disorders—Most ailments functional and due to disturbance of general health or fault of professional exercise—*Catching cold*, 271—*Sore throat or relaxed throat*, 272—*Pharyngitis*, or inflamed throat, 273—*Clergyman's sore throat*, 274—Useless advice of rest without treatment, 275—*Elongated or relaxed uvula*, 275—Symptoms and treatment—Refutation of objections to snipping in appropriate cases—*Enlargement of the tonsils*, 278

—Its injurious effects on the voice, articulation, and respiration, and on senses of hearing, smell, and taste—Operation, and testimony in support of its advisability—*Laryngeal troubles*, 281—Reasons for not considering them at length—*Loss of voice*, 281—Symptoms and treatment—Cautions as to dangerous and patent remedies—*Common head cold*, 284—*Nervousness*, 285—Concluding remarks, 286. ... 268—287

ON DEFECTS OF SPEECH: STAMMERING AND STUTTERING .. 288—303

Present position of the subject in public estimation—Brief consideration of vowels and consonants—Oral teaching of deaf mutes result of more perfect knowledge of physiology of speech—Distinctions between *stammering and stuttering*, 293—Fault of respiration the most frequent cause, 297—Defective state of health of stutterers and stammerers—Treatment—*Mechanical—Surgical*, 299, and *educational*, 301—The last both mental and physical.

APPENDIX I.—THE PROCESS OF PHOTOGRAPHY OF THE VOCAL ORGANS IN THE ACT OF SINGING .. .. 304—307

APPENDIX II.—COPY OF LETTER FROM DR. WYLLIE ON APPROXIMATION OF THE POCKET LIGAMENTS IN TONE PRODUCTION .. .. 307—308

INDEX .. .. 309—322

ADVERTISEMENTS (xvii—xxxviii)

LIST OF PLATES.

※ All Illustrations of this work which have been borrowed or adapted from other authorities are duly acknowledged. Those not so named are either original, or, as the result of actual dissection and experience, have been modified to such an extent as to justify claim to originality. The laryngoscopic drawings have been made by Mr. Lennox Browne, and the other figures have been drawn under our joint direction by Mr. Sherwin, of 4 Staple Inn Buildings, whose care and skill we are happy in having secured. We also gratefully recognise the painstaking intelligence with which Mr. Royle, of 2 Newman's Row, Lincoln's Inn, has engraved the woodcuts.

Acknowledgment of obligation in the matter of the photographs is accorded in the appendix on Photography of the Larynx, page 304.

PLATE		PAGE
I.	Original and untouched Portrait illustrating the process of Photography of the Larynx. (*Copyright*)	*Frontispiece*
II.	A Reed (*from Tyndall*)	30
III.	Section of the Human Body (*Adapted from Küss and Czermak*.)	39
IV.	Framework of the Chest	40
V.	Chest and Lungs	42
VI.	The Lungs, &c. (*adapted from Niemeyer*)	43
VII.	Side View of the Voice-box or Larynx	52
VIII.	Front View of the Voice-box or Larnyx	54
IX.	Side View of the Voice-box or Larynx, showing the interior of it, the right plate of the shield having been removed	57
X.	Side View of the Voice-box or Larynx, showing the interior of the left half	60
XI.	Side View of the Voice-box or Larynx, showing the external muscles	62
XII.	A. Glottis in Repose B. Glottis in Deep Breathing C. Glottis in the Production of Tone	65

PLATE		PAGE
XIII.	View of a Section of the Voice-box or Larynx from above	66
XIV.	Side View of the Voice-box or Larynx, showing the left Pocket and Mucous Folds	69
XV.	View of the Voice-box or Larynx cut open from behind	72
XVI.	The Voice-box or Larynx seen from behind	73
XVII.	The Soft Palate	80
XVIII.	Natural Waist (*adapted from Flower*)	110
XIX.	Deformed Waist (*adapted from Flower*)	111
XX.	Natural Position of Organs in Unconfined Chest (*adapted from Roth*)	112
XXI.	Distorted Position of Organs in Body deformed by Stays (*adapted from Roth*)	113
XXII.	Dr Tobold's Laryngoscope	150
XXIII.	Dr. Foulis's Auto-Laryngoscope	155
XXIV.	Laryngeal Image showing Reversion of the Reflected Image	158
XXV.	,, ,, in Gentle Breathing	160
XXVI.	,, ,, ,, Deep Breathing	160
XXVII.	,, ,, ,, Tone Production	160
XXVIII.	,, ,, "Lower Thick" Register	163
XXIX.	,, ,, "Upper Thick" Register	164
XXX.	,, ,, "Lower Thin" Register	167
XXXI.	,, ,, "Upper Thin" Register (Female Larynx)	168
XXXII.	,, ,, "Small" Register (Female Larynx)	169
XXXIII.	The Registers of the Human Voice	171
XXXIV.	Repetition of the Laryngeal Images in the Various Registers	178
XXXV.	Photographs of the Larynx in the Production of Different Mechanisms (*Copyright*) .. *to face page*	178
XXXVI. A. B. C. XXXVII. A. B. C.	Illustrating the varying capacity of the chest according to the method in which the lungs are inflated	183
XXXVIII.	Section of the Voice-box or Larynx showing the shape of the Vocal Ligaments in the "Thick" Register (*from Merkel*)	200
XXXIX.	Section of the Voice-box or Larynx showing the shape of the Vocal Ligaments in the "Thin" Register (*from Merkel*)	200
XL.	Photographs of the Soft Palate in the production of Different Tones (*Copyright*) .. *to face page*	215

PREFACE.

EACH of the Authors of the following pages has already contributed something towards the store of literature on the Human Voice. These contributions have had a large circulation and have so far been successful, but they have been necessarily one-sided and therefore incomplete; for while the surgeon was unable to touch on matters musical, the teacher found himself in a similar difficulty on many points of hygiene and health.

The one, after many years of experience, came to the conclusion that wrong production of voice or abuse of its function was the chief cause of most of the cases of vocal failure, and even of throat disease, occurring to professional voice-users, which came under his notice.

The other had become equally convinced that the scarcity of fine voices in singers as well as in speakers, generally acknowledged to exist, was due, less to dearth of material, than to faults in its cultivation and exercise.

The want of a complete work from both these points of observation had been repeatedly urged upon us, and as we had for some years been in the habit of collaborating in the treatment of patients and pupils, and had found that our experience on all points of physiology and of hygiene, of precept and of practice, in so far as we could form an opinion, was in entire concord, we agreed to write conjointly something which should, if possible, supply the want indicated, and, containing the combined experience of vocal surgeon and of voice trainer, become a complete manual for all voice-users.

Probably it will not be difficult for readers to identify the separate authorship of certain chapters and passages, but the work is offered as essentially a joint one; for there is not a chapter or illustration, and hardly a paragraph, but has been the subject of frequent mutual consideration and discussion.

We trust that, as a result of this intimate collaboration, our aim has been attained; and for the same reason, we desire to acknowledge equal responsibility for any shortcomings.

Lennox Browne

36 *Weymouth Street,*
   Portland Place.

Emil Behnke.

12 *Avonmore Road,*
~~35 Talgarth Road,~~
   West Kensington, W.

NOVEMBER, 1883.

PREFACE TO THE THIRD EDITION.

THE first edition having been exhausted within a month of publication, and the second with almost equal rapidity, the authors desire to repeat their grateful acknowledgment of so marked an appreciation of their labours.

April, 1884.

PREFACE TO THE FOURTH EDITION.

SINCE the last edition the authors have endeavoured, by publication of a separate monograph on "The Child's Voice," to supply a want frequently expressed by the readers of this volume. One of them has also treated with more detail than appeared convenient in a handbook the question of the value of Stimulants in relation to Voice-use.

These little appended essays render it unnecessary to make any change in this new edition, and the authors have only to once again express their recognition of the continued favour with which their work is received.

December, 1885.

OPINIONS OF THE PRESS.

"THE extract we have quoted will be sufficient to show that this is a book to be studied, not to be merely read."—*The Times*, Dec. 27, 1883.

"Their book is absolutely epoch-making."—*Cologne Gazette*, Feb. 24, 1884.

"The book is written with clearness, simplicity and directness, and, though scientific in method and thorough in execution, is devoid of all unnecessary technicalities. . . . It is indeed a work that will not fail to reward its reader with liberal gifts of exceptionally useful information."—*The Daily Telegraph*, Dec. 29, 1883.

"Is not only easily understood, but is interesting reading."—*The Daily News*, Dec. 20, 1883.

"In providing the means for a better knowledge of vocal physiology the writers have thrown the onus of ignorance in this matter upon the shoulders of those singers and speakers who neglect this important branch of their education."—*The Morning Post*, Dec. 25, 1883.

"A work of high practical and scientific utility, which ought to be invaluable to all who use their voices for public speaking or singing."—*Pall Mall Gazette*, March 14, 1884.

"Every singer, actor, and ordinary public speaker, should possess a copy, and take its teachings well to heart."—*Echo*, Jan. 22, 1884.

"The precepts of the Voice-trainer in the book are of undoubted value to the teacher of singing; and many of them, especially in the chapter on 'Voice Cultivation,' are of wider application still."—*The Saturday Review*, Jan. 12, 1884.

"The authors have produced a treatise of eminent usefulness to clergymen, and to all who are called upon to use their voices in public; and a copy should be placed in the library of every Theological College in the kingdom."—*The Record*, Dec. 28, 1883.

"The book is, indeed, a fascinating one, and, once begun, is with difficulty relinquished."—*The Observer*, Jan. 27, 1884.

"In fine, Messrs. Lennox Browne and Behnke have given to the world a book, every page of which is worth learning by heart, and in which there is not a single superfluous line."—*Sunday Times*, Jan. 6, 1884.

"In 'Voice, Song and Speech,' are very happily combined the experience of a successful throat specialist, who has the reputation of being, above everything, practical, and of a singing-master who is qualified by scientific attainments to understand what he teaches. The result is a work of great interest and utility, not only to the voice-user, but to the general reader."—*Truth*, Jan. 3, 1884.

"To sum up in a few words the leading characteristics of 'Voice, Song, and Speech,' it is full of valuable information, intelligibly imparted, never tiresome, and frequently very amusing; a mine of learning, the measures of which are not offered to the public in rough-hewn blocks, but daintily polished and fashioned into attractive shapes by skilled and artistic hands."—*The Theatre*, Dec. 1883.

"A treatise of a composite nature, of great value as a guide for singers and speakers. All who study it and follow its teachings, may benefit both physiologically and artistically."—*Illustrated London News*, Jan. 26, 1884.

"Mr. Lennox Browne speaks with authority on the medical side of the question, while his *collaborateur* combines laryngeal science with a knowledge of music."—*The Graphic*, Dec. 29, 1883.

"The results of two such earnest investigators of the subject here presented to the public cannot fail to produce a most salutary effect upon the art of voice-training, and we sincerely hope the book will be extensively read. . . . The volume will assuredly remain as the most perfect manual for singers and speakers ever published."—*The Musical Times*, Feb., 1884.

"The whole book, in point of fact, is full of that which the student ought to learn for his own self-guidance. We commend it heartily to all vocalists, amateur or professional. A careful reading will open their eyes to many things now, perhaps, unsuspected."—*The Lute*, Jan. 15, 1884.

"This volume is the most complete work on the voice for the use of the musician, the singer, and the general reader, valuable for its clearness of treatment and for the trustworthiness of its information."—"Many excellent books there have been before this on the subject, but this belongs to our day, and advances the reader to the level of present knowledge."—*Musical Opinion*, Dec. and Jan., 1884.

"Their book is interesting from cover to cover, and cannot fail to be the standard work on the subject of which it treats."—*The Tonic Sol-fa Reporter*, January, 1883.

"The book is written so that he who runs may read. . . . The two sections, on the daily life and the ailments of the voice-user, contain much good advice without giving that little knowledge (more particularly of medicines and prescriptions) which is dangerous."—*Edinburgh Medical Journal*, March, 1884.

"The photographs, of which there are many, both of the larynx and soft palate, in the act of singing, may be accepted, quite irrespective of their value to the singer, as triumphs of photographic art, and are of very great interest from many varied points of view."—*Medical Press and Circular*, Dec. 5, 1883.

"The warmest encomium we can offer to the two well-informed and experienced authors of this excellent work is simply to invite the public to *read* the production of their joint labours. Its merits will prove so self-evident to all as to render any panegyric on our part superfluous."—*Student's Journal and Hospital Gazette*, Dec. 22, 1883.

"This work is a step in the right direction, and we wish the authors every success."—*Public Opinion*, Dec. 29, 1883.

"We can most highly recommend it to all who are interested in the training of the 'Voice.'"—*Journal of Education*, Feb., 1883.

"A very imperfect idea has after all been given of the varied information stored within its pages. There seems to be nothing omitted, as there might seem to be nothing to criticise. . . . The reader will close the book with the feeling that he has been reading the opinions of authors who are possessed in a singular degree of the merit of thinking and writing in a clear, common-sense manner."—*St. Cecilia Magazine, Edinburgh*, Jan., 1884.

"The most comprehensive treatise that has appeared."—*Edinburgh Musical Star*, Feb., 1884.

"We can cordially recommend this work as the most thoughtful and suggestive treatise on the Voice known to us."—*Knowledge*, Feb. 8, 1884.

"Now that the work has appeared, we have no hesitation in declaring it superior to any of its predecessors."—*Health*, Feb. 29, and March 7, 1884.

"The book is copiously illustrated, and it forms a very complete work of reference and study. The subject is threshed out thoroughly, every detail is alluded to with copious references to authorities, and the value of the book is greatly enhanced by the clear and comprehensive style adopted by the two joint authors."—*London Figaro*, Dec. 15, 1883.

VOICE, SONG, AND SPEECH.

A PLEA FOR VOCAL PHYSIOLOGY.

"If any one doubts the importance of an acquaintance with the principles of physiology as a means to complete living let him look around and see how many men and women he can find in middle or later life who are thoroughly well."—*Herbert Spencer.*

WE have only to demand application of the above pertinent question of our great modern philosopher on the subject of general physiology to the more special one, the title of which heads this chapter, to explain why it seems strange to us that there is any necessity to plead for a knowledge of vocal physiology amongst singers and speakers. Such knowledge should be universally admitted as an indispensable branch of vocal culture. The result would be twofold: first, the full beauties of the vocal organ would be developed with intelligence and ease; and secondly, fewer voices would be ruined in the training, or be prematurely worn out, since both teachers and pupils of singing and of elocution would know better the construction, capabilities, and delicacy of the instrument on which they wish to play.

Some have ridiculed the idea that an acquaintance with this subject is of any more use to the vocalist than is the anatomy of the hand to the pianist. But the examples are not analogous, inasmuch as the pianist obtains his instrument ready made for him, and if he wear it out or injure it he can purchase another, while the vocalist has to form his voice, and if he wrongly use it, it may be gone for ever.

A pupil on going over an exercise or piece is told by the master, "You are singing with nasal, or throaty, or muffled quality," as the case may be; "let the tone be a pure vocal one." The master imitates the fault with exaggeration, then (presumably) patterns correctly; but although the pupil recognises the defect he is unable to remedy it, because singing cannot be learned exclusively by imitation, any more than painting by copying the works of masters, however great. The teacher's injunctions serve but to bewilder the anxious student, who would be only too thankful to produce pure and beautiful tone did he understand the process, and were the master possessed of sufficient practical knowledge of vocal physiology to rightly instruct him in control of the individual or various muscles whose imperfect action causes the defects in question. Analogies must not, then, be sought for between the practice of a living and of a mechanical art, which latter might be applicable to certain rules for the education of a pianist and a violinist. The true analogy is to be found in the two arts of singing and painting, whereas the likenesses and differences of practice with two instruments might be illustrated by the kindred mechanical graphic arts of engraving and lithography. We wish to urge that the singing pupil should not be asked to make a copy of any master, but to produce an original with all the differences and individualities thereof. But what would be said of an art student who attempted a figure subject without knowledge of anatomy so as to understand the action of the various muscles? Who dreams of painting costumed figures until he has mastered the mysteries of form in the nude and the consequent meaning of every fold of drapery? Who, again, would sanction the painting of a landscape without previous knowledge of the laws of light and shade, of composition and, above all, of perspective? And supposing such were attempted, who would look at the resulting works or give them a place on wall or in portfolio? All teaching of laws of Art must be *preliminary* and not supplementary to practical teaching; for the knowledge of how nature works should be recognised as a foundation, not as a superstructure. Vocal instruction in the direction indicated before practice is attempted is therefore preferable, because it leads to prevention of faults of style, and indeed of diseased conditions which would otherwise, through ignorance, result. In other words, we urge that "prevention is better than cure," and we would add that when "cure" is effected a relapse will occur under return to predisposing and exciting causes.

No serious reply is really required to those who object to scientific teaching on the ground that many of our greatest singers in the past knew nothing of these things. That may be; but, in the first place, they would have been none the worse for such knowledge; and in the second place, the same objection would apply to extension of scientific research and knowledge in all and every other direction. It is a question worthy of consideration whether failure or scarcity of good voices in the present may not be in a measure due to inability to transmit the gift simply because the greatest possessors in the recent past have been unable, or unwilling, to give the necessary time to teach by imitation, and have possibly also been ignorant of any other method of education. Here, again, the analogy of painting and singing may be used in illustration of our argument. We do not advance that now and again a great genius in either art has not shone on the world who appeared to have been self-taught; but treatises and rules must be made for the average capacity, not for the exceptional. It may be true that there is a present dearth of the finest voices, but it is undeniable that there is, in late years, a greater average excellence in the musical qualities and scientific attainments of singers, and also in the elocutionary qualifications of many members of parliament, clergymen, actors, and other public speakers. We deny, however, the assumption that many great artists are "self-taught," and Leslie, in his 'Handbook for Young Painters,' combats this idea with great vigour, and by ample illustration proves its fallacy. All that he says could, by mere change of the word "painting" into "singing," apply to our contention. Constable also very pertinently remarks that "a self-taught artist is one taught by a very ignorant person." The fact is that a genius may be said to illustrate a gift by which the possessor absorbs almost, as it were, naturally, and imitates immediately, all the fundamental essential laws of his art, and he will even originate ideas—possibly without knowledge of the laws on which they are based, but always in conformity therewith. He will not have to work with less industry, but his industry will always be rightly directed; and the degree of facility with which teaching is absorbed, digested, and assimilated, constitutes the difference between genius and talent, and also the different grades of talent.

We cannot better enforce this portion of our argument than with a quotation from a recent work by Leo Kofler entitled 'The Old Italian School of Singing' (E. S.

Werner, Albany, N.Y.), a book full of valuable information, and one to be strongly recommended. He asks the question: "How shall we account for the sentiments of a great musician and teacher like F. H. Truhn, of Berlin, who, in his pamphlet 'About the Art of Singing,' expresses himself in the following manner: 'Mozart knew nothing of Chladni's and Helmholtz's researches; who, then, need to have studied physiological analysis of the vocal organs to become a singer or a teacher of singing?' The great masters of the old Italian school were of the opposite opinion. The renowned Italian singer, composer, and musical writer, Giovanni A. Buontempi, who died before he could get a glimpse of the glorious era of the old Italian school, informs us in his 'History of Music,' of which Dr. Burney gives a great many and long abstracts, that at his time the daily study of the physical laws that govern the singer's tones was required of the pupils. The same is told by Arteaga of his times. J. F. Agricola, in his translation of Tosi's important work, gives in the first chapter a description in detail of the larynx and its functions. Dr. Marx, in his noteworthy book, 'The Art of Singing,' in section ii., treats upon vocal physiology with such a thorough knowledge that we wonder how it was possible to achieve such scientific results thirty years before Garcia first saw the vocal ligaments in operation in a living body. The study of vocal physiology is surely a very essential duty of the singing-teacher; without it he cannot conscientiously be a vocal trainer. Would you trust a physician of whom you know that he has not acquired the necessary knowledge of the mysteries of the human body? Why, then, would you pin your faith upon a voice-trainer who makes a boast of his ignorance of the natural laws that govern the vocal organs? These organs are the most delicate, vital, and complicated parts of our body. Is it reasonable, then, to say that a man can train them without knowing their natural conditions? No rational being can decline the advice given by Agricola in his previously mentioned translation of Tosi: 'The knowledge of the vocal organs is always very useful to the singer, and especially to the teacher, and in many cases indispensable. For even when nature has adorned a singer with the best qualities, the knowledge of physiology is necessary to prevent all damages that might be done through ignorance. But when a teacher finds natural faults and defects in a voice, how can he successfully battle with them if he is unacquainted with the seat of the evil?' Dr. Haertinger remarks: 'As in all other arts and sciences man can only reach the truth and perfection by walking in those paths along which he can follow the footprints of nature, so also in voice-training. If the student of the art of singing receives no insight into the mysterious workshop of his vocal organs, then he will not only make no advance in the cultivation of his voice, but, on the contrary, will positively distort it and lose all naturalness.' This shows the fallacy of the popular belief, that if a man or a woman is only a great singer they must necessarily be the best teachers. If they have not studied the art of training voices, the first chapter of which must contain the science of the natural conditions of the vocal organs, they are unfit to train others, for the same reason that the best pianist—just because he has learned to play the piano—cannot be considered to have thus fitted himself to become a manufacturer of pianos. For this he would have to undergo considerable extra training."

That all teachers, however empirical, realise in a certain degree that the vocal machinery is capable of being brought under control may be proved by the advice given on this subject in so-called treatises on the voice. It is amusingly varied and contradictory.

Thus, singing pupils are told by different authorities: To breathe by the descent of the diaphragm; by drawing in the abdomen and raising the ribs; to swell out the sides while drawing in the abdomen as a support to the chest!— To control the expiration by means of the abdominal and the chest muscles; to control it by contraction of the ventricles of Morgagni.—To breathe through the nostrils; through the mouth; through both at the same time.—To keep the larynx fixed; to hold it in a high position; to hold it in a low position; to make it rise gradually; not to attempt to control it at all.—To hold the mouth, the neck, the palate, and the pharynx very stiff and tense; to hold all these parts quite loosely.—To tighten the under lip; to depress the tongue; to practise the soft palate till it becomes as hard as a bone.—To sing with closed mouth before attacking the tone, and with a strong nasal quality m—m—maw, &c.; to say "pm" with closed mouth, letting the sound pass through the nostrils, resulting, we are assured, in a wonder-working stroke of the epiglottis. —To focus the sound; to direct the voice towards the roof of the mouth; against the hard palate; against the upper front teeth; into the head; to the bottom of the chest; to lean the tone against the eyes! to sing all over the face!

Well may the puzzled student ask which of all these recommendations are right and which are wrong! The teachers who give these quasi-physiological directions feel that the voices with which they have to deal are wrong in some important respects and must be changed, and that mere imitation will not effect the change. They are, indeed, unconsciously groping for a knowledge of the mechanism of the vocal organ, which is as necessary for the proper development of a healthy voice as it is for the restoration of a lost or ruined one. But there need be no groping where science can light up the way.

This is true of the speaking voice as well as of the voice in singing, the same mechanism being called into play in both cases. All public speakers, as well as singers, should receive scientific training in the mechanism and right employment of the organ of voice. It is precisely here, on the threshold of their art, that many elocutionists fail. They occupy themselves with articulation, pronunciation, intonation, modulation, emphasis, and gesture, and having but little, if any, physiological knowledge are therefore unable to form a true basis of voice-production. It is clear that a teacher of singing or of elocution who is thoroughly and practically acquainted with the anatomy and physiology of the parts over which he is to give his pupils control, and who can skilfully examine a pupil's larynx, and direct its movements, is, other qualifications being equal, in a position to produce better results than one who is deficient in such skill.

Unfortunately but little attention is paid to this fundamental training; and it is only when singers, and especially speakers, find their voice fail that they begin to think they have not used the organ aright, and seek for information which should have been theirs before the commencement of their public career, whether it be in the senate, the pulpit, the law-court, the concert-room, or the stage.

It is true that no person ever attempts to use the singing voice in public without special training of some sort; yet there are still members of parliament, clergymen, and other public speakers, who commence and continue their important work without any previous vocal discipline.

"When a man is called upon to address a large assembly for the first time in his life, he is all at once made aware that the vocal production to which he is habituated fails him utterly. He makes a variety of impromptu experiments in pitch and intensity, some of them ludicrous, and all unsuccessful; and having soared to heights unsustainable by human throat and insupportable to human ear, he drops past that mean elevation at which alone he might have poised himself securely, and plunging 'deeper than ever plummet sounded,' is lost in an incomprehensible growl." ('The Cultivation of the Speaking Voice,' by John Hullah. London: Macmillan & Co., p. 23.)

In this matter of vocal training we are in a retrogade condition; for we find that the development of the voice was considered by the ancient Greeks a part of the proper education of every student, and essential to health. "The discipline for the formation and improvement of the voice among the Athenians was so comprehensive that, as we are informed by Roman writers, not less than three different classes of teachers were employed for this purpose, viz., the vociferarii, phonasci, and vocales. The object of the first class seems to have been to strengthen the voice and to extend its compass; the office of the second to improve its quality, so as to render it full, sonorous, and agreeable; while the efforts of the third, who, perhaps, were considered as the finishing masters, were directed to the proper intonation and inflection." ('Philosophy of Voice and

Speech,' by James Hunt. London, 1858. Longman, Browne & Co., p. 350.) This training, in which all youths of respectability participated, was distinct from that of the rhetorician which followed the more scientific teaching just described.

The advisability of imitating the Athenians by establishing classes for voice training on scientific principles is earnestly commended to those in authority in our universities, and in our musical and theological colleges. A preacher is something more than a sermon-maker, he is a "thought-creator" and a "thought-conveyer," and it is his duty to convey his thoughts to his auditors in a suitable and impressive manner. But if his tone-production be faulty, rendering his voice unmusical and unsympathetic; if he put upon it an unnatural strain and use an unnecessary expenditure of force; or if his speech be weak and unintelligible, then his most beautiful thoughts and profoundest learning will be powerless to elevate and instruct his congregation. For himself, he will be fortunate if he escape some of the many throat troubles which are only peculiar to clergymen because they, of all voice-users of the higher grades, speak most frequently in an unnatural voice.

No man who is conscious of the ability to speak effectively can undervalue the power of a pleasant voice; and no hearer of a melodious voice but will acknowledge its influence. We have, probably, all been charmed and our attention riveted by such a voice, even when the discourse was not above commonplace. The converse of this is, alas, more often met with. It is a fact that many of the greatest thinkers, scholars, and writers use in public speaking and reading a heavy, low monotone, or they rasp the ear with a high and strident pitch. Their "thoughts that breathe and words that burn" fall lifeless and cold, nay, even weary, and repel their listeners, who experience a sense of relief when the inharmonious voice ceases; the speaker also being thankful that his painful struggle to be heard is over. How much the influence of the unfortunate possessor of such a voice is nullified! If a statesman, how small must be his success in directing the fortunes of a nation! If a clergyman, painfully will he feel that his earnest endeavours avail him nothing. If a barrister, he sees judge and juryman sleeping, and to the detriment of his client he may lose his carefully prepared case. Yet in almost every instance a voice which has no inherent beauty may, by correct training, become attractive and pleasant, and obtain clearness, smoothness, and commanding resonance.

The following quotation, taken from a lecture by Cull, on 'Reading Aloud,' is much to the point: "By the term a highly cultivated voice I do not mean the application of those rules of reading which are taught by elocution masters, but a cultivation of the voice on sound acoustic and physiological principles, analogous to those which are so eminently successful in cultivating the voice of song. This is not mere theory. Voices have been cultivated on such principles with great success. Weak ones have been strengthened and improved in flexibility and tone; and even those supposed to be permanently silenced by long-continued clergyman's sore throat have been restored to public usefulness." ('King's College Lectures on Elocution,' by Charles John Plumptre. London: Trübner & Co. Appendix II., p. 448.) It is to be hoped that the time is not far distant when there will be at our universities and training colleges a chair of vocal physiology. Wealthy and benevolent persons have here a noble object for their liberality, presenting to them an opportunity of preventing for all time much suffering, both physical and mental; and of enabling numbers of devoted and talented men to continue to the end their valuable services in the cause of the commonwealth and of religion. By furnishing the means of instruction, and by making obligatory to each student a course of practical study on the formation, management, and preservation of the voice, clergyman's sore throat and other cognate disorders which now seriously mar the prospects and hinder the usefulness of many public speakers will be much less frequent.

Clergymen and other public speakers break down with injured or ruined voice and enfeebled health, more frequently through simple ignorance of the true method of voice-production than from all other causes combined.

For, alas. there is a sadder phase than that already sketched. The habitual faulty use of the respiratory and vocal muscles produces congestion of the vascular supply to the mucous membrane, disorder of the secreting follicles, irritation of the sensory nerves of the throat and uncertainty of action of the vocal muscles, each resulting in hoarseness, and deterioration of power both to produce and to control the desired tones; so that all functional exercise occasions fatigue and nervous depression, with the addition of injury to the general health. Chronic throat disorder is thus established, which, if neglected, is obstinate of cure. Singers who occupy a middle place in art, and more frequently the clergy, seem to be peculiarly liable to these maladies; and it is painful to see them thus broken down in health, sometimes to even a vital extent, as well as in voice for want of proper knowledge as to a right use of their vocal organs. It ought not to be. Clergymen should not be sent to their high calling unprepared for the physical part of their vocation, ignorant of the mechanism and management of the wonderful instrument upon which they play in speaking.

It has been our great gratification to have restored to vigour by the use of scientific vocal gymnastics, sometimes even without any medical treatment, many voices which had utterly broken down under faulty production; but if speakers and singers would start on their public career properly prepared for the physical part of their work, no voice restoration would be required. Knowing how to produce their voice they would avoid errors which destroy that most perfectly constructed and, under fair use, most lasting of all musical instruments.

Stammering and stuttering, which afflict more persons than is perhaps imagined, would be much more frequently cured than they now are if a correct knowledge of the physiology of the vocal apparatus were possessed by those who undertake their treatment; but this point can only be alluded to here, and will be dealt with in detail in the special section treating on this question.

Many intending students of singing who read this chapter will probably ask, "How is true vocal culture to be obtained, seeing that not only is a thorough knowledge of the art of music needed, but also an intimate acquaintance with vocal physiology?" Doctors, especially those who make affections of the throat a specialty, have the requisite knowledge of the anatomy and physiology of the voice; but a doctor whose time is occupied in the cure of disease cannot give attention to the vocal culture of his patients. Neither has every doctor musical knowledge and taste. Doctors are all naturally on the outlook for symptoms of disease, and the specialist, no less than the generalist, seeks for the original cause in the general constitutional fault; he goes even farther, and tries to put his finger on the exact local seat of trouble, and his remedial measures are not confined to the drug or the knife, but also include correction of both general and local trouble. Yet all this has nothing to do with scientific vocal culture, for which there is a wide field outside the province of the physician, although the work runs somewhat on parallel lines. Teachers are needed who have gone through a regular course of physiological and anatomical training; who have learnt the way in which all the muscles of the vocal apparatus act, so that on hearing a faulty voice they may be able to say which muscle or set of muscles requires to be brought into play, or subdued in action, as the case may be. Nor must they be unpractical and satisfy themselves with merely theorising on the subject. They must also, having discovered the fault, know how to correct it; for though the physician has gone far to success when he has made a correct diagnosis of disease, he will not cure his patient unless he pursues a proper remedial treatment. Above all, and before all, the scientific teacher must be able to apply his anatomical knowledge to the development of the respiratory organs to their full capacity.

It is possible that few will have a sufficient liking for physiology to study this portion of the subject in the dissecting room as well as from books, and to verify in their own and other living persons' throats the discoveries already made. Yet but little good will be effected without this practice, especially that of laryngoscopic investigation of the vocal organs in the performance of the various functional acts; for the dead and excised larynx cannot be made to act as a living one.

An intelligent use of the laryngoscope and application of its teaching will give a greater facility in the art of voice-cultivation than has hitherto been enjoyed. Inexpert manipulators who are unable to use the laryngoscope properly, and therefore cannot produce a good tone while seeking to investigate with it, illogically come to the conclusion that only forced and unnatural sounds can be made while using the laryngoscope, and that, in consequence, its teachings are unreliable. We know that a bad workman generally blames his tools instead of his own inefficiency; and here the fault lies solely with the operator. Doubtless there are difficulties to be overcome, but none that are insuperable, and in the proper place we shall give such detailed and plain directions as will greatly facilitate pursuance of this interesting study. Let not the earnest worker be discouraged by a few failures; ultimate success is surely attainable, and the result will abundantly reward his patience and perseverance.

It must, however, be understood that in thus advocating a scientific basis for the production, cultivation, and preservation of the voice we are not thinking of laryngoscopy alone. It is a mistake to speak of this as though it were the one and all of vocal physiology. It is, on the contrary, only a small part of it, and would avail the student but little were he not also fully acquainted with the vocal apparatus as a whole, which, as will be seen further on, comprises separate mechanisms for production, emission, and resonance, with many other minor factors to regulate the qualities of clearness and beauty of sound, and distinctness of utterance. The immediate origin of the voice is, it is true, in the vocal ligaments; but as the surgeon has, in the cure of all disease, whether of the throat or of any other part, to go far beyond the seat of local manifestation, so the teacher and student of voice-production must not think of the voice simply as the result of the vibrations of the vocal ligaments. Such a narrow view of the subject would necessarily lead to error and failure, and men who are continually talking or writing about the action of the "vocal cords" or of the "ventricles of Morgagni," or indeed of any other part of the mechanism, instead of viewing the instrument as a whole, do not deserve the name of scientists. The greatest attention to even the minutest details is certainly indispensable in this as in any other field of research; but details are important only in their respective places, and they should never be so magnified as to assume undue proportions, or to distort our view of the subject in its entirety. Though much of singing is due to automatic muscular action in the vocal organ, yet physiological instruction as to the best method of filling the lungs so as to set the cords in vibration, as to economy of expiration so as to produce efficient and even vocal tone, and the many facts to be hereafter detailed, bearing on the altogether voluntary control over the tongue, lips, and soft palate, are not only of essential service to the singer, but of great independent interest to all students of the art, and cannot fail to lead to a more intelligent exposition of their capabilities.

This being agreed, we have to study the construction of all these parts in detail and as a whole, and to deduce from this study how to govern their movements. With the knowledge thus acquired, muscular efforts can be explained, directed, or controlled; weakness can be changed into strength, and harshness into sweetness. It is, in short, the business of teachers of singing and of elocution to commence where scientific investigators have left off; to acquaint themselves with the physiological and acoustic laws governing the voice; and then to turn these to practical account in drilling their pupils. Such at any rate is the task that we set ourselves to accomplish in the following pages, and, indeed, we propose to go somewhat further. There can be no doubt that, as a result of the non-scientific character of much of the instruction in the art of singing and speaking, very false and ignorant ideas exist amongst voice-users as to their mode of life, and as to the ailments which affect their sanitary well-being, both general and professional. We shall endeavour, without transgressing beyond the bounds of reason, to give such information on the more prominent points of hygiene and health which affect the voice-user in his daily career as will render his work more easy, and will lead to the detection and remedy of some of his health defects. There cannot be a doubt that want of such knowledge is at the root of many a vocal failure. We shall feel ourselves happy indeed if we can supply that want.

THE LAWS OF SOUND BEARING UPON THE VOICE.

MUSICAL SOUND is the result of vibrations which occur at regular intervals, and with a sufficient rapidity of succession. We can *see* the vibrations by watching a sounding string. Or we can demonstrate them by drawing a sounding tuning-fork, with a style attached to one of the prongs, over a piece of smoked glass, when the style will not produce a straight but a wavy line, revealing the to-and-fro motion of the prong. But the most striking manner in which sonorous vibrations can be rendered visible consists in Chladni's interesting experiments, which show that when sand is scattered over a sounding plate of glass or of metal, fastened with a clamp in the centre, the sand is driven from the vibrating parts of the surfaces and collects along the lines remaining stationary, which are called *nodal lines*. By drawing a bow over the edge of such plates, and by interrupting the vibrations at various points, by pressing a finger against them, sand-figures of extreme beauty may be produced.

We can also *feel* sonorous vibrations by gently touching with the finger a suspended sounding bell. Hang up a little piece of cork in such a manner as to make it just touch the rim of the bell and it will be thrown into motion. In order to prove that sound *is* the result of vibrations touch the bell heavily enough to stop the vibrations, and you also stop the tone. Strike a tuning-fork and touch one of its prongs with the tip of your tongue, the vibrations will cause a tickling sensation so strong as to send a shock through your whole body. Or again, if the vibrating tuning-fork be held so as to touch a lightly suspended button, the latter will be violently dashed aside.

These vibrations do not give rise to the sensation *sound*, unless they throw our hearing apparatus into similar vibrations. There is consequently a medium required to communicate them to the ear. This medium is the air-ocean by which we are surrounded on all sides, and that it really is the sound-conveying medium may be inferred from the fact that without air we do not hear. Suspend a bell connected with clockwork under the receiver of an air-pump, exhaust the receiver as perfectly as possible, and then set the clockwork going. You will see the hammer striking the bell, but no sound will be heard. As you re-admit the air gently by degrees you hear the sound, very faintly at first, but louder and louder as the air surrounding the bell becomes more and more dense; the vibrations being transmitted by the air inside the receiver to the glass, and thence to the air outside.

The vibrations of the sounding body are communicated to the air, not by propelling individual particles of it through space like a shot, but by setting up to-and-fro motions which knock, so to speak, one particle against its neighbour, after which it rebounds and finally returns to its original position; just as the excursions of a pendulum get smaller by degrees, until at last they cease entirely. The neighbouring particle imparts the motion to another one, and also returns to its original position, and so on. Alternate condensations and rarefactions of the air are thus produced, travelling outwards from the sounding body, each condensation together with its succeeding rarefaction being termed a sound wave. Let it be understood that while these waves are travelling along, the particles of which they are formed merely execute a very limited movement to and fro. It must further be observed that the sound waves do not only travel in one direction, but in every direction all around. We have therefore to think of them as hollow spheres whose diameter increases in size as they proceed on their journey.

We have thus seen how a vibratory motion is communicated to the air and transmitted through it in the form of waves. These waves, striking the drumhead of the ear, cause it to vibrate; the vibrations thus set up are transmitted by the auditory nerve to the brain where they are perceived as sound.

Now as sound travels in waves like light, we should expect to see it reflected like light; and that such is really the case is proved by the echo. When the sound waves strike against a wall, a cliff, or any other opposing surface, they return to us provided the reflecting surface is at right angles to a line drawn from the point where we stand. If this is not the case the echo will be sent in another direction, and it may be heard by other persons, but not by him who produced the original sound. The reflecting surface must also be far enough away to allow the ear to distinguish the echo from the original sound, or the two will merge into each other. If two reflecting surfaces are inclined towards each other in such a way as to throw the reflection of the same sound to and fro, the echo is repeated—in some cases, over and over again, each time, of course, less loudly, until at last it dies away altogether. There are wonderful instances of this on record, one of the most famous being the echo between the wings of a castle not far from Milan, which repeats the report of a pistol sixty times.

An illustration of the reflection of sound by curved roofs or ceilings may be found in the whispering gallery of St. Paul's, where the faintest sound is conveyed from one side of the dome to the other, but is not heard at any intermediate point. Inconvenient secrets have been thus revealed, an instance of which has been cited by Sir John Herschel. "In one of the cathedrals in Sicily the confessional was so placed that the whispers of the penitents were reflected by the curved roof, and brought to a focus at a distant part of the edifice. The focus was discovered by accident, and for some time the person who discovered it took pleasure in hearing, and in bringing his friends to hear, utterances intended for the priest alone. One day it is said his own wife occupied the penitential stool, and both he and his friends were thus made acquainted with secrets which were the reverse of amusing to one of the party." ('On Sound,' by Tyndall. London: Longmans & Co., 2nd ed., p. 16.)

VIBRATIONS may be either simple or compound. *Simple* vibrations follow the laws of a pendulum, and are, therefore, also called *pendular* vibrations. An instance of *compound* vibrations is furnished by a string, which swings not only up and down and from side to side, but also in segments. Every form of compound vibration may be analysed into, or may be said to be composed of, simple or pendular vibrations, but no explanation of this very complicated matter can be attempted here.

SIMPLE TONES, such as the highest notes of the pianoforte, or tuning-forks mounted on suitable resonance boxes, are the result of *simple* vibrations.

COMPOUND TONES are the result of *compound* vibrations. The ear has the power of analysing a compound tone, and of dividing it into its component parts. This amounts to saying that when we hear a compound tone "the ear experiences the same effect *as if* a certain series of simple tones having definite musical pitches and very different degrees of loudness were sounded together. Of course, no such tones are really sounded, but as the mental effect is the same as if they were, it becomes convenient to speak of *compound* musical tone as *consisting* of a series of *simple partial* tones, and to reason upon these partial tones as if they alone existed, instead of the compound tone itself." ('Pronunciation for Singers,' by Alexander J. Ellis. London: J. Curwen & Sons, p. 8.)

THE FORCE OR LOUDNESS of a tone depends upon the amplitude or largeness of the vibrations. This is easily proved. Draw a bow smartly over a string. You will see large vibrations and hear a loud tone, and in the same proportion as the vibrations grow smaller, the tone will become fainter, until at last both will die away. Loudness also depends upon the distance at which the tone is heard; the nearer the instrument producing the tone is to the ear the greater is its force. This is a matter of every-day experience, and needs no demonstration.

And lastly, loudness depends upon the density of the air in which the tone is generated. We have already had a proof of this by observing that the sound of a bell under a receiver is fainter the more the receiver is exhausted, and that it becomes louder the more air is re-admitted. In a similar manner the loudness of a tone generated in the rarefied air of a high mountain is less than that of a tone generated under otherwise identical conditions in the denser air of a valley below. It must be observed that the loudness of a tone does not depend upon the density of the air in which it is *heard*, but upon that in which it is *generated*. Hence a cannon fired in the rarefied air of a high mountain will not be heard in the denser air of the valley; while the sound of the same cannon with the same charge when fired below will be distinctly heard above.

THE PITCH or height of a tone depends solely upon the rate of vibration; the greater the number of vibrations in a given time the higher being the pitch.

Fewer than sixteen vibrations per second are not perceived by the ear as a tone, but merely as a succession of separate shocks; and more than 38,000 vibrations per second altogether cease to produce a sensation of sound.

The following table shows the vibrational number of a few extreme tones used in music:—

Large organs	C_{IV} .	$16\frac{1}{2}$	vibrations per second.
Latest grand pianos	A_{IV} .	$27\frac{1}{2}$	,, ,,
Ordinary modern pianos . . .	C_{III} .	33	,, ,,
Double bass	E_{III} .	$41\frac{1}{4}$	,, ,,
Pianos with usual compass . .	A^{III} .	3520	,, ,,
Pianos with exceptional compass .	C^{IV} .	4224	,, ,,
Piccolo flute	D^{IV} .	4752	,, ,,

The lowest of these tones are too near the point at which the ear perceives sound only as a series of successive shocks; they are therefore musically imperfect, and can only be used in connection with their higher octaves. The highest tones of the above table on the other hand are shrill and unpleasant. The tones which can be used in music to best advantage have from 40 to 4000 vibrations per second, and cover a compass of seven octaves.

The lowest tone of a bass voice is probably F_{III} with 44 vibrations per second, and the highest limit on record is that of "Bastardella," who is said to have sung B^{11} with 1980 vibrations per second. According to these figures the entire range of the human voice covers about five octaves and a half.

COMPOUND TONES, as we have seen before, consist of a number of partial tones. These the human ear is capable of distinguishing, and the faculty of thus analysing a tone may be greatly increased by properly directed practice. But Helmholtz has provided us with "resonators" enabling us to reinforce each of the partials separately and thereby to recognise each one of them without any difficulty. These resonators consist of hollow globes made of glass or of metal, with two openings at opposite points. One of these openings is large and has sharp edges, while the other one passes through a sort of nipple suitable for insertion in the ear. If we stop one ear and put the nipple of a resonator in the other, most of the tones produced about us will be made very dull; but if the proper tone of the resonator be sounded it will strike the ear most powerfully. A series of such resonators, tuned to different notes, will enable even musically untrained ears to distinguish faint partial tones, though accompanied by others which are very strong.

Upon analysing a number of compound tones, we find the arrangement of the partials as follows :—

I. The prime tone by which the pitch of the compound is generally allowed to be determined.

II. A partial an octave above the prime.

III. A partial a fifth above No. II., or a twelfth above the prime.

IV. A partial a fourth above No. III., or two octaves above the prime.

V. A partial a major third above No. IV., or two octaves and a major third above the prime.

VI. A partial a minor third above No. V., or two octaves and a fifth above the prime.

VII. A partial almost exactly a minor third above No. VI., or two octaves and a sub-minor seventh above the prime.

VIII. A partial one tone above No. VII., or three octaves above the prime.

The compound tone C would consequently be expressed in musical notation thus:—

There are many more higher partials in some compound tones than the above eight. The low tones of a harmonium, for instance, have at least twice the number, and the tones of a good bass voice have at least twenty partials. But those mentioned above are the most important of the series.

The partials occur in every compound tone in the same relative position. This does not mean that they are all present in every case; it simply means that the order in which the series is established is unchangeable; thus a tone may contain only partials Nos. 1, 3, and 5, or Nos. 1, 2, 4, and 8, all the others being absent; but no partial can, under any circumstances, crop up out of the regular order, say between Nos. 1 and 2, or between Nos. 2 and 3, and so forth.

We have so far only touched upon two properties of

---

* Slightly below the pitch here indicated.

tone, namely *loudness* and *pitch*. We are now in a position to discuss the third, which is *quality*.

THE QUALITY of a tone is "that peculiarity which distinguishes the musical tone of a violin from that of a flute, or that of a clarionet, or that of the human voice, when all these instruments produce the same note at the same pitch." ('The Sensations of Tone,' by Helmholtz. Translated by Alexander J. Ellis. London: Longmans, Green & Co., p. 17.) The quality of tone is generally described as depending upon the *form* of the vibrations. "This assertion which physicists hitherto based simply upon the fact of their knowing that the quality of tone could not possibly depend on the periodic time of vibration, or on its amplitude, will be strictly examined hereafter. It will be shown to be so far correct, that every different quality of tone requires a different form of vibration; but on the other hand it will also appear that different forms of vibration may correspond to the same quality of tone." (Helmholtz, op. cit., p. 32.)

If we could detach the prime tones of compounds from their upper partials we should find them, loudness and pitch being alike, undistinguishable from each other, no matter by what instrument they were produced; and it is the co-existence with the prime tone of its upper partials, their relative position and their relative degree of loudness, which make the difference between the tones produced by various instruments. That such is really the case Helmholtz has demonstrated by experiment in the following manner: he arranged a series of tuning-forks, corresponding to the partials of a compound tone as described before. He kept them in constant motion by electro-magnets, and a resonator was attached to every one of them which he could open and shut at pleasure by simply touching the digitals of a little keyboard. He was thus in a position to reinforce any or all of the tones of the tuning-forks in various degrees of loudness; and he found that he could by these means imitate, not only the quality of most musical instruments, but also that of several vowel sounds.

We therefore come to the conclusion that the quality of a tone depends—

1. Upon the number of partials of which the tone consists.
2. Upon their relative position.
3. Upon their relative degree of loudness.

This subject is further illustrated by the following rules:

1. "*Simple Tones* have a very soft, pleasant sound, free from all roughness, but wanting in power, and dull at low pitches."

2. "*Musical Tones*, which are accompanied by a moderately loud series of the lower upper partial tones, up to about the sixth partial, are more harmonious and musical. Compared with simple tones they are rich and splendid, while they are at the same time perfectly sweet and soft if the higher upper partials are absent."

3. "If only the uneven partials are present, the quality of tone is *hollow*, and, when a large number of such upper partials are present, *nasal*. When the prime tone predominates, the quality of the tone is *rich* or *full;* but when the prime tone is not sufficiently superior in strength to the upper partials, the quality of the tone is *poor* or *empty*."

4. "When partial tones higher than the sixth or seventh are very distinct, the quality of the tone is *cutting* and *rough*. The degree of harshness may be very different. When their force is inconsiderable the

higher upper partials do not essentially detract from the musical applicability of the compound tones; on the contrary, they are useful in giving character and expression to the music." (Helmholtz, op. cit., p. 172.)

Hitherto we have only spoken of what may be described as the *inherent* quality of tone. But in addition to this there are other peculiarities of which notice must be taken, namely, the various ways of *beginning* and of *ending* a tone, and those more or less noticeable *accompanying noises* from which no tone is absolutely free.

Most people know that it makes a great difference to a tone whether it is attacked abruptly or gradually, with a thump or with a gentle touch. Striking the string of a piano with a felt hammer or with a stick does not produce the same tone. In a similar manner a tone is greatly affected by being allowed to die away gradually or by being stopped suddenly. Thus while the tone of a pianoforte string struck in the ordinary way is fuller and more lasting than that of a pizzicato tone on a violin, yet the latter is much more piercing and penetrating. But the differences of attack and of release are in no case more characteristic than in the human voice, where they are noted in the form of different letters, as for instance the consonants B, D, G, P, T, and K.

The accompanying noises, independently of what we have called the *inherent* quality, by which one tone may be distinguished from another, is illustrated in wind instruments by the hissing of the air striking against the sharp edge of the mouthpiece, and in string instruments by the scraping of the bow. Similar effects are produced in the human voice by pronouncing the letters F, V, S, Z, TH, R, and L. Even the vowels themselves are accompanied by faint noises similar to those produced by whispering the same sounds.

STRINGED INSTRUMENTS produce tone by the vibrations of the strings. The number of these vibrations within a given time depends (1) on the length, (2) on the tension, (3) on the thickness, and (4) on the density of the strings; that is to say, the shorter, the tighter, the finer, and the lighter the string, the more rapid will be the vibrations in a given time; in other words the higher will be the pitch of the tone produced.

FLUTE or FLUE PIPES produce tone by the vibrations of the elastic column of air in the tube caused by a stream of air being driven against the sharp edges of some opening. The number of these vibrations within a given time depends almost entirely upon the length of the column, and is but slightly modified by its diameter and by the nature of the mouthpiece. The shorter the column the greater the number of vibrations, and *vice versâ*. If, therefore, we take two pipes, one half as long as the other, the short one will produce a tone an octave higher than the long one. We are all familiar with an illustration of this by the pipes of an organ; there is a separate pipe for every tone, and their length increases on a regular scale.

REED INSTRUMENTS may have stiff or flexible reeds or tongues.

STIFF REEDS are made of metal. They do not produce tone by any vibrations of their own, but by cutting the air which is driven past them into puffs. The pitch of these tones is regulated by the length and elasticity of the reeds. A different reed is therefore required for every new tone. Such reeds may be used free, as in the harmonium, concertina, accordion, &c., or they may be used in connection with tubes, as in the organ. When this is the case the reed governs the vibrations of the column of air. If, therefore, the tone is to derive any advantage from the association of the reed with the tube, the length of the tube must be such that one of its partial tones corresponds with the vibrations of the reed.

FLEXIBLE REEDS are generally made of wood and they are always associated with a tube of some kind. They produce tone by their own vibrations which, however, is overpowered and governed by the vibrations of the column of air. The pitch of these tones therefore depends chiefly upon the length of the tube, and is but little influenced by the length and elasticity of the reed.

Professor Tyndall says: "Perhaps the simplest illustra-

II.—A REED. (*From Tyndall.*)

tion of the action of a reed commanded by its aërial column is furnished by a common wheaten straw. At about an inch from a knot I bury my penknife in this straw, *s r′* (Pl. II.), to a depth of about one-fourth of the straw's diameter, and, turning the blade flat, pass it upwards towards the knot, thus raising a strip of the straw nearly an inch in length. This strip, *r r′*, is to be our reed, and the straw itself is to be our pipe. It is now eight inches long. When blown into, it emits this decidedly musical sound. I now cut it so as to make its length six inches; the pitch is higher: with a length of four inches, the pitch is higher still. I make it two inches, the sound is now very shrill indeed. In all these experiments we had the same reed, which was compelled to accommodate itself throughout to the requirements of the vibrating column of air." (Op. cit., p. 194.)

THE CLARIONET is an instrument of this kind in which the tone of the reed is overpowered and governed by the vibrations of the column of air; but the pitch in this instance also depends, to some extent, upon the narrowing by the lips of the slit between the reed and its frame.

THE HAUTBOY AND THE BASSOON are similar instruments, but they have *double* reeds with a slit between them through which the air is forced.

IN THE HORN AND TRUMPET the lips of the performer supply the double reeds. The lips are but very slightly elastic, and therefore cannot produce tone by their own independent vibrations; but they are easily set in motion by the pressure of the vibrating column of air. In the older instruments of this class the tones are limited to the prime tone, with its harmonic upper partials, of the tube, and the particular tone to be produced depends upon the tension of the lips and upon the power of blast. Modern horns and trumpets, &c., are perfected by the addition of keys supplying the tones which were formerly wanting.

THE HUMAN VOICE is also generally described as a reed instrument, a statement which requires some qualification. We shall, however, be in a better position to enter into this question after the mechanism of the vocal apparatus has been explained, and we defer until then a discussion of the subject.

RESONANCE is caused when a sounding body communicates its vibrations to another body; or when, in other words, the second body is thrown into co-vibrations with the first body. The following is an illustration with which most persons are familiar. Strike a tuning-fork and it will produce a tone, but a very faint tone only. Now put the vibrating tuning-fork with its handle upon a table. The vibrations of the fork will be communicated to the table, that is to say, the table will be thrown into co-vibrations with the tuning-fork, with the result of greatly increasing the sound. The sound of strings in the piano, harp, violin, &c., is reinforced in a similar manner, i.e. by direct communication of the vibrations of the strings to the sounding-board or to the body of the instrument. In these cases the loudness of the resulting sound is increased because a larger body of air is set vibrating.

The vibrations of a sounding body may, however, also be communicated to another body without being in contact with it at all. This may be distinguished as *sympathetic* resonance. The following illustrations will make the matter clear.

Roll up a sheet of paper so as to form a tube six inches long, and about one inch in diameter. Strike an ordinary C tuning-fork and hold it close to one of the ends of the tube. The tone, which was at first scarcely audible, will now be heard all over the room. We can, to some extent, shorten or lengthen the tube, and yet get resonance, but we obtain the greatest amount of reinforcement for the sound of our high C by a column of air six inches long.

If we convert the open pipe into a closed one by putting one end of the tube upon the table, and then hold the vibrating fork over the aperture, we find the resonance produced by it very insignificant. But if we substitute for the high C tuning-fork another one producing the C an octave lower we get again a very strong resonance. We here find that with a closed pipe the best resonance is produced by a tone an octave lower than is necessary for getting the best resonance with an open pipe of the same length. This is equal to saying that by opening a closed pipe we raise its pitch by an octave. Another very simple and instructive experiment in the same direction is this: Take a *tall* bottle with a wide neck, such as is generally used for preserving fruit; strike a high C tuning-fork, and hold it over the empty bottle. There will be no reinforcement, and the vibrating fork will produce as little sound over the bottle as away from it. Now pour water into the bottle gently, and with as little noise as possible, thereby shortening the air-column inside, and you will find the sound of the tuning-fork intensified by degrees, until at last, continuing to pour in water, the tone will, at a certain point, burst forth quite loudly. If still more water is poured in, the tone will decrease again as gradually as it was at first intensified, until at last it dies away altogether.

In a similar manner jars of different height may be operated upon with tuning-forks of different pitch. Or the experiment may be altered as follows: Strike a C tuning-fork, and hold it over an ordinary tumbler; then push a piece of cardboard over the glass, reducing its aperture. The result will be a gradual reinforcement of the tone of the tuning-fork, until at a certain point it is heard quite loudly. Push the cardboard *beyond* this point and the tone will become gradually fainter, until it quite dies away.

All these trials show that there is, for every tone, an air column of a certain size which most powerfully reinforces that tone.

There is yet another illustration of sympathetic resonance

which is very interesting. If the strings of two violins are tuned exactly alike, and a string of one is bowed, the corresponding string of the other violin will also begin to vibrate, though the two instruments are not in contact with each other.

"Tuning-forks are the most difficult to set in sympathetic vibration. To effect this they must be fastened on sounding boxes which have been exactly tuned to their tone. If we have two such forks of exactly the same pitch, and excite one by a violin bow, the other will begin to vibrate in sympathy, even if placed at the farther end of the room, and it will continue to sound when the first is damped. The astonishing nature of such a case of sympathetic vibration will appear if we merely compare the heavy and powerful mass of steel set in motion, with the light yielding mass of air,* which produces effect by such small motive power that it could not stir the lightest spring which was not in tune with the fork. With such forks, the time required to set them in full swing by sympathetic action is also of sensible duration, and the slightest disagreement in pitch is sufficient to produce a sensible diminution in the sympathetic effect. By sticking a piece of wax to one prong of the second fork, sufficient to make it vibrate once in a second less than the first—a difference of pitch scarcely sensible to the finest ear—the sympathetic vibration will be wholly destroyed." (Helmholtz, op. cit., p. 63.)

* Steel is, bulk for bulk, about 6000 times as heavy as air.

SPEAKING AND SINGING.

VOICE is sound originated in the larynx, and may be produced by any animal possessing that organ.

SPEAKING is voice modified in the cavity of the mouth. The medium of conveying his thoughts, it is the attribute of man alone, raising him above all animals.

SINGING is a higher development of the same power, being, in fact, sustained musical speaking.

It is not possible to draw a clear line between singing and speaking, as both are actions of the same organs. There must be speech in song, or it would lose all the charm attached to the distinct rendering of the words. There must also be a *certain amount* of song in speech, or it would soon become unbearable by its dreariness and monotony.

Nevertheless, singing and speaking differ from each other, and are in some respects even antagonistic. Mr. Ellis (op. cit., p. 1) distinguishes the following points :—

1. "SINGING AND SPEAKING DIFFER IN COMPASS.—In singing, a good and fine quality of tone is sought to be attained at pitches varying by at least a twelfth, and sometimes two octaves or even more. In speaking, an audible quality of tone is desired, but one which is not strictly musical, at pitches generally within a fifth, and only occasionally extending to an octave."

2. "SINGING IS AT SUSTAINED, SPEAKING AT GLIDING

PITCH.—In singing, a tone has to be sustained for a considerable time at an invariable pitch. In speaking, not only is the length of time for which any sound is sustained much less, sometimes necessarily very short indeed, but the pitch at which it is delivered is uncertain and variable, and constantly rising or falling, sometimes first rising and then falling, or first falling and then rising, for the same spoken sound."

3. "SINGING REQUIRES A CLEAR, SPEAKING AN IMPEDED PASSAGE FOR THE BREATH.—In singing, a good quality of musical tone can only be attained by peculiar adjustments of the cavities between the larynx and the lips, which generally imply that they are unchoked or unimpeded; and by a peculiar arrangement of the larynx itself, which implies, on the contrary, that it is so choked and impeded that the wind has to force its way through it from the lungs. In speaking, the upper cavities have to be choked and impeded in many ways more or less injurious to musical qualities of tone, and sometimes entirely destructive of any musical tone whatever, allowing mere noise to pass, or actually preventing any sound at all from passing. And the larynx has occasionally to be so open that no musical sound whatever can be produced, except by a further adjustment of the lips and tongue to produce whistling, an effect not admitted in speech."

4. "SINGING HAS TO BE RAPID AND SLURRED, WHERE SPEAKING CANNOT BE SO.—In singing, the melody often requires the notes to be sung with great rapidity, and at other times to be slurred into each other. In any languages, as the English, where the vowels are separated by numerous consonants, this rapidity is impossible, and the slurring becomes equally impossible from the necessity of separating the musical by unmusical sounds."

The English language is generally supposed to offer greater difficulties to the singer than either Italian, Portuguese, Spanish, French, or German.

"What a stumbling block English proves to foreigners was exemplified by Duprez, who, in the recitative in 'William Tell,' used to say 'My country and my *face*' (faith)." ('Dramatic Singing,' by W. H. Walshe, M.D. London: Kegan Paul, Trench & Co., p. 77.)

What beauties, on the other hand, it possesses with regard to speaking may be best seen from the following opinion of Jacob Grimm, the greatest philologist of modern times. "The English language possesses a power which probably never stood at the command of any other nation. This singularly happy development and condition has been the result of an intimate union of two of the noblest languages, the Teutonic and the Romance; the former supplying the material ground-work, the latter the spiritual conceptions. In truth, the English language, which by no mere accident has produced and upborne the greatest and most predominant poet of modern times (I can, of course, only mean Shakespeare) may with all right be called a world language; and, like the English people, appears destined hereafter to prevail with a sway more extensive than its present one, over all portions of the globe. For in wealth, good sense, and closeness of structure, no other of the languages at this day spoken deserves to be compared with it—not even our own German, which is torn even as we are torn, and must rid itself of its defects before it can enter into the lists as a competitor with English." (James Hunt, op. cit., p. 226.)

THE ANATOMY AND PHYSIOLOGY OF THE VOCAL ORGAN.

THE HUMAN VOICE considered as a musical instrument consists of four parts:—

1. THE CHEST OR THORAX and the LUNGS containing the air which is the *motor element*.

2. THE WINDPIPE OR TRACHEA, in which the air is carried up and down.

3. THE VOICE-BOX OR LARYNX, in which are situated the vocal ligaments forming the *vibrating element*.

4. THE UPPER PART OF THE THROAT OR PHARYNX, THE MOUTH AND THE NASAL PASSAGES forming the *resonator*.

THE CHEST OR THORAX is an air-tight chamber formed by the *spine* at the back, by twelve *ribs* on either side, by the *breast-bone* or *sternum* and the *collar-bones* or *clavicles* in front, by the *root of the neck* above, and by the *midriff* or *diaphragm* below. Each higher rib being a little shorter than the one below, it follows that the shape of the chest as a whole must be conical. The chest is, in other words, considerably broader below than above.

THE RIBS are, with the exception of the two lowest on each side, which are called the *floating ribs*, attached behind to the spine, and in front to the breast-bone, just as a bucket handle is fastened to the bucket; and the ribs are capable of being raised or lowered just as the bucket handle may be moved up and down. In a state of rest,

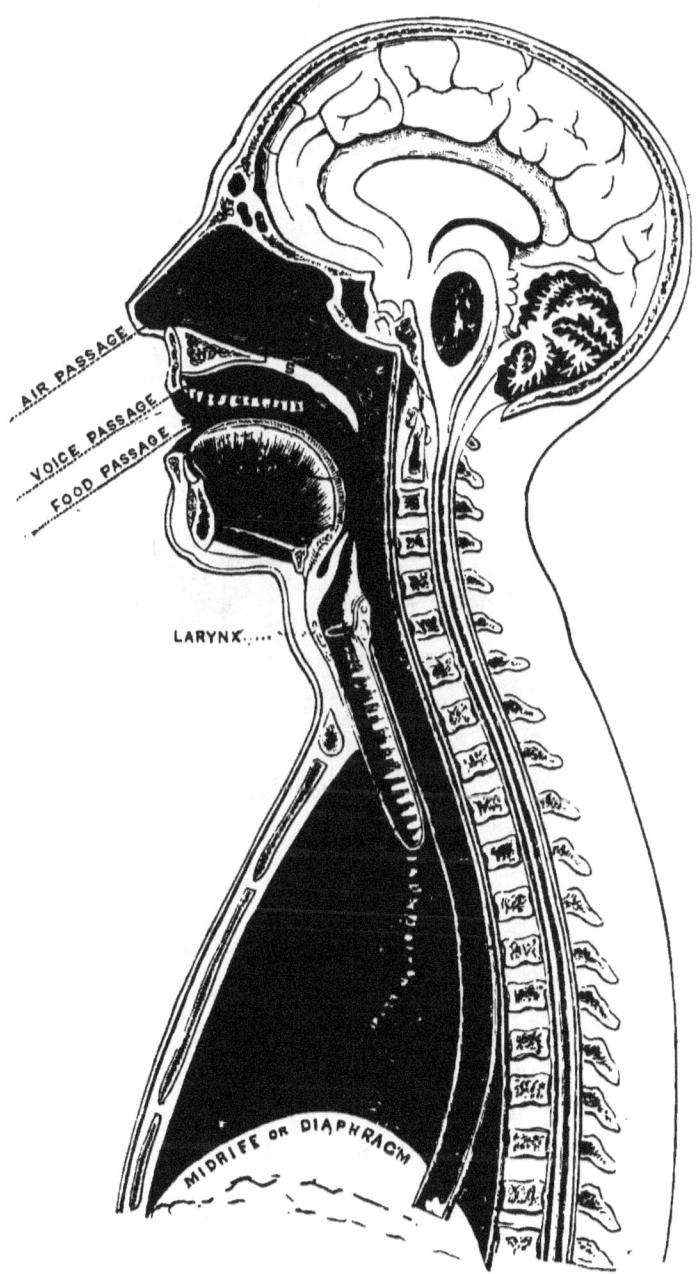

III.—SECTION OF THE HUMAN BODY. (*Adapted from Küss and Czermak.*)
N, Nasal passages ; H, Hard palate ; S, Soft palate ; E, Eustachian tube.

however, they take a position slanting forwards and downwards.

THE MIDRIFF OR DIAPHRAGM (*see* Pl. III.) is a large powerful muscle which, as implied by the name, serves as a *partition* dividing the chest from the abdomen. In a state of rest the midriff has the shape of a basin put upside down, that is to say, it arches up into the chest. It has a number of fibres extending from the centre of the lower surface downwards and outwards to the ribs, and we must particularly notice two very strong bundles called the *pillars* of the midriff which go from the middle of the

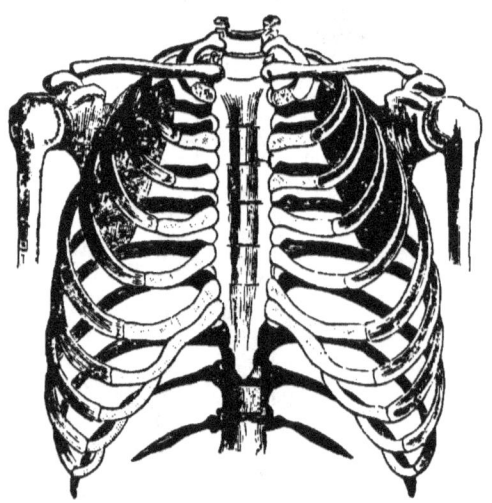

IV.—FRAMEWORK OF THE CHEST.

diaphragm to the spine. When these fibres and pillars contract, the midriff is not only considerably flattened, thereby increasing the capacity of the chest at the expense of the abdomen, it is also pulled down in its entirety, so that its action somewhat resembles that of a piston in the cylinder of a pump.

But more: its outer rim is attached to the lower ribs,

and as these are moveable the arched-up centre of the midriff cannot possibly be directed downwards without its circular edge being elevated, thereby forcing the ribs forward and outward. It is quite clear, therefore, that the chest is, by this action of the diaphragm, enlarged in three directions, namely, in height, in depth, and in width.

When the muscular fibres which have just been described relax, the midriff arches up again as before, and it is assisted in this act by the return of the stomach and of the intestines to their original position. The result of this is, of course, the reduction of the chest to its original dimensions.

THE MUSCLES OF THE CHEST.—Each pair of ribs is united by two sets of muscles, the outer *intercostals* and the inner *intercostals*. The *outer* intercostals by their contraction raise the ribs, and they are assisted by various other muscles connecting the ribs with parts of the spine above them. If these muscles relax, the ribs will, by their own weight, resume their former position, and in this they are assisted by the contraction of the *inner* intercostals and of other muscles connecting the ribs with that bony ring between the spinal column and the lower extremities called the *pelvis*. By these agencies the dimensions of the cavity of the chest from back to front and from side to side are alternately increased and diminished.

We must notice in addition a set of muscles uniting the ribs with the shoulders and the shoulder-blades, enabling us to raise and to lower the upper part of the chest and the collar-bones in conjunction with the shoulders. By the action of these the height of the cavity of the chest may also be alternately increased or diminished, though only to a very limited extent.

THE LUNGS are contained in the chest, which they fit

exactly, and of which they occupy by far the largest part, leaving but a small portion for the heart and blood-vessels. They are two separate bodies united only by means of the branches of the windpipe called the *bronchi*. The lungs

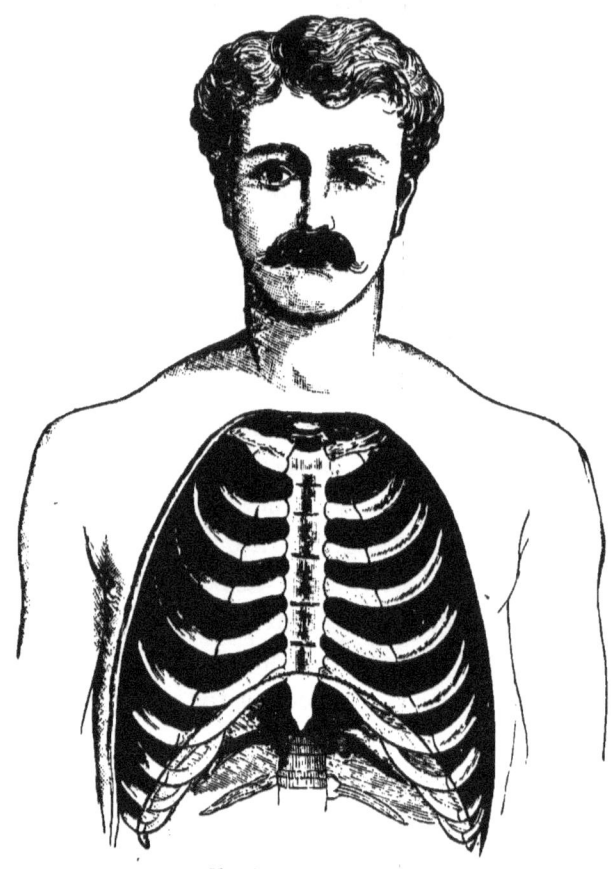

V.—CHEST AND LUNGS.

The curved line at the bottom of the drawing indicates the Midriff or Diaphragm.

are coneshaped, the pointed part being above, and the broad part below. They consist of different divisions called *lobes;* these are made up of sub-divisions called *lobules*, and these again consist of little clusters of minute air-cells resembling bunches of grapes. It has been calculated that there are no less than *six hundred millions* of these air-cells in the lungs of a full-grown man. Between these air-cells there are, circulating in all directions, the *capillary vessels* receiving the blood from the heart. The right lung is larger than the left, and it has

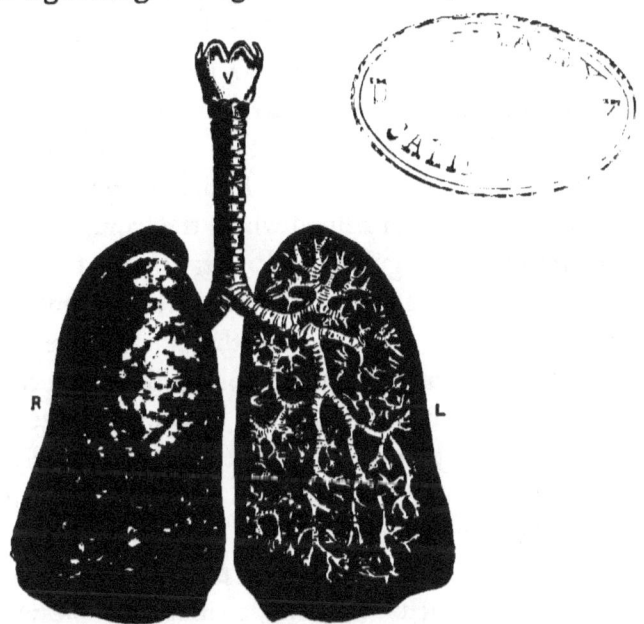

VI.—THE LUNGS, ETC. (*Adapted from Niemeyer.*)

V, Voice-box or larynx; W, Windpipe or trachea; R, Right lung; L, Left lung. In the section of the left lung are indicated the ramifications of the left bronchus.

three lobes, the upper, the middle, and the lower; the left lung has but two lobes, the upper and the lower.

THE PLEURÆ.—Each lung is enclosed in a double bag called the *pleura*. Take a bladder, expel the air from it, and double it up by putting the fist into it. The fist represents the lung, and the doubled bladder a part of the pleura; both together will give a tolerably clear idea of the whole arrangement. The outer bag forms a lining to the walls of the chest, and the inner one serves as a covering to the lung to which it closely adheres. The lobes of the lungs are separated from each other by infoldings of the inner bag. The interior surfaces of the two bags which are thus in close contact are very smooth, and they are kept moist with a lubricating fluid which enables them to move upon each other without friction. It is the main object of the pleuræ to keep the lungs in position, and to facilitate the working of the chest and of the lungs in respiration.

THE WINDPIPE OR TRACHEA (*see* Pl. VI.) is the tube by means of which the air is carried into and out of the lungs. It descends from the upper part of the throat, and is kept open by from 18 to 20 rings formed of gristle or cartilage. The rings are open behind where the windpipe comes into contact with the gullet or *œsophagus*, and the ends of the rings are united by the same fibrous membrane which unites them in front and at the sides. The windpipe is capable of being slightly prolonged or shortened, and widened or narrowed, and its interior is covered with a mucous membrane. This tube may be readily felt and handled through the skin, and it will be understood from the above description why it is that, though firm and capable of resisting injury, it possesses at the same time sufficient elasticity to yield to moderate pressure and to movements from all directions.

THE BRONCHIAL PASSAGES OR BRONCHI (Pl. VI.)—The windpipe having, in its downward course, entered the chest, it there divides into two branches, one for each lung; these are called the *bronchi*. Each bronchus enters the lung, and divides shortly afterwards into two lesser ones. These again divide and subdivide, spreading out, like the roots and fibres of a tree, until at last their ramifications end in the microscopic air-cells of the lungs.

THE MUCOUS MEMBRANE with which the windpipe is lined extends upwards through the upper part of the throat into the nasal cavities, and downwards into the smallest bronchial tubes in the lungs. It is covered with a multitude of mucous glands, secreting that thin glairy fluid called *mucus*, which keeps the membrane in a moist state. It is soft, smooth, more or less red, and protected by a layer of minute cells. These, again, are studded with innumerable, extremely fine, hair-like projections called the *cilia*, all pointing in an outward direction, and continually swaying backwards and forwards, thus removing out of the air-passages any excess of mucus which would otherwise accumulate in them and obstruct them.

RESPIRATION.—The function of the lungs is respiration, which may be considered from a chemical and from a mechanical point of view. The *venous* blood is driven from the right lobe of the heart into the capillary vessels of the lungs, which are separated from the air-cells by a skin so exceedingly fine that it does not prevent the blood receiving from the air the oxygen which it wants in exchange for the carbonic acid which it wishes to get rid of. The result of this interchange is that the dark-blue venous blood is found, on leaving the capillaries, to have been changed into bright-red *arterial* blood. This then passes into the left lobe of the heart whence it is pumped up the main artery through the whole system.

The object of respiration, therefore, chemically considered, is to bring into the blood the oxygen, without which we could not live, and to carry away the carbonic acid which, if retained, would soon poison us. The importance of this cannot be overrated, for life or death depends upon it, and respiration from a mechanical point of view, as in the production of the voice, is, comparatively speaking, but a small matter.

In this section we have mainly to deal with breathing mechanically considered. This subject is best studied in a pair of calf's lungs, which may easily be obtained in any butcher's shop under the name of *lights*. The calf's lungs are very similar to those of man, and a few experiments upon them will be found more instructive than any descriptions and explanations that could possibly be given. It is, of course, necessary to make these investigations immediately after the animal has been killed, and before the lungs have become cold.

We see that the calf's lungs are, as in those of human beings, two separate bodies, united only by means of the windpipe and its branches. We also notice how much broader they are below than above. This point ought to be carefully verified, for reasons which will appear later on. If we press upon the lungs we find that they are elastic and yielding to the touch; also that they emit a peculiar whizzing sound. Insert a tube into the windpipe, and blow into it, when the lungs will very considerably increase in size. Tie the windpipe up with a piece of string, and the lungs will remain in this inflated condition. Remove the string, and the air previously blown into the lungs will escape again, and they will dwindle down to their original size. Observe that only that air escapes which you blew into the lungs. There was air in them before you commenced your experiment, and this remains in them. You may squeeze some of it out by pressing upon the lungs, but even after doing that a large quantity of air will remain in them.

These experiments upon the calf's lungs give us some conception of the nature of respiration which is carried on in our own bodies under very similar circumstances. If we draw a breath we inflate our lungs as we inflated the calf's lungs by blowing into them. By holding our breath we keep our lungs inflated as we kept the calf's lungs inflated by tying up the windpipe, and by letting our breath go we allow our lungs to dwindle down as the calf's lungs dwindled down when we removed the string with which we had tied up the windpipe. As after this a large quantity of air remains in the calf's lungs, so it also does in our own; and as even with a great deal of squeezing and of pressing we cannot remove all the air out of the calf's lungs, so we are also unable, even by making the greatest effort, to eject all the air from our own lungs.

The air which cannot be ejected from the lungs by any effort is called *residual air*.

The additional amount remaining in the lungs after an ordinary expiration is called *supplemental air*.

The air over and above this passing into and out of the lungs in quiet breathing is called *tidal air*.

And finally the air which may be inhaled by the deepest possible inspiration is called *complementary air*.

We may consequently look upon the lungs as divided into zones, and we shall find that—

1. In the bottom zone the air is nearly stagnant, and never pure.
2. In the middle zone it is fairly flowing, and less impure.
3. In the top zone it is continually renewed, and nearly resembles the air we inhale.

RESPIRATION, as we have thus seen, consists of two acts, *inspiration* and *expiration*. Let us now consider how these two acts are accomplished.

The lungs have not the power of inflating themselves;

they are quite passive. But the chest enlarges, and the lungs are obliged to do the same, because they are pressed by the air to the chest walls, and compelled to follow their every movement, just as a stone is held to a boy's leather "sucker." In other words, when the chest enlarges, the air rushes into the lungs, thereby inflating them, in order to prevent the formation of a vacuum which would otherwise be created in the pleural cavity, that is to say, between the two bags in which, as we have seen before, the lung is enclosed, and one of which adheres to the lung and the other to the chest. This constitutes *in*spiration.

This act of *in*spiration is quickly followed by the expulsion of the air. The lungs are very elastic, and they have a constant tendency to return to their original form. As soon as the contraction of the inspiratory muscles ceases, this elasticity, which till then has been opposed, re-asserts itself, and the lungs contract. The diaphragm and the chest walls follow the lungs just as the latter adhered to the former in inspiration. In addition to this there is the natural impulse of the chest walls, of the midriff, and of the walls of the abdomen, &c., to return to their original position. The air is by these acts expelled, and this constitutes *ex*piration.

While, then, in ordinary breathing *in*spiration is the result of muscular contraction, and, therefore, *active*, *ex*piration is the result of the elasticity of the organs which had been opposed by *in*spiration, and consequently *passive*. But as we have the power of forced *in*spiration, so we have also the power of forced *ex*piration; and if we make use of this power, *ex*piration ceases to be passive, and also becomes the result of muscular contraction. The muscles called into play in inspiration as well as in expiration have already been described on p. 41.

We have seen that the chest may be enlarged in three different ways.

1. By the descent of the midriff or diaphragm. In this method the abdomen is pushed out of the way and the chest walls are gradually dilated from below upwards, but the shoulders remain unmoved. This method of chest expansion is known as *midriff, diaphragmatic,* or *abdominal* breathing.

2. By sideways extension of the ribs. In this method also the shoulders remain unmoved. This constitutes *rib* breathing, or *lateral* or *costal* breathing.

3. By raising the shoulders with the collar-bones, the shoulder-blades, and the upper part of the chest. This is *collar-bone, clavicular,* or *scapular* breathing.

In taking a full, deep inspiration, midriff and rib breathing take place almost together and assist each other—that is to say, the midriff contracts and flattens, and immediately afterwards the ribs extend sideways—with this difference, however, that in men the action of the midriff takes a larger share in the work than the ribs, while in women, on the contrary, the movement of the ribs is greater than that of the midriff.

" By way of illustrating this curious difference of breathing in men and women the following anecdote, which has the recommendation of being strictly true, may perhaps amuse the reader. Some time ago a troupe of 'Female Minstrels,' calling themselves, I believe, 'The American Amazons,' made a tour in this country. Their faces were blackened in the orthodox fashion, and they were in male attire, wearing tight-fitting garments of a peculiar kind. Two friends, both medical men, went to hear them (or perhaps to see them, I am not sure which), when Mr. A. remarked that two of the performers were men. Mr. B.

E

did not see it, even when the individuals were pointed out to him, and asked his friend for the reasons for his opinion. 'Why,' said Mr. A., 'I see it by their abdominal breathing.' And sure enough Mr. B. now saw it too, and there was no mistake about it; for in the two suspected individuals the abdomen was evidently moving in respiration, while in all the others no movement was perceptible excepting that of their chests." ('The Mechanism of the Human Voice,' by Emil Behnke. London: J. Curwen & Sons, 3rd. ed., p. 16.)

For further elucidation of this most important subject of respiration the reader is referred to the chapter bearing on its hygienic aspects, which commences at page 102, and also to the illustrations XXXVI A., B., and C., and XXXVII A., B., and C., printed at page 183, where this question is again considered in relation to its direct effect on voice cultivation. In the portion treating of the ailments of the voice-user, as well as in that on speech defects, it will be seen that the method of respiration has the most important bearing on the general as well as on the professional well-being of the class for whom we write. It is difficult, therefore, to exaggerate its importance on the whole teaching of this treatise.

THE VOICE-BOX OR LARYNX.

THE VOICE-BOX OR LARYNX is the central organ of the vocal apparatus, and is situated on the top of the windpipe. Its front corner or angle (Pl. VII., 1) may be both seen and felt in the throat, and the general position of the voice-box is thereby at once indicated.

This position is not by any means a fixed one, but the larynx may, on the contrary, easily be pushed on one side. It also moves upwards and downwards in the fulfilment of various functions which will be described in another chapter.

The voice-box is, roughly speaking, a short tube, three cornered above and cylindrical below. It is, moreover, larger at the top than at the bottom, and may therefore be said to resemble a funnel, the upper part of which has been bent into a triangular shape.

The larynx is composed of cartilages or pieces of gristle held together by various ligamentous bands, and moved by numerous muscles. The scientific names of these pieces of gristle are chiefly derived from Greek words signifying in some cases the different objects which the cartilages were supposed to resemble, and in others their position or purpose; while again, certain cartilages and other parts of the larynx are sometimes named after the anatomists who first described them. All these designations are more or less arbitrary, and they are calculated to increase the difficulties of the student instead of helping to remove them. We have considered this matter the more carefully, as the present work is intended for readers some of whom may not have had a scientific education, and we have accordingly decided upon the following plan of nomenclature, which will appeal to all classes:—

1. We shall, as in the preceding pages, make use of English terms, conveying to the general reader some idea of the form or nature of the part to be described.

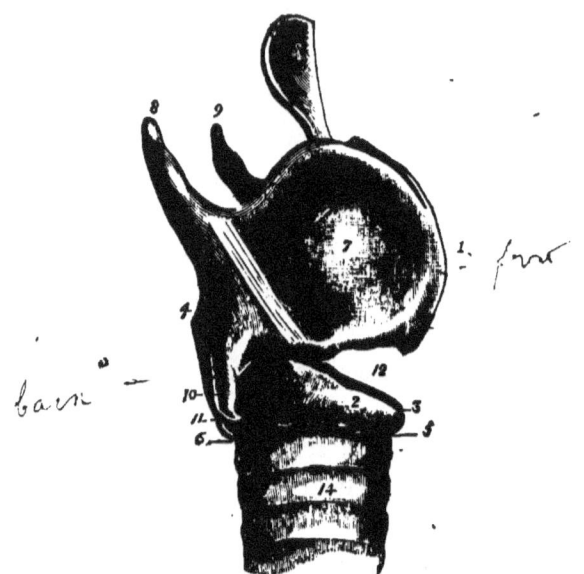

VII.—Side View of the Voice-box or Larynx.

1. Front corner or angle of the voice-box (Adam's apple).
2. Ring (cricoid) cartilage.
3, 4. Upper border of the ring.
5, 6. Lower border of the ring.
7. Shield (thyroid) cartilage.
8, 9. Upper horns (superior cornua) of the shield.
10. Right lower horn (inferior cornu) of the shield.
11. Point where the shield moves upon the ring.
12. Ring-shield (crico-thyroid) aperture.
13. Lid (epiglottis).
14. Windpipe (trachea).

2. These English names, when used for the first time and in all diagrams, &c., will be followed by the scientific terms of which, in most cases, they are translations.

3. We shall also add the names which Professor Ludwig has given to the cartilages in accordance with their functions. These designations will, we believe, greatly assist the reader

in finally forming a clear conception of that marvellously beautiful little piece of mechanism now to be described.

THE FRAMEWORK of the larynx consists of five cartilages or pieces of gristle.

1. The Ring (*cricoid*) cartilage, or Foundation cartilage.
2. The Shield (*thyroid*) cartilage, or Tension cartilage.
3. The Lid (*epiglottis*), or Cover cartilage.
4 and 5. The Pyramids (*arytehoid* cartilages), or Position cartilages.

THE RING (*cricoid*) cartilage (Pl. VII., 2) is situated on the top of the windpipe, of which it forms the finishing part. It has the shape of a signet ring, being narrow in front and having behind a broad plate corresponding to the seal. The upper border (Pl. VII., 3, 4) rises very considerably towards the back, where the ring is about four times as high as in front. The lower border (Pl. VII., 5, 6) runs about parallel with the rings of the windpipe, that is to say, its general direction is horizontal; but it is often united with the top ring of the windpipe by means of extensions of various sizes which give it a more or less irregular appearance. In Plate VII. the ring cartilage is partly hidden, but it will be shown again in another illustration, and we shall then see it in its entirety. The ring forms the basis of the larynx, because the whole of that structure is, as it were, built upon it. It is for this reason that it is also called the *foundation* cartilage.

THE SHIELD (*thyroid*) cartilage (Pl. VII., 7) is so called because it serves as a shield or protection to the more delicate parts of the vocal apparatus which, as we shall find later on, are concealed by it. It consists of two symmetrical plates or "wings," united in front by means of a narrow centre-piece at a more or less acute angle, which forms the prominence referred to just now as that corner of the triangular funnel (Pl. VII., 1) which may be both seen and felt in the throat, and which is commonly called the "Adam's apple." This name has been given to it because in the opinion of the superstitious anatomists of the dark ages the prominence was caused by the sticking in the throat of the apple, from the forbidden tree, which Adam had eaten. *But Adam ate the app (not the tree.)*

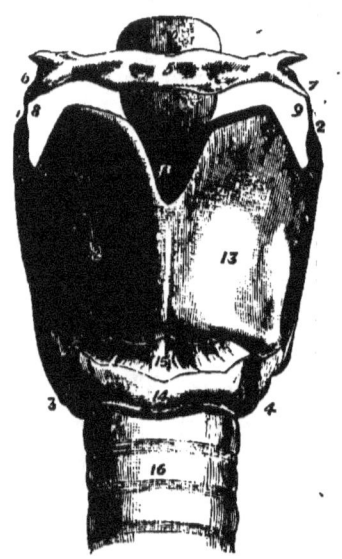

VIII.—FRONT VIEW OF THE VOICE-BOX OR LARYNX.

1, 2. Upper horns of the shield.
3, 4. Lower horns of the shield.
5. Tongue (hyoid) bone.
6, 7. Horns of the tongue bone.
8, 9. Bands uniting the shield with the tongue bone.
10, 11. Lid.
12, 13. Plates of the shield.
14. Ring.
15. Elastic band uniting the shield with the ring.
16. Windpipe.

The plates or wings of the shield have each at the back two horns—the upper and the lower. With the upper horns (Pl. VIII., 1, 2) the shield cartilage is attached by means of bands (Pl. VIII., 8, 9) to the corresponding projections (Pl. VIII., 6, 7) of the tongue bone (Pl. VIII., 5). With the lower horns (Pl. VIII., 3, 4) it moves upon the ring cartilage as upon a pair of hinges. The preceding diagram (Pl. VII., 11), although it shows only one of the lower horns, will make this clearer still.

If the shield cartilage (Pl. VII., 7) were gradually drawn downward and forward, the distance between the front of the shield (Pl. VII., 1) and the highest part of the back of the ring (Pl. VII., 4) would be increased, and the space which we now see between the shield and the ring (Pl. VII., 12) would get smaller and smaller, until at last it quite disappeared.

Authorities differ as to whether the shield moves upon the ring, or the ring upon the shield, and some even maintain that both are moved at the same time. But it is sufficient for our purpose to know that a movement as upon a hinge takes place whereby, as just explained, the distance between the front of the shield and the highest part at the back of the ring is increased. Supposing for the moment the ring cartilage to remain stationary, and the shield cartilage to be moved upon it downward and forward, the tension of the vocal ligaments, as will be seen presently, would chiefly depend upon the lever-like action of the shield, and this cartilage therefore receives the additional appellation of the *tension* cartilage.

THE LID (*epiglottis*) or cover cartilage. Reference to the section of the human body (Pl. III., p. 39) will show that the food we take has to pass over the voice-box and then through the gullet (*œsophagus*) into the stomach. But the larynx is open at the top, so that a contrivance is required which will 'close it during the act of swallowing. This is done by the lid, an elastic cartilage which allows itself to be drawn over the voice-box, thereby protecting it against any intruding foreign substances. It is a thin, pliable, leaf-shaped cartilage (Pl. VIII., 10), and is attached with its tapering basis (Pl. VIII., 11) to the inner side of the shield just below the point where the two plates or wings are united.

The epiglottis, therefore, must not be thought of as a flat lid such as that of a box, but as a soft substance closing the aperture of the larynx with its overlapping edges and its interior cushion-like projection. Owing to these peculiarities it is also spoken of as the *cover* cartilage, which is a very appropriate name for it.

It sometimes happens, especially if we are laughing or talking while taking our meals, that the lid does not exactly close the aperture of the voice-box, thereby allowing a particle of food to enter it. When such a thing happens we say the food has "gone the wrong way," and there is then no peace until the intruder has been got rid of, generally by a violent fit of coughing. The result of a foreign body entering the larynx is sometimes a very serious matter, and there are cases on record where small objects as a coffee-bean or a cherry-stone lodged in the voice-box have rapidly caused death.

The lid is, however, not the only means of protection which the larynx possesses; there are some parts immediately below it which can be pressed together, thereby helping to prevent anything from getting into the voice-box. Persons have been known even to have had no lid from birth, or to have lost it by disease, and yet they never experienced any difficulty in swallowing. But "exceptions prove the rule," and, in spite of a few cases of this description, the fact remains that the lid is obviously the first and most natural protector of the voice-box.

We have thus far become acquainted with three cartilages out of the five. Let us now remove one plate of the shield as though cutting it off with a knife (Pl. IX.), in order that we may look inside and see the remaining two cartilages which have hitherto been hidden by it. These are :—

THE PYRAMIDS (*arytenoid* cartilages), or position cartilages. When taken together they are supposed to resemble a "pitcher," though it requires a very fanciful imagination to recognise the form; it is, at all events, in accordance

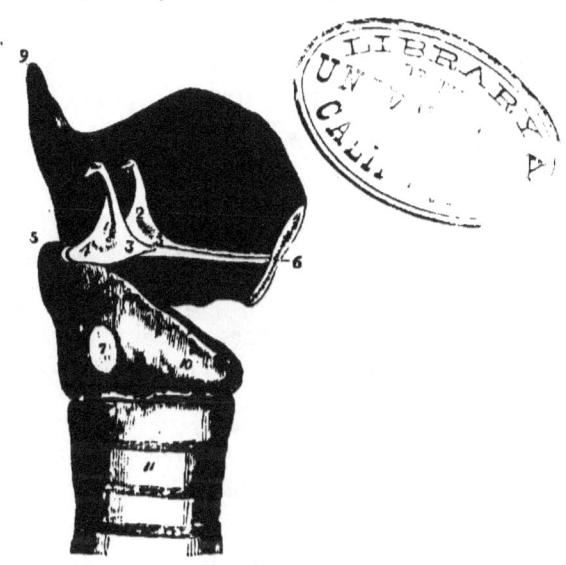

IX.—SIDE VIEW OF THE VOICE-BOX OR LARYNX SHOWING THE INTERIOR OF IT, THE RIGHT PLATE OF THE SHIELD BEING REMOVED.

1, 2. Pyramids (arytenoid cartilages).
3, 3. Vocal processes of the pyramids.
4. Muscular process of the right pyramid.
5. Upper border of the ring.
6, 3, 3. Vocal ligaments.
7. Place of attachment for the shield.
8. Left plate of the shield.
9. Left upper horn of the shield.
10. Ring.
11. Windpipe.

with this real or imaginary shape that the Greek name *arytenoid* cartilages was bestowed upon them. They are really two triangular little bodies, each broad at the base and tapering up towards the top. They are consequently also called the pyramids. Of the five cartilages forming the framework of the larynx, the two pyramids undoubtedly play the most important part, and it is unfortunate, therefore, that it is almost impossible to give a clear idea of them without the aid of a working model such as we use in our lectures, by means of which their movements can be imitated.

The shape of the pyramids is shown very plainly on our drawing (Pl. IX., 1, 2). Their bases are three-cornered, and slightly hollowed out, so as to fit easily upon the upper rim of the ring. Each basis points one corner forwards (Pl. IX., 3, 3), and one sideways (Pl. IX., 4). Of the latter we can in our drawing, of course, only see the corner pointing to the right. The two corners pointing forwards are called the *vocal processes*, and those pointing outwards are called the *muscular processes*.

The sides of the pyramids correspond with the outlines of their bases; each pyramid has, therefore, one surface at the back, a second at the inner, and a third at the outer side. The inner surfaces are, in fact, opposite to and parallel with each other. This is, however, only the case while the pyramids are in the position they occupy in diagram IX., and they are capable of executing a variety of movements with surprising freedom and rapidity. Their inner sides may be made to run parallel or to diverge. In addition to this they can be drawn away from each other, or towards each other, so that their summits may either be widely separated or brought close together. We shall see very shortly that the shape and the width of the chink of the glottis, and also to some extent the tension of the vocal ligaments, depend largely upon the position of the pyramids. No better name could therefore have been chosen for these little bodies than that of *position cartilages*.

THE VOCAL LIGAMENTS (Pl. IX., 3, 3–6) are two ledges of elastic tissue, covered with a very delicate membrane.

Each of them is connected on one side along its whole length with the shield cartilage. The vocal ligaments are attached by their hinder ends to those little forward pointing projections of the pyramids which are called the vocal processes (Pl. IX., 3, 3), and by their front ends to the centre of the shield (Pl. IX., 6), where the two plates meet under a more or less acute angle.

The vocal ligaments are generally called the vocal *cords*, but this term is misleading, as it implies strings like those, for instance, of the violin, which are attached only at either end, and are free at every other point. This, as we have just seen, is not the case, the "cords" being free only along their inner edges. The left vocal ligament in our next drawing (Pl. X., 1, 2, 3, 4) shows this very distinctly, and it forms, together with a muscle constituting a part of it, a triangular ledge attached with its broad basis to the shield cartilage. The name "vocal bands," which German physiologists have substituted for "vocal cords," does not mend the matter, as it is open to exactly the same objections. The term "vocal lips," also used by some writers, conveys an equally wrong idea of these parts, and as there is no name directly descriptive of the thing to be designated we prefer the word "ligament," which has at least the negative advantage of not conjuring up a false image. We shall, consequently, in these pages always speak of the tone-producing element as the "vocal ligaments."

The vocal ligaments having met are struck by the air blown against them from below, and being elastic they yield, allowing themselves to be forced upwards. A little air is thereby set free, and the pressure from below diminished, in consequence of which the vocal ligaments resume their former position, and even move a little more downwards. The renewed pressure of the air once more overcomes the resistance of the vocal ligaments, which again recede as soon as another escape of air has taken place, and this process is repeated in rapid and regular succession.

We have here two sets of vibrations—primary and secondary; the primary vibrations being those of the vocal ligaments, and the secondary vibrations being those

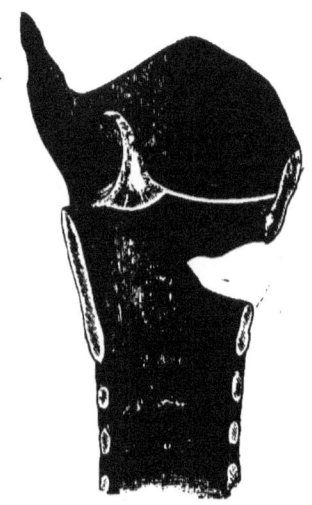

X.—Side View of the Voice-box or Larynx showing the Interior of the Left Half.

1, 2, 3, 4. Left vocal ligament and shield-pyramid muscle (thyro-arytenoideus).
5. Left pyramid.
6, 7. Ring.
5, 7. Side ring-pyramid muscle (lateral crico-arytenoideus).

of the column of air passing between the vocal ligaments. The result of these vibrations is *vocal tone*. The tone so produced does not, as will be more fully explained in another place, constitute the human voice in its entirety, but merely the original sound of it. All authorities are, however, now agreed that this original sound is the result of the vibrations of the vocal ligaments.

Quotations in support of the above statement might be

given to any extent, but the following one from Professor Marshall's 'Outlines of Physiology,' which is conclusive, may suffice: "Experiments on living animals show that the vocal ligaments are alone the essential organs for the production of voice, for so long as these remain untouched, although all the other parts in the interior of the larynx be destroyed, the animal is able to emit vocal sounds. The existence of an opening in the larynx of a living animal or of man, *above* the glottis,* in no way prevents the formation of vocal sound; such an opening, if situated in the trachea, causes total loss of voice, but by simply closing it vocal sounds can again be produced. Such openings in man are met with either as the results of accidents, of suicidal attempts, or of operations performed on the larynx or trachea for the relief of disease."

The vocal ligaments in the adult male are, in a state of rest, about three-quarters of an inch long, and in the female about half an inch. They are, as pointed out before, attached in front to the shield (Pl. IX., 6) and behind to the pyramids (Pl. IX., 3, 3). Let it now be borne in mind (1) that the pyramids in their turn are fastened to the upper border of the ring, and (2) that by drawing the shield downward and forward upon the ring, or by in any other way approximating these two cartilages in front (*see* p. 55), the distance between the upper border of the ring (Pl. IX., 5) and the front of the shield (Pl. IX., 6) is increased, and it will be easily seen that either of these movements must, of necessity, have the effect of stretching the vocal ligaments, thereby *raising* the pitch of the voice.

The drawing of the shield downward and forward upon

---

* Glottis means the vibrating element of the voice-box.

the ring is brought about by a pair of muscles ascending on either side, in the shape of a fan, from the ring to the shield (Pl. XI., 1, 2, 3). These muscles are called the "ring-shield muscles," or *crico-thyroidei*. In opposition to them there is another pair inside the shield, running parallel with the vocal ligaments of which, indeed, they may be said to form the most important part (Pl. X., 1, 2, 3, 4).

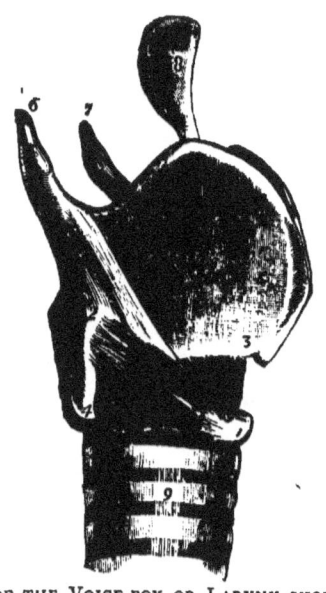

XI.—Side View of the Voice-box or Larynx showing one of the External Muscles.

1, 2, 3. Ring-shield muscle (crico-thyroideus).
4. Right lower horn of the shield.
5. Shield.
6, 7. Upper horns of the shield.
8. Lid.
9. Windpipe.

They are attached, like the vocal ligaments, in front to the shield cartilage, and behind to the pyramids, in consequence of which they are called the "shield-pyramid muscles" or *thyro-arytenoidei*. It is one of their functions to counteract the ring-shield muscles, and, having overcome their resistance, to pull the shield cartilage up again, thereby, of course, relaxing the vocal ligaments, and *lowering* the pitch of the voice. The ring-shield muscles, therefore (Pl. XI., 1, 2, 3), *stretch* the vocal ligaments, and the shield-pyramid muscles (Pl. X., 1, 2, 3, 4) *relax* them.

But the relaxing of the vocal ligaments is not the only function of the shield-pyramid muscles. Their action is indeed so exceedingly complicated as to make a clear description of it almost impossible. There is, probably, comparatively speaking, no muscle in the human body with so many varied points of origin and insertion of its fibres; these fibres going in all directions, and enabling the muscles to alter their tension, density, elasticity, and shape. It would be quite beyond the scope of this manual to enter into minute details of their structure, nor do we think we should make matters at all more comprehensible by following the example of some authors who divide these muscles in two bundles, and speak of them as the *ex*ternal and the *in*ternal shield-pyramid muscles. This distinction is anatomically difficult, and would in the end serve to puzzle and to confuse the reader instead of enlightening him.

Most of the fibres run parallel with the vocal ligaments, taking the same somewhat curved line (Pl. X., 1, 2, 3, 4); many run right up into the pocket ligaments, and the rest run in almost every other direction, the whole being so entangled as to make it a hopeless task to classify them. The action of the shield-pyramid muscles is fourfold:—

1. They relax the vocal ligaments.

2. They twist the pyramids by pulling at the *muscular* processes, thereby approximating the *vocal* processes.

3. They press towards the interior, thereby bringing larger portions of the vocal ligaments in contact with

each other, thus reducing the length of the vocal chink; and,

4. Their outer vertical fibres, by contracting, diminish the diameter of the inner portion of the shield-pyramid muscles and of the vocal ligaments, making them flatter and thinner.

That the last described action is not, as might perhaps be imagined, merely a matter of speculation will be proved in another chapter, and it will then be seen that this action is of the greatest importance in connection with the formation of one of the so-called registers of the voice. In the meantime it will be observed that while in some ways it is the function of the shield-pyramid muscles to lower the pitch of the voice, it is also their function under other conditions to raise the pitch.

In accordance with the structure just explained the shield-pyramid muscles have, in these later days, been called the "sphincter* muscle" of the glottis. They have also been called the "vocal muscles," since they play so important a part in the formation of all vocal tone that a paralysis of them causes total loss of voice.

These two pairs of muscles, then, namely the ring-shield muscles (Pl. XI., 1, 2, 3) and the shield-pyramid muscles (Pl. X., 1, 2, 3, 4), by stretching, slackening, and compressing the vocal ligaments, mainly govern the pitch of the tones produced by their vibrations. The ring-shield muscles receive some assistance in stretching the vocal ligaments from another quarter, of which we shall speak later on.

We have now had a view of the vocal ligaments, and we have seen by what means their tension is altered. As,

---

* *Sphincter* is an anatomical term applied to circular muscles which constrict or close certain natural orifices.

however, in a state of repose the ligaments diverge behind, they must be brought parallel to each other before they are ready for the production of sound. In order to explain how this is done let us imagine that we have cut off that part of the pyramids which is standing out above the vocal ligaments (Pl. IX., p. 57), and let us now have a look at these parts from above. You see the ligaments (Pl. XII., A, 1, 2), a section of the pyramids (Pl. XII., A, 3, 4), and uniting these an elastic band (Pl. XII., A, 5). These parts are commonly called the "glottis," and anatomists distinguish a *ligamentous* glottis formed by the vocal liga-

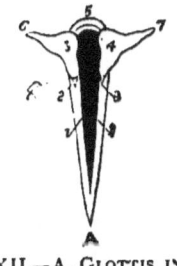 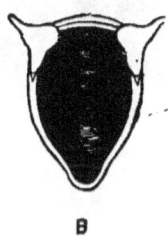 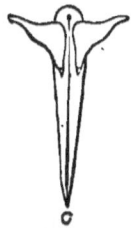

XII.—A, Glottis in Repose.   B, Glottis in Deep Breathing.   C, Glottis in the Production of Tone.

1, 2. Vocal ligaments.
3, 4. Section of the pyramids.
5 Elastic band.
6, 7. Muscular processes.
8, 9. Vocal processes.

ments, and a *cartilaginous* glottis formed by the pyramids.

The term glottis really signifies the "tongues" or "tonguelets" (*lingulæ laryngis*) of the larynx, and as the pyramids do not, by any vibrations of their own, take a part in the production of tone, the appellation belongs, strictly speaking, to the vocal ligaments alone. Unfortunately matters are still further complicated by the additional use of the name glottis for the chink between the ligaments, and this leads to unnecessary difficulties and incongruities. Medical men speak of "spasms of the glottis," and singing masters of the "shock of the glottis," which terms are quite meaningless when applied to a space. The chink just spoken of is also called in physiological works the "aperture of the glottis" or "rima glottidis," and there appears to be no reason why such an appellation should not be exclusively used for it, reserving the term glottis for the vocal ligaments.

Here, as in all other cases, it is most desirable to have a clear definition of terms, and we shall therefore use the

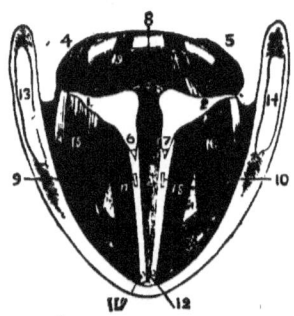

XIII.—VIEW OF A SECTION OF THE VOICE-BOX OR LARYNX FROM ABOVE.

1, 2. Muscular processes of the pyramid cartilages.
3, 3. Ring cartilage.
4,1 & 5,2. Back ring-pyramid muscles (Posterior crico-arytenoidei).
6, 7. Vocal processes of the pyramid cartilages.
6,11 & 7,12. Vocal ligaments.
8. Pyramid muscle (arytenoideus transversus).

9 & 10. Elsberg's "vocal nodules."
11 & 12. Sesamoid cartilages.
13, 14. Shield cartilage.
15 & 16. Side ring-pyramid muscles (lateral crico-arytenoidei).
17 & 18. Shield-pyramid muscles (thyro-arytenoidei).
19 & 20. Bands by means of which the pyramids are attached to the ring.

word "glottis" only to designate the vibrating element of the larynx, while distinguishing the space enclosed by it as the "chink of the glottis," when referring to variations of its shape in production of tone, or the "vocal chink" when alluded to generally.

On Plate XIII. are seen all parts in a state of rest. This illustration, which has given us more trouble to perfect than any other, should be very carefully studied by the reader, as it gives a very complete view of the dissected larynx seen from above, and if thoroughly comprehended will greatly aid interpretation of the others. To the muscular processes of the pyramids (Pl. XIII., 1 and 2) a pair of muscles is attached, the bases of which are fixed upon the back of the ring cartilage below (Pl. XIII., 4 and 5). The action of these "back ring-pyramid muscles," or *posterior crico-arytenoidei* (Pl. XIII., 4, 1 and 5, 2), is to contract as soon as we take breath, thereby drawing together the pyramids *behind* and separating them in front, at the same time stretching the elastic band behind. By this movement the chink of the glottis is thrown *wide open* into the shape depicted on Pl. XII. B. During expiration the back ring-pyramid muscles relax, the elastic band contracts, and the vocal chink resumes the shape as on Pl. XII. A. These movements go on from the beginning of our lives to the end, whether we are asleep or awake, with more or less vigour, according as we take a slight or a deep inspiration. The back ring-pyramid muscles (Pl. XIII., 4, 1 and 5, 2) have consequently the all-important function of keeping open the gate through which the air we breathe enters the lungs. They have, therefore, been poetically called the "guardians of the portal of life." By their action of pulling the pyramids backwards, they also assist the ring-shield muscles (Pl. XI., 1, 2, 3) in stretching the vocal ligaments.

In opposition to these "opening muscles" there is another pair rising from the side borders of the ring (Pl. XIII. 3, 3), which are fastened to the front part of the muscular processes of the pyramids (Pl. XIII., 1 and 2), serving to draw together the vocal processes (Pl. XIII., 6 and 7) to which the vocal ligaments are attached, and which are thereby brought parallel with each other.

These "side ring-pyramid muscles" or *lateral crico-*

arytenoidei (Pl. XIII., 15 and 16; see also Pl. X., 5, 7, p. 60) are assisted by a single muscle uniting the pyramids behind the elastic band which we have already noticed. This muscle we will call the "pyramid muscle" or *arytenoideus* (Pl. XIII., 8). By the united action of the muscles which have just been described, and which may be termed the "closing muscles," the vocal chink is thrown in the shape shown on Pl. XII. C., and the vocal ligaments are now in a proper position for the production of tone.

Before proceeding farther it will be well if we once more glance at the muscles with which we have become acquainted, so that we may be quite sure about their functions.

MUSCLES.

I. GOVERNING THE SHAPE OF THE VOCAL CHINK.

THE BACK RING-PYRAMID MUSCLES or *posterior crico-arytenoidei*. } Opening the vocal chink.

THE SIDE RING-PYRAMID MUSCLES or *lateral crico-arytenoidei*, and the PYRAMID MUSCLE or *arytenoideus*, assisted by the SHIELD-PYRAMID MUSCLES or *thyro-arytenoidei*. } Closing the vocal chink.

II. GOVERNING THE PITCH OF THE VOICE.

THE RING-SHIELD MUSCLES or *crico-thyroidei*, assisted by the back RING-PYRAMID MUSCLES or *posterior crico-arytenoidei*. } Stretching the vocal ligaments.

THE SHIELD-PYRAMID MUSCLES or *thyro-arytenoidei*. } Slackening or compressing the vocal ligaments.

The Pocket Ligaments or *false vocal cords* are a pair of horizontal projections running above and parallel with the vocal ligaments. In order to get a clear conception of this as well as the remaining parts of the voice-box, some of which are very minute, it will be necessary to study

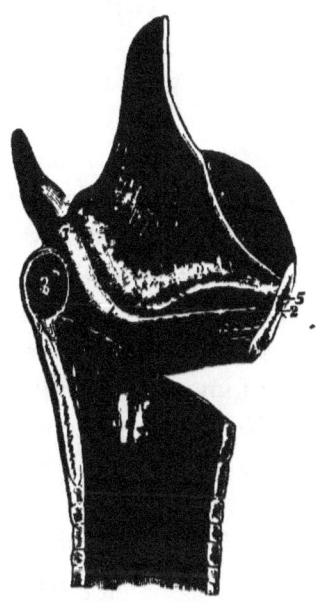

XIV.—Side View of the Voice-box or Larynx showing the Left Pocket and Mucous Folds.

1,2. Left vocal ligament.
3. Elevation indicating the left buffer cartilage (cartilage of Santorini).
4,5, 2,1. Entrance to the left pocket.
4,5. Left pocket ligament.
6. Elevation indicating the left cartilage of Wrisberg with the prop cartilage (cuneiform cartilage) running down to 4.
7. Mucous fold (ary-epiglottic) connecting the pyramid cartilage with the lid.
8. Pyramid muscle.

them in detail. Let us therefore look at the annexed drawing, showing the interior of the left half of the larynx, which we now see, for the first time, covered with mucous membrane, that is to say, in its natural state.

We recognise the vocal ligament (Pl. XIV., 1, 2), and we see its insertion in the shield cartilage (Pl. XIV., 2), but the pyramid for which we look on the left of the draw.ng, and to which, as we know, the other end of the vocal ligament is attached, is hidden from our view though we can just trace its curved outline slanting upward and backward (Pl. XIV., 1, 3).

Above the vocal ligament we see another horizontal projection (Pl. XIV., 4, 5), which, like the vocal ligament, is attached in front (on the right of the drawing) to the shield cartilage, and behind (on the left of the drawing) to the pyramid. It must be observed, however, as a matter of some practical importance, that while the two points of insertion in front (Pl. XIV., 2 and 5) are vertically in a straight line, or, in other words, one exactly above the other, the two points of insertion behind (Pl. XIV., 1 and 4) are *not* so placed, No. 4 being inserted more outwardly than No. 1. Let it be noticed also that the upper projection (Pl. XIV., 4, 5) does not form a straight line, but a curve, resembling that of the lid of the open eye. This curved, horizontal projection, the position of which has thus been indicated, is the left pocket ligament.

THE POCKETS OF THE LARYNX or *ventricles of Morgagni* are two cavities, the functions of which are described by various writers in the most conflicting manner. The space between the vocal ligament and the pocket ligament (Pl. XIV., 1, 2, 4, 5) is the entrance to the left pocket, the pocket itself being behind. Professor Struthers, of Aberdeen University, compares this arrangement to a fireplace with the chimney behind. The fireplace enters the wall in a horizontal direction, and merges into the chimney, which runs behind it in a vertical direction. The opening 1, 2, 4, 5, corresponds to the fireplace, and the pocket behind it to the chimney, with this difference, that the chimney is open at the top and passes out of the house, while the pocket is closed at the top and remains in the larynx. The height of different pockets varies greatly; as a rule it does not exceed two-fifths of an inch, so that their terminations do not reach the upper border of the shield cartilage. But there are instances in which the pockets are nearly three-quarters of an inch high; and where such is the case they, as a necessary consequence, reach beyond the shield. Sometimes they are so high as nearly to touch the root of the tongue, while in other cases they are quite shallow. Their outer walls are chiefly formed of loose, fatty, cellular tissue, and they are almost entirely surrounded by a multitude of minute glands.

THE CARTILAGES OF SANTORINI, so called after their discoverer, are two small pliable cartilages attached to the summits of the pyramids which they protect from the pressure of the lid striking against them in the act of swallowing. In accordance with this function they have been named the "buffer cartilages." ('The Throat and its Functions.' Louis Elsberg, M.D., &c. New York: G. P. Putnam & Sons, p. 31). In our drawing (Pl. XIV., 3) we see an elevation of the mucous membrane, indicating one of them on the top of the left pyramid.

From the buffer cartilage (Pl. XIV., 3), running up to the lid (Pl. XIV., 7), there is a fold of mucous membrane (*aryteno-epiglottic fold*), and there is, of course, a corresponding fold in the right half of the larynx. These folds of mucous membrane are stiffened by two little strips of gristle called the *cuneiform* cartilages which consequently also go by the appropriate name of the "prop cartilages" (Elsberg, op. cit., p. 31). The enlarged upper terminations of the prop cartilages are called the "cartilages of WRISBERG." The left one of these is shown in our drawing (Pl. XIV., 6), and the prop itself may be traced through the mucous membrane running in a downward direction (Pl. XLV., 6, 4).

We are now in a position to understand the next drawing (Pl. XV.), and to examine it in detail. It represents an entire larynx cut open from behind, and we have no difficulty in recognising the parts described above. If we

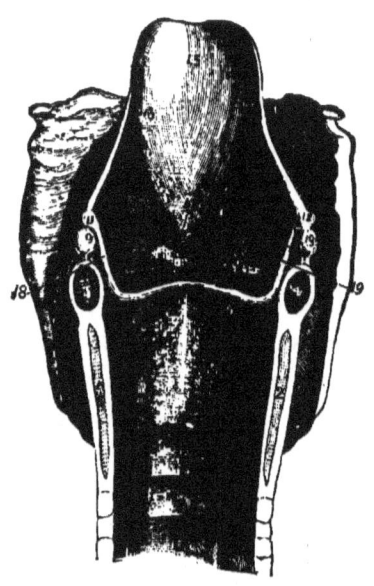

XV.—View of the Voice-box or Larynx cut open from behind.

1, 2. Ring cartilage.
3, 4. Pyramid muscle.
5 & 6. Vocal ligaments.
5, 7, 6, 8. Entrances to the pockets.
7 & 8. Pocket ligaments.
9, 10. Cartilages of Santorini.
11 & 12. Cartilages of Wrisberg.
11, 13 & 12, 14. Ary-epiglottic folds.
15. Lid.
16. Windpipe.
17. Cushion of the lid.
18 & 19. Prop cartilages.

could bend it so as to unite the two ends of the ring cartilage (Pl. XV., 1 and 2), and the two ends of the pyramid muscle (Pl. XV., 3 and 4), we should give the larynx its natural shape. The vocal ligaments (Pl. XV., 5 and 6) and the pocket ligaments (Pl. XV., 7 and 8) would run in a forward direction, meeting in front, and diverging a little behind, and above these there would be a kind of tube called the "vestibule of the larynx."

The upper rim of the vestibule is formed by the two buffer cartilages (Pl. XVI., 12 and 9), by the two cartilages of Wrisberg (Pl. XVI., 10 and 13), the two folds of mucous membrane running up to the lid (Pl. XVI., 10, 11, 13 and

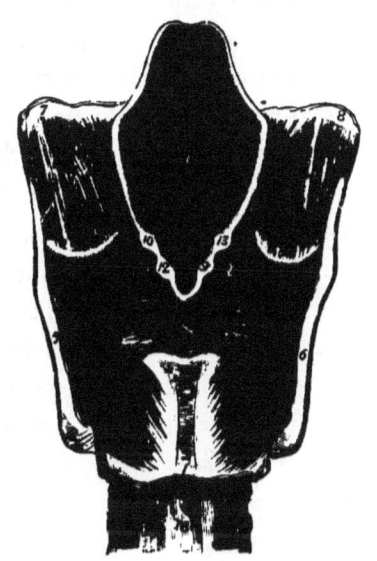

XVI.—THE VOICE-BOX OR LARYNX SEEN FROM BEHIND.

1, 2. Ring cartilage.
3, 4. Pyramid muscle.
5 & 6. Shield.
7 & 8. Tongue bone.
9 & 12. Cartilages of Santorini.
10 & 13. Cartilages of Wrisberg.

11, 15, 14. Lid.
16. Windpipe.
17. Cushion of the lid.
18 & 19. Back ring-pyramid muscles.
20, 21 & 22, 23. Constrictors of the vestibule.

14), and by the top of the lid (Pl. XVI., 15). The vestibule of the larynx extends downwards as far as the pocket ligaments, and we observe in its sides the prop-cartilages (Pl. XV., 18 and 19), which, as we have seen above, help to keep it open. We also notice, just above the point at which the pocket ligaments meet, an elevation (Pl. XV., 17) which is called the "cushion" of the epiglottis.

Through the vestibule (Pl. XVI., 12, 10, 11, 15, 14, 13, 9) the air passes in respiration, and the sound in singing and speaking, and we have to look down this tube with the laryngoscope when we wish to study the conditions of the larynx in the act of producing tone. The food we take passes *over* this tube, and we know that its mouth is covered for this purpose by the lid. But we have also seen that the upper free part of the epiglottis (Pl. XVI., 15), which could alone cover it, is entirely wanting in some persons, and that they, nevertheless, do not experience any difficulty in swallowing. There must, therefore, be additional safeguards, and we discover, upon closer examination, an arrangement which is as simple as it is effective, and which consists in the pressing together of the vocal ligaments and of the pocket ligaments. The closure of the pocket ligaments is effected by the vertical bundles of the outer portions of the shield-pyramid muscles, and by contraction of the "constrictor" of the vestibule (*arytenoideus constrictor vestibuli laryngis*) (Pl. XVI., 20, 21 and 22, 23), which passes up from the bases of the pyramids to the lid encircling the tapering points of the pyramids just below the buffers, and then stretching itself over the prop cartilages.

Plate XVI. will explain this matter more clearly than any verbal description, and we have now learnt that the closure of the larynx is brought about by three factors, namely, the vocal ligaments, the pocket ligaments, and the lid. Although, therefore, the lid must ever be regarded as the chief means of closing the larynx, yet we can easily understand how, in its absence, the other parts just enumerated can supply its place, and effectually protect the voice-box from any intruding foreign substances.

It will be useful to point out here that the closing of

the *larynx* and the closing of the *glottis* are two very different things. The larynx is closed in swallowing, in vomiting, and by the effort of squeezing or pressing together the throat, as when making violent efforts of straining or of lifting; but it is doubtful whether in any case the pocket ligaments can be sufficiently pressed together behind to make the closure really airtight, because their points of insertion are not, as we have before remarked, in the middle line of the larynx, but a little to the right and left of it, and we shall see what elaborate means are necessary to bring them into entire contact in experiments upon dead larynges (see p. 143). But however this may be, *it is quite certain that in the production of tone the pocket ligaments, while in a healthy state*, NEVER MEET, and that the glottis alone is closed. This is a fact of which there cannot be the shadow of a doubt in the mind of the merest tyro with the laryngoscope.

The pockets are the means of isolating the vocal ligaments, thus affording them room to range themselves and to vibrate freely and without hindrance. They also allow the sound-waves to expand sideways; and lastly, they produce, with their many little glands, moisture for the lubrication of the vocal ligaments, without which moisture, according to the investigations of J. Müller, the production of tone cannot be carried on. ('Ueber die Compensation der physischen Kräfte am menschlichen Stimmorgan,' p. 8. Berlin, 1839).

The prop cartilages (Pl. XV., 18 and 19) now require a little additional attention. They have, according to some writers, the shape of the letter L; and their little horizontal arms extend into the vocal ligaments, enabling them to remain partly closed and to let only a part of their length vibrate in the production of tone. The little horizontal arms of the prop cartilages are, in fact, by one of these authors considered to constitute the mechanism of the so-called "head voice," i.e. the highest register of the female voice.

Madame Seiler says that they " reach to the middle of the vocal ligaments by which they are enveloped." ('Voice in Singing.' Philadelphia: J. B. Lippincott & Co., p. 189.)

Dr. Witkowski ('The Mechanism of Voice, Speech, and Taste.' Translated and edited by Lennox Browne. London: Baillière, Tindall & Cox, p. 12) gives a description of these cartilages which corresponds very closely with that of Madame Seiler. Speaking of some of the glands of the voice-box he says: " They are arranged in the form of an L, whose vertical branch goes along the arytenoid cartilages, *the horizontal branch following the direction of the vocal cords. There is often found situated in the midst of this group of glands the cuneiform cartilage of Wrisberg*, sometimes reduced to a mere cartilaginous granule."

Dr. Elsberg (op. cit., p. 37) calls them the "posterior vocal nodules," and describes them as " elongated nodules " in the hinder portion of the vocal ligaments, and says they are found " more often in the female than in the male sex " (Pl. XIII., 9 and 10, p. 66).

A description of the larynx would not be complete without mentioning yet another pair of very minute cartilages called the " anterior vocal nodules," or *sesamoidea anteriores* (Pl. XIII., 11 and 12), although it is not clear what function they have beyond, perhaps, toughening the vocal ligaments at their points of attachment to the shield cartilage.

THE RESONATOR OF THE VOCAL ORGAN.

THE RESONATOR consists of—
1. The pockets;
2. The pocket ligaments;
3. The vestibule;
4. The lid;
5. The upper part of the throat, or pharynx;
6. The cavities of the nose; and,
7. The mouth.

It has already been pointed out on p. 75 that the pockets allow the tone-waves to expand sideways. This must undoubtedly have some influence upon the quality of the tone; and the size of the pockets, which, as we have seen before, greatly varies in different persons, may therefore safely be assumed to be of some consequence in this direction. They are compared by some authors with the membranous bladders which protrude from the necks of certain frogs when croaking; or with the enormous pouches of the *mycetes*, or howling monkeys of America, whose voices are louder than the roaring of lions. The pockets of the human larynx, in proportion to the neighbouring parts, are, however, so small that there is no justification for these fantastic comparisons, which are the more easily shown to be valueless when it is remembered that such animals as the tiger, or the ox, which are certainly not deficient in voice power, have no laryngeal pockets at all.

Let us now suppose the tone to emerge from the pockets; in its upward course it next strikes against the edges of the pocket ligaments, and their thinness or thickness, sharpness or roundness, cannot fail in some way to affect it. The tone next passes through the vestibule, which, as we know, is capable of being contracted or dilated, and it then comes into contact with the lid or epiglottis, which probably varies more in size, shape, and position in different persons than any other part of the vocal apparatus. In some it is scarcely three-quarters of an inch high, while in others it is of such a size as to project over the tongue, so that it may be seen as soon as the mouth is opened. It may be barely turned over a little at the top, or it may be rolled up like a piece of cinnamon bark. It may stand up nearly perpendicularly, leaving the larynx quite free, or it may slant backwards so as to hang over the voice-box. While, however, the shape, size, and position of the lid varies in different persons, its position is also continually varying in the same individuals.

It is quite plain from the foregoing considerations that the lid is the means of more or less suddenly and abruptly turning the tone-waves and of directing them under one angle or another against the back of the throat whence they are reflected into the mouth. We are therefore justified in concluding that the lid has some considerable influence upon the quality of the voice. It may thus be the cause of certain characteristics which enable us to recognise the voice of a friend though we do not see him; and it may also account for some similarities of voice which are found in many families, just as there are similarities of features. We put this forth, to a considerable extent, as a matter of conjecture, which has nevertheless sufficient foundation in fact to be interesting as a problem in the production of voice which may one day be satisfactorily solved.

THE UPPER PART OF THE THROAT, otherwise called

in medical works the *pharynx*, is a cavity, the largest part of which may be seen through the arch at the back of the open mouth. The gullet and the larynx open into it from below, and the mouth and the nostrils from above; it also communicates with the drums of the ears by means of two narrow channels called the " Eustachian tubes."

THE CAVITIES OF THE NOSE have for their base the hard and soft palate (Pl. III., H and S, p. 39), and they are divided by a bony partition. Each cavity consists of three channels, of which we are here only concerned with two, as the third answers a purpose outside our present subject. These channels are very irregular in construction, and they are so contrived as to temperate the air we inhale so that it may not strike cold into the vocal apparatus. They are also, like the air-passages below, lined with a mucous membrane provided with those wonderful little hair-like projections called *cilia*, pointing in an outward direction and continually executing to-and-fro movements from back to front. This arrangement, combined with the glairy fluid secreted by the innumerable tiny glands of the mucous membrane, enables the nasal cavities to arrest all impurities of the air which would otherwise find their way into the larynx and the wind-pipe or even into the lungs. The cavities of the nose, therefore, temperate and purify the air we inhale, and they may be regarded as a natural "respirator."

THE MOUTH or *buccal cavity* is the space between the lips in front and the pharynx behind. We are all familiar with the shape of the lips, the tongue, and the teeth, and we are also acquainted with their movements and functions. The only part of the mouth, therefore, of which it is necessary here to give a description is the palate. This is divided into two portions, namely, the *hard* palate in front, and the *soft* palate behind.

THE HARD PALATE is the hard bony portion of the roof of the mouth, and is bounded in front and at the sides by the sockets of the teeth in the upper jaw, while behind it terminates in the soft palate. It is covered with mucous membrane, and having the shape of a dome, not

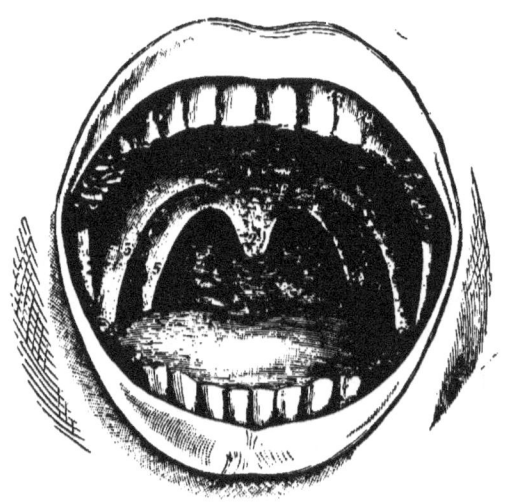

XVII.—THE SOFT PALATE.

1. Soft Palate.
2. Uvula.
3 & 4. Anterior pillars of the fauces.
5 & 6. Posterior pillars of the fauces.

7 & 8. Tonsils.
(The space between the pillars 3, 4 and 5, 6, is called the "fauces.").

only forms the roof of the mouth, but also the floor of the nasal cavities.

THE SOFT PALATE (Pl. XVII., 1) is the movable partition we see at the back of the mouth, and it is formed by a variety of muscles which are covered by a continuation of the mucous membrane which lines the hard palate. It has the shape of an arch with two curved muscular ridges on either side which are called the "pillars of the fauces."

The *anterior* pillars (Pl. XVII., 3 and 4) contain a pair of muscles (palato-glossi) which by their contraction straighten and tighten them, thereby bringing them closer together and narrowing the space between them called the "isthmus of the fauces."

The *posterior* pillars (Pl. XVII., 5 and 6) contain another pair of muscles (palato-pharyngei) which rise from the upper horns of the shield cartilage, and which, by their contraction, not only approximate the posterior pillars of the fauces, but also the plates of the shield, thereby narrowing the space between them.

THE UVULA (Pl. XVII., 2) is the little grape-shaped pendant hanging down from the centre of the soft palate. It chiefly consists of a muscle (azygos-uvulæ) which runs into the middle line of the soft palate, and which has the power of shortening, elevating, and retracting the uvula. The reader will get a clear idea of its action by carefully comparing the photographs facing page 215, which show the uvula in different stages of contraction.

In addition to the muscles described above we have still to notice the "tensor" and the "elevator" which, as indicated by their names, serve to tighten and to raise the soft palate.

Having thus studied the various parts of which the soft palate is composed, we can readily understand that it is of a highly mobile nature. It is, in fact, a movable partition, by means of which either the mouth or the nasal cavities can be almost completely separated from the throat. In order fully to understand this the reader is recommended to look at the lines indicating the "voice passage" and the "air passage" on Plate III., p. 39. If the nasal cavities are to be shut off from the throat the soft palate is *raised* and pressed against the back of the pharynx. The closure is aided by a sort of cushion being formed upon the back of the uvula by the contraction of the muscle which elevates that body. If the mouth is to be shut off from the throat, the soft palate is *lowered,* and rests closely upon the back of the tongue.

The soft palate plays a most important part in vocalisation. In the formation of all pure vowel sounds it is *raised,* thereby more or less tightly closing the nasal cavities, and it has been found that the closure is modified for the different vowel sounds as follows :—

It is loosest for *ah,* tighter for *ai,* tighter again for *oh,* tighter still for *oo,* tightest of all for *ee.*

This has been clearly shown by Czermak in the following manner. Lying down on his back, he had the nasal cavities filled with tepid water. He then uttered the various vowel sounds, and ascertained from the quantity of water required to force open the closure formed by the soft palate the degree of tightness for each vowel. He afterwards constructed a very ingenious apparatus, by means of which, in one of his lectures, he demonstrated this fact to his audience.

The soft palate also gradually rises as we sing up the scale, and it occupies a different position for every different pitch; it stands, however, lower in "falsetto" than in the corresponding high "chest" tones. It must also be observed that the closure of the soft palate is never sufficiently tight entirely to prevent the setting up of co-vibrations in the nasal cavities with those passing from the pharynx into the mouth.

DIFFERENCES OF THE LARYNX IN CHILDREN, WOMEN, AND MEN.

THE larynx of a newly-born baby is about a third the size of that of a woman, but it appears smaller because it is closer to the tongue-bone than at a later period, and its outer surface, consisting of the two plates of the shield cartilage, forms a very insignificant curve instead of that acute angle which we notice in the larynx of men. The voice-box grows very rapidly up to the third year, and less quickly up to the sixth, and from this time up to the fourteenth or fifteenth year there would seem to be no alteration in its proportions, and it is very much the same in boys as in girls. The voice remains all this time the same in pitch though it increases in compass, and its vibrational number does not exceed that of grown-up women.

At the time of puberty, which generally takes place at the age of fourteen or fifteen, but sometimes a couple of years sooner or later, the larynx grows rapidly during a period of from six months to two or three years, until it attains its final size. In boys it alters in the proportions of from 5 to 10, and in girls from 5 to 7. The larynx is at this time more or less red, and the tissue loose; the vocal ligaments increase not only in length but also in thickness. In boys the shield cartilage loses the gentle curve, and forms the prominence which goes under the name of the "Adam's apple;" the larynx in its entirety increases more in depth than in height, with the result of adding to the length of the vocal ligaments, thereby producing lower tones. In girls the larynx increases more in height than in depth and width, and the horizontal outline of the shield does not lose its evenness. The vocal ligaments remain shorter and thinner than in the male voice-box. At this time the voices are said to be breaking, and it will easily be understood from the above explanation why the child's voice of the boy changes into the tenor or bass of the man, while the difference in girls is but slight and so gradual as frequently to be almost imperceptible. The uncertainty of the boy's voice during the time of mutation is a curious phenomenon, and, assuming the growth of the larynx to take place in all its component parts at the same rate, not easily accounted for. The explanation is probably that the cartilages grow faster than the muscles, and that the muscles consequently lose control over the cartilages until everything is finally and permanently re-adjusted.*

We have thus seen that while before the period of puberty the voice-box is materially the same in both sexes, there are afterwards considerable differences noticeable, not only with regard to size, but also with regard to shape. Of this we can, to a large extent, satisfy ourselves by simply comparing the throat of a woman with that of a man, as the one is round and smooth, while the other shows a more or less marked protuberance. These differences may be more clearly observed in exsected larynges, i.e. in voice-boxes cut out of dead bodies; and we find:—

* "It is said that the celebrated Lablache found his voice changed into an excellent bass in a single night, after having, on the previous day, taxed his voice to the utmost at a festival of the church." (James Hunt, op. cit., p. 111.)

1. That the female larynx is about one-third smaller than the male.

2. That all its cartilages are thinner and more delicate.

3. That the outer horizontal contour of the female shield cartilage is round and even, while that of the male forms an acute angle.

4. That the part from the pocket ligaments upwards is comparatively lower in the female voice-box than in the male, and much less developed.

5. That the upper horns of the female larynx are comparatively shorter than those of the male.

6. That consequently the female larynx is much more closely attached to the tongue-bone than the male, which causes the position of the voice-box to be altogether higher in women than in men.

The following average measurements, taken from Luschka's great work on the larynx ('Der Kehlkopf des Menschen.' Hubert v. Luschka, M.D., &c. Tübingen, 1871. H. Laupp), and reduced from centimètres and millimètres to inches (Behnke, op. cit., p. 64), show at a glance the difference in the proportions of the male and of the female larynx :—

	Male.	Female.
Height of voice-box in front with the lid raised	$2\frac{4}{5}$ in. (7 cent.)	$1\frac{9}{10}$ in. (4·8 cent.)
Greatest width between the plates of the shield cartilage	$1\frac{3}{5}$ in. (4 cent.)	$1\frac{2}{5}$ in. (3·5 cent.)
Depth between the lower border of the shield cartilage and the opposite point of the ring cartilage	$1\frac{1}{5}$ in. (3 cent.)	1 in. (2·4 cent.)
Length of the vocal chink	1 in. (25 mm.)	$\frac{3}{5}$ in. (15 mm.)

If there were no difference between the male and female larynx except that of size, all their proportions would, of course, be the same. But we see from the above table that this is not the case, and we now append the result.

Differences between the proportions of male and female voice-boxes :—

In height	$\frac{9}{10}$ of an inch.
In width	$\frac{1}{5}$ "
In depth	$\frac{1}{5}$ "
In length of the vocal chink	$\frac{2}{5}$ "

With age the cartilages of the male larynx ossify, while in women a kind of second mutation takes place, and in consequence of these changes the voice loses in power, beauty, and flexibility. But continual practice appears to counteract this process to a great extent; at all events, there are many exceptions to the rule, as most of our readers know from their own personal observation.

MOVEMENTS OF THE LARYNX WHICH CAN BE SEEN OR FELT.

The larynx of men in a state of rest occupies a position in the middle of the throat, while that of women stands, for reasons already explained in the last chapter, considerably higher. We have also seen, on a former occasion, that the voice-box is attached by ligaments to the tongue-bone, and that the tongue-bone is firmly connected with the root of the tongue. The consequence is that every movement of the tongue affects the position of the larynx. In addition to this there are the so-called *ex*-trinsic laryngeal muscles which may be briefly described as the "elevators" and the "depressors," and which have the power, as implied by their names, of raising or lowering the larynx.

The larynx goes down in *in*spiration, reaching a lower

point and falling more rapidly the deeper and the more vigorous the inflation. By opening the mouth more or less widely we cause the voice-box to execute corresponding downward movements. In singing, a gradual lowering of it is noticeable as we go down the scale. But the descent of the larynx is complete in the acts of sucking and of yawning, when it assumes so low a position in the throat that the whole of the windpipe and even a part of the ring cartilage disappears in the chest.

The larynx goes up in *ex*piration, when the extent and speed of the movement obviously, to a great extent, depend upon the nature of the preceding inspiration. It is also clear that we must be raising the larynx by shutting the mouth, if by opening it we had previously lowered the voice-box. In singing up the scale the larynx gradually rises, though in changing the mode of tone production it stands lower for the first tones of the higher "register" than for the last tones of the corresponding lower register. It must be also borne in mind that it is quite possible, and under certain circumstances even necessary, to limit these movements to a considerable extent. The highest position is occupied by the larynx in the act of swallowing, when it rises so completely as to be no longer noticeable in the throat.

Further, the larynx occupies different positions in the throat in *whispering* various vowel sounds. It stands lowest for *oo* and highest for *ee*, the succession being as follows: *oo, oh, ah, ai, ee.*

THE HUMAN VOICE AS A MUSICAL INSTRUMENT.

"Physiologists," says Dr. Witkowski (op. cit., p. 1), "are quite at issue when they endeavour to determine what kind of instrument the vocal organ resembles; indeed Galien compares it to a flute, Magendie to a hautboy, Despinez to a trombone, Diday to a hunting-horn, Savart to a bird-catcher's call, Biot to an organ-pipe, Malgaigne to the little instrument used by the exhibitors of "Punch," and Ferrein to a spinet or harpsichord. The last named compared the lips of the glottis to the strings of a violin; hence was given the name *vocal cords*, which they have since retained. The current of air was the bow, the thyroid cartilages the *points d'appui*, the arytenoids the pegs, and, lastly, the muscles inserted in them the power which tensed or relaxed the cords."

Of the above theories there are three which seem particularly plausible, and which we must therefore examine.

1. THE STRING THEORY.—The vocal ligaments were compared 200 years ago by Ferrein to vibrating strings, and as the sounds of both are raised by tension there seem, at first sight, to be good grounds for this comparison. We have since learnt, what Ferrein did not know, that the tone of the vocal ligaments may be raised, like that of strings, by shortening, which fact goes a long way towards confirming his theory. Nevertheless, the comparison breaks down as soon as we examine it at all carefully, for it is found by experiments that the scale of changes produced by the tension of strings is totally different from that of the same process applied to the vocal ligaments. But apart from this it is manifestly impossible for strings as

short as the vocal ligaments to produce the resonant low tones of deep bass voices. The theory that the human voice is a stringed instrument must therefore be dismissed as untenable.

2. THE FLUTE-PIPE THEORY.—We have seen in the chapter on sound that the pitch of tones produced by flute-pipes is mainly governed by the length of the tube. Now the larynx, as a general rule, stands lower in the throat in the production of low tones than in the production of high tones, which, of course, means that the vocal tube is longer in the production of low tones and shorter in the production of high tones. There would, consequently, seem to be some justification in comparing the human voice to a flute-pipe. But when we consider that it requires an open tube of about six feet to produce the low G of any ordinary bass voice, we see at once that this comparison cannot for a moment be seriously maintained, and it is therefore unnecessary to enter into details concerning the alterations of pitch, &c.

3. THE REED THEORY is the one most generally accepted by modern writers, and so far as the actual production of the original tones of the voice is concerned it is absolutely correct, because the vocal ligaments cut up the column of air passing between them into a quick and regular succession of puffs, just the same as reeds. If nothing else were required to prove the case the human voice would undoubtedly have to be considered a reed instrument. Let us therefore look into this matter carefully. We have seen in the chapter on sound (p. 29) that there are two kinds of reeds, namely, stiff reeds and flexible reeds. Our attention can, of course, only be claimed by the latter. The pitch of their tones is, as we have learnt, almost entirely governed by the length of the tube to which they are attached. That is to say, the vibrations of

the column of air in the tube overpower those of the reed and compel it to vibrate in sympathy with themselves. What this really means will be seen most clearly when it is remembered that in instruments like the clarionet and the oboe the *same reed* producing the *same tone* serves for the whole compass, and that the alterations in pitch are *solely* brought about by alterations in the length of the tube.

Nor is this all. Not only are instruments such as the above mentioned *capable* of producing low tones of a very different pitch from those high tones corresponding, or nearly corresponding, to the proper tones of their tongues, but these high tones are not used in music at all, because they are shrill and unpleasant, and their pitch cannot be maintained with sufficient certainty.

There is yet another kind of reed instrument which is formed by the human lips in brass instruments, and as these form *membranous* tongues it might be supposed that their action, in conjunction with the tube to which they are attached, corresponds most exactly to that of the vocal ligaments with the cavities above and below them.

But the lips cannot produce tone by any vibrations of their own. "Babies may be often heard to 'trill the lips,' and German coachmen use a very audible lip-trill to stop their horses, but in each case the real tone is produced in the larynx, and the vibration of the lips only serves to interrupt it; these examples, however, allow us to judge of the rate of vibration natural to the lips." (Helmholtz, op. cit., p. 147. Footnote by Alexander Ellis.) We also know that in horns and trumpets, &c. (without keys), the range is limited to the prime tone, with its harmonic upper partials, of the tube. "In the use of brass instruments the different form and tension of the lips of the player act only to determine which of the proper tones of the tube shall speak; the pitch of the individual tones is almost entirely independent of the tension of the lips." (Helmholtz, op. cit., p. 149.)

We have thus fully reviewed the nature of reed instruments with flexible and with membranous tongues, and we must now compare their leading characteristics with those of the human voice. We see at once the vast difference between reeds and the vocal ligaments, inasmuch as the latter " have the advantage over all artificially constructed tongues of allowing the width of their slit, their tension, and even their form to be altered at pleasure with extraordinary rapidity and certainty" (Helmholtz, op. cit., p. 147), which is equally true of the vocal ligaments as compared with the human lips in playing upon brass instruments.

With regard to the vocal tube we think the truth is this: the resonator of the human voice, commencing with the pockets of the larynx (or ventricles of Morgagni) and ending at the lips and the nostrils, " admits of much variety of form, so that many more qualities of tone can be thus produced than on any instrument of artificial construction." (Helmholtz, op. cit., p. 147.) It has also *some* influence on the pitch. This is proved without the shadow of a doubt by the fact, first discovered by Donders, and afterwards worked out more accurately by Helmholtz, Merkel, Koenig, and others, that the cavity of the mouth for different vowels is tuned to different pitches. We are not, as everybody knows by practical experience, hereby prevented from hearing the various vowels except on tones the partials of which are reinforced by different shapes of the cavity of the mouth; but certain pitches are unquestionably more favourable to some vowels than to others.

Again, the soft palate contracts more and more, and the

arch between the pillars of the fauces gets narrower and higher, as we sing up the scale, relaxing again visibly when we change, for instance, from "chest" to "falsetto," just as the larynx falls under the same circumstances after it has previously risen in the throat. The contraction of the pillars of the fauces cannot take place without drawing together the upper horns of the larynx, thereby narrowing the space between the wings of the shield cartilage; and this movement has the effect of raising the pitch of the voice, as any one can prove to himself by imitating it with his fingers in the act of singing a tone.

Finally, we must bear in mind that the windpipe has the power, to some extent, of varying its length and calibre, and of assuming different degrees of tension. "The experiments of Savart have shown that a cavity which only responds to a shrill note when its walls are firm and dry, may be made to afford a great variety of lower tones when its walls are moistened and relaxed in various degrees. This observation may probably be applied also to the trachea." ('Principles of Human Physiology,' by Dr. Carpenter. London: John Churchill, 7th ed., p. 791.)

"Sir Charles Wheatstone more than forty years ago drew attention to this relation of the variation in tension of a tube to a free reed, and illustrated it by the instrument known as the jew's harp, in which the reed, being set in motion, produces one steady bass sound. The variation of sounds is produced wholly in proportion as the skill and will of the performer varies the cavity of the mouth so as to present a succession of volumes of air calculated to vibrate the different multiples of the primary bass sound. This influence of the tube is by experiment found to be the same whether the tube is placed after the reed, as in several wind instruments or before *and* after it, as in the vocal organs." ('Medical Hints on the Production and Management of the Singing Voice,' by Lennox Browne, F.R.C.S. London: Chappell & Co., p. 27.)

Under these circumstances we are justified in declining to believe that the alterations in the length, shape, and tension of the tubes above and below the vocal ligaments are *entirely* without influence upon the pitch of the voice; but we are obliged to admit that it plays only a secondary part in the matter. The question is admirably summed up by Helmholtz in the following words: "In the larynx the tension of the vocal chords, which here form the membranous tongues, is itself variable, and determines the pitch of the tone. The air chambers connected with the larynx are not adapted for materially altering the tone of the vocal chords. Their walls are so yielding that they cannot allow the formation of vibrations of the air within them sufficiently powerful to force the vocal chords to oscillate with a period which is different from that required by their own elasticity. The cavity of the mouth is also far too short, and generally too widely open, to serve as a resonance chamber which could have material influence on the pitch." (Op. cit., p. 149.)

It is evident from the foregoing considerations that the human voice, the original action of the vocal ligaments notwithstanding, is in its entirety no more a reed instrument than a flute, pipe, or a string instrument.

There are authors who, having come to the same conclusion, try to compromise matters by asserting that the human voice *combines* the properties of the above-named three classes of instruments; but the laws governing reeds, flute-pipes, and strings are so totally different as to make such a combination a physical impossibility. The fact is that the human voice is so immeasurably superior to any instrument made by human hands that all attempts at defining its nature must necessarily fail. "The *vox humana* of the Divine Artificer is an incomparably more complex, as it is an incomparably more beautiful, instrument than any of its compeers. Fearfully and wonderfully is it made. Not only is its mechanism more intricate, not only are its constituent parts more numerous and delicate than those of any artificial organ, but the action of these is complicated by conditions from which every other instrument is free." ('The Cultivation of the Speaking Voice,' by John Hullah. London: Macmillan & Co., p. 9.)

PHYSICAL CAUSES OF THE DIVISION OF VOICES.

We now come to the question how the various classes of voice—i.e. soprano, contralto, tenor, and bass—are to be accounted for by physical differences. Tone is produced by the vibrations of the vocal ligaments; unquestionably, therefore, a voice must be high or low according to the number of vibrations the ligaments are capable of producing within a given time. This is in accordance with the laws of sound, and admits of no objection. When, however, we endeavour to ascertain upon what conditions this vibrational number depends, we are met by great difficulties, because the subject is still to a great extent shrouded in mystery.

But as a logical consequence of the conclusion at which we arrived when discussing the question whether the human voice is a reed instrument or not, we are now driven to admit that the chief, though not the only, cause of the differences between the different classes of voices must be sought in the vocal ligaments.

When we compare the vocal ligaments of a soprano with those of a bass we see so great a difference in the dimensions of the two pairs of ligaments, i.e. in their length, width, and thickness that no one would hesitate as to which of the two produced the high voice and which the low one. This difference of size is even more striking in exsected larynges than in living persons, because in the former we can carefully examine the vocal ligaments, not only from above, but also from below; and we cannot fail to be struck with the fact that the proportions of the male larynx as a body are much larger in every direction than those of the female.

So far, then, the matter is clear enough, and goes a long way to confirm the principle of small vocal ligaments for high voices and of large vocal ligaments for low voices. But the difference between the vocal ligaments of soprano and contralto on the one hand, and between those of tenor and bass on the other, are not always equally marked. It is true that, as a rule, the vocal ligaments of soprano and tenor are shorter than those of contralto and bass; but it is also true that sometimes the very opposite is the case.

When the ligaments of contralto and bass are comparatively short, they are thick in proportion; their tension is also small because their thickness is due to the large bulk of the shield-pyramid muscles which are contained in them, and this enables them to yield less to the stretching influence of the ring-shield muscles than would otherwise be the case.

When the ligaments of soprano and tenor are comparatively long, they are thin in proportion; their tension is also relatively great because their thinness is due to the small bulk of the shield-pyramid muscles, and this prevents them from resisting the stretching influence of the ring-shield muscles, as much as would otherwise be the case. Under these circumstances the vocal ligaments occupy a very slanting position, which causes them to "speak" very readily, i.e. little power of blast is required to set them in vibration. Soprano and tenor voices with such a mechanism are of a light and flexible kind, and their higher registers are readily united with the lower ones.

The above statements are confirmed by that great authority, Prof. Merkel, of Leipzig, who most minutely explains the subject in his latest work on the larynx. ('Der Kehlkopf,' by Carl Ludwig Merkel, M.D. Leipzig: J. J. Weber.) There are, however, without any doubt, other factors besides those enumerated above, which are of consequence in determining the particular kind of voice to be produced by this or that vocal apparatus, as for instance the tube above the vocal ligaments, or the windpipe, or both. Thus we have seen that a pressing together of the upper portion of the shield cartilage has the effect of raising the pitch of the voice. It is, therefore, but reasonable to infer that larynges in which this part is naturally narrower than in others, will produce a higher voice.

With regard to the trachea, Dr. Jagielski has suggested that, " following a general law, the calibre and length of the windpipe is less in short people than in tall, and that, therefore, persons with high voices are generally short in stature. Where the singer is tall, with tenor or soprano range, he believes that the windpipe branches off very high up, and so the tube is lessened in length, and that the wind-pipe and larynx are disproportionate to the stature, and *vice versâ* where persons of short stature have low voices." (Lennox Browne, op. cit., p. 29.) It is possible that the capacity of the chest, the structure of the whole body, or even, as imagined by some, the complexion, may have something to do with the kind of voice a person possesses; but we have not as yet any knowledge with regard to such influences, and they consequently remain for the present a matter of speculation.

To what an extent such speculation is carried by some writers may be seen from the following amusing paragraph in *Musical Opinion*, March 1st, 1883: "The voice is more acute among the inferior than in the higher orders of animals, in the birds than in the mammalia, in the smaller species than in the larger. The ancient nations must have had higher voices, because the Adam's apple, which is the more prominent the lower the voice, was regarded as a deformity. In proportion as races are developed the antero-posterior diameter of the larynx is increased. The Adam's apple becomes more and more pronounced, and the voice tends constantly to become lower. The primitive peoples of Europe must have had nothing but tenor voices; their actual descendants are baritones; our posterity in the future, according to the doctor's theory, will be all bassos. We are descending the scale of sounds. The races which are still in the rear of civilisation ought, therefore, at the present moment, says Dr. Delaunay, to have higher voices than the white races. This, he affirms, is the case with the negroes and the Mongolians. The height of the voice, he continues, is so clearly a characteristic of the stage of evolution, that as age advances, the limits of the human voice continue to remove from the acute to the grave, consequently one may be a tenor at sixteen, a baritone at twenty-five, and a bass at thirty-five years of age.

"In general—it is always the doctor who speaks—sopranos and tenors are blonde, while the contraltos and basses are brown. Tenors are thin, basses are fat. The voice is grave in men of seriousness and intelligence. It is fluty—we are still quoting Dr. Delaunay—among the frivolous and empty-headed.

"The voice is higher before eating than after. This is the reason why tenors and sopranos dine early. Stimulant foods and strong liquors, by provoking a certain congestion of the larynx, make the voice lower. Therefore tenors are sober and avoid alcoholic drinks; on the other hand, the bassos can with impunity eat and drink what they like.

"The action of singing, again, determines a congestion of the organs of phonation. A tenor who uses his voice too much loses his high notes, and becomes a baritone. All singers, whether male or female, can go higher in the morning than in the evening. The music of matins is higher than vespers. The voice is higher in the south than in the north. The majority of French tenors come from the departments which border on the Mediterranean or the Pyrenees. On the other hand, in the north we find the basses. At the Russian Church in Paris there are basses who can give the *contre-ut-de poitrine*.

"The voice is somewhat higher in summer than in winter. The pitch is affected by the variations of temperature. M. Delaunay might have added that it depends also on the variations of the barometer."

THE HYGIENIC ASPECT OF THE VOCAL APPARATUS.

To those who have studied carefully the foregoing chapters, and have rightly appreciated the importance of accurate knowledge of their vocal organ as a whole and in a state of health, little need be said to enforce attention to Nature's simple laws for the general sanitary well-being of the singer and speaker; nor need much argument be employed to prove that only second in the importance of a sound body for a sound mind is the necessity for such a condition to possession of a pure voice. The reader may, however, be encouraged to learn at the commencement of our remarks, that in direct proportion as he takes care of his body will his vocal health and strength be maintained, and, on the other hand, that the better the voice the better usually is the general health, and the more robust the vocal organ; for above everything does good tone production imply high oxygenation of the tissues; and a delicate condition of the throat is, if not invariably, most frequently the result of wrong use or abuse of its functions.

Physical strength and digestion by no means universally interfere with the force of brain of the writer or composer, nor with the hand of the painter, and though naturally either pen or brush is wofully handicapped where the health of him who wields it is impaired, much good literary and artistic work—and even the very best—has been achieved by the feeble and delicate. For singing, however, the body is an essential part of the voice, it is the very encasement of the instrument, and if at any time disordered in health, impairment of vocal function is a direct and immediate result. For in voice production alone can no correction of faults be made when the tone has once been uttered, and unlike the written phrase or painted work it must tell its own tale at the very moment it issues from its possessor.

We trust to the reader's good sense not to think any direction as to diet, exercise, or health unworthy of attention because at first sight it may appear trivial. The successful singer's life must be one long practice of self-denial. Articles of diet which, if not beneficial from a food point of view, may be harmless to the ordinary individual, will often prove detrimental to the due capacity of breathing power necessary for the vocalist, or they may from their piquancy act as direct irritants of the fauces and impair *timbre* and resonance, or as reflex irritants affect volition and certainty of utterance. Violent or even moderate athletic exercise must be avoided, or indulged in only with rigid precautions against a too sudden lowering of the increased body temperature. Indulgence in dancing and other innocent amusements, from the additional reason that they occasion exposure to inhalations of dust and too late hours, will often have to be abjured, or enjoyed only at the risk of impairment of the singer's great possession. While it is an undoubted fact that many grand voices have been irretrievably ruined by neglect of this quality of self-abnegation, it is equally true that thousands find themselves cheerfully abstaining from luxuries of the table and the so-called pleasures of their non-singing relatives and friends for the sake of retaining their one great and heaven-bestowed gift, and with the result of materially conserving their general health and vitality as well as their voice.

For reasons already stated there is indeed nothing to be said as to the rule of life of a voice-user that would not be beneficial to the health of every individual, only while to the one attention to detail is essential for the performance of daily duty, to others it is, though always advisable, only absolutely necessary when warned by illness that a law of nature has been transgressed.

Health management of the human voice must be viewed then from very many and various, but equally important, standpoints. In the first place it should be considered in relation to hygiene as affecting elements of its composition already considered when treating of its mechanism; and this will be the purpose of this chapter. It will comprise consideration of (1) the motor portion representing the lungs and their function of respiration; (2) the vibrating portion representing the larynx and the share it takes in the production of various pure vocal tones by varied use of the registers; (3) the resonant cavity as comprised in the pharynx, fauces, cavity of the mouth, and nasal passages; and lastly, the articulating apparatus in which are included the tongue, palate, lips, teeth, &c.

To render more complete the discussion of all points connected with these different portions of the vocal organ from initial force to articulate emission it will be further necessary to consider the influence of fashion, dress, diet, and many simple points of hygiene on the general health, matters which may be considered as part and parcel of the daily life of the voice-user, and in conclusion we will say something as to the commoner diseased conditions in so far as they may be recognised as a cause of vocal impairment, or as remediable by means within the reach of the non-medical reader. We do not desire for one moment to invite the reader to be constantly doctoring himself—in fact, nothing could be more pernicious than such a practice, both to the vocal organ itself and to the mental happiness of its possessor. On the contrary, we hope to be able to prove that defects in voice-production from the medical point of view, no less than from the teacher's, depend in by far the majority of instances, on general and not on local causes; and if we can indicate these we shall confer great benefit on the class for whom we write, by inducing them to seek for a cause instead of treating symptoms by quack nostrums whose effects are almost always, when not negative, actually harmful.

I.—THE HYGIENIC ASPECT OF MANAGEMENT OF THE MOTOR PORTION—RESPIRATION.

The question of *breathing* has been very fully considered in its physiological aspect, and very complete directions as to the best methods of exercising the act are contained in the chapter on practice; but something may be said in viewing it from a medical aspect, as to the chemical act of respiration; that is, how does it affect the general vitality independently of its action on the vocal ligaments? And then, how from the mechanical point of view does it affect the health or perfection of the vocal mechanism in part and as a whole?

RESPIRATION CHEMICALLY CONSIDERED.—Dry air consists of four volumes of nitrogen, one volume of oxygen, a very little carbonic acid, and a mere trace of several other substances.

Oxygen is by far the most active constituent of the air, and to the agency of it are owing the existence of animal life, the maintenance of combustion, &c.

Nitrogen forms the bulk of the air. It possesses few

chemical properties of consequence, but performs the important part of diluting the oxygen which, if inhaled alone, would act with too great intensity.

The following graphic description of the process of breathing and of its effects upon the general economy, is condensed from Dr. Paul Niemeyer's 'Die Lunge,' Leipzig. J. J. Weber, 1872 :—

"The *Lungs* (1) swallow the air; (2) digest it, and (3) throw it out again after it has become useless."

"The *Air* we breathe *out* is (1) warmer than when inhaled; of this we have a proof in winter when our lungs seem positively to be steaming; (2) it carries water which we can condense on a cold pane of glass, and which in very cold weather freezes in our beards, on ladies' veils, &c.; (3) it is also otherwise chemically altered, as we perceive on entering a close room full of people, when we instinctively hurry to the nearest window and throw it open. We have an impression that the air in the room is very different from that we have just been inhaling out of doors; and that this is true would be proved if one of those present were to blow through a little glass tube into a bottle filled with lime-water, or if we left a wide-mouthed bottle of this fluid standing open in the room. The limewater would very soon become thereby clouded, the cause of which change is that the lime uniting with the carbonic acid from the breath produces white carbonate of lime, or in plain English, chalk. *A change of gases* therefore takes place in the lungs, which is brought about in 'this way: the blood consumes the oxygen and throws out carbonic acid in return."

The result of this is that our dark-blue blood is changed into bright-red blood without which we cannot perform the simplest muscular act, such as lifting an arm or moving a finger; and this is what is called the chemical aspect of breathing.

Oxygen, as we thus see, is the oil in the lamp of life, and the necessity of always having fresh air is therefore self-evident. The question, then, of the purity of the air to be breathed is one of immeasurable importance, but one very generally neglected. The difference between the air of the practice-room of the singer in daylight and of the gas-heated and often dust-laden concert-room and theatre is undoubtedly the cause of many a failure and disappointment of both vocalist and *entrepreneur*, who have, as the result of rehearsal, anticipated a success not always realised on the public platform. Supposing all that was necessary in breathing in air to the lungs was for the individual to take in a large amount at a time irrespective of considerations of temperature and dust, particles of organic and inorganic matter such as are always floating about in the atmosphere of cities and habitations, there would be no reason why he should not inhale with the open mouth; but since nature has provided, in the nostrils, an apparatus both for warming and filtering the air, it is important that this passage should be used, and that it should be quite open and unimpeded. Nasal breathing is also desirable because the muscles of the mouth and throat to be used in articulation, must not be fatigued by unnecessary and contrary actions. This point has been insisted on by both of us in previous works, and its importance has been recognised by many leading authorities. In point of fact, however, much misapprehension exists on the question. While we urge the importance of nose-breathing for full inflation, which is an act to be performed slowly, steadily, and gradually, we do not deny that for rapid half-breaths occasionally demanded by the singer or speaker, inspiration by the mouth is not only justifiable but unavoidable. Habitual practice, however, in mouth-breathing can only lead to great discomfort, if not to actual and direct mischief of the throat, windpipe, and chest; and such is very probable to result in the foggy and cold-damp weather of spring, autumn, and winter, three parts of the year as experienced in this country. As Dr. Elsberg remarks (Op. cit., p. 17), "The natural mode of quiet breathing is through the nose; mouth-breathing is an acquirement. A new-born infant would choke to death if you closed its nose; it does not immediately know how to get air into the lungs through the mouth until after, by depressing the tongue, you have once made a passage for it." Those who have had a cold in the head, which obstructs the nostrils, know the great temporary discomfort occasioned, and there is probably no affection more irksome and depressing than a constant closure of the nasal passages, as caused by polypus or any other obstruction. It may be added that even asthma and other serious chest diseases are induced from this cause, and that the purity and resonance of all vocal tone is diminished or destroyed in proportion to the amount of closure. In another place we answer the absurd objections of those who think that pursuance of the natural practice which we advocate leads to production of a disagreeable tone-quality which is called "nasal."

As these pages pass through our hands for press we read, and here make note, of a very instructive case reported in the *Lancet* of April 21, 1883, by Mr. Walsham, in which the singing voice had been quite lost for some few years, as the result of the septum of the nose being strongly bent to the right side. After an operation for the cure of this defect "the nasal intonation was lost, the patient is now able to sing with pleasure and his friends consider he has a very good voice."

Mr. Curwen, in his admirable 'Teachers' Manual,' has well said, "the singer's purpose necessitates a larger use of breath than is needed for ordinary respiration," as indeed it is for all muscular efforts requiring extra exertion, as those of lifting weights, running, &c., but it does not follow that the effort to increase the lung capacity for any of these actions is injurious; on the contrary it is beneficial, for the very act implies, unless the muscles be wrongly used or strained, and provided also that the inhaled air be pure, that the blood is so much the more purified, and consequently the general bodily strength is so much the more increased. Hence we see that from a health point of view, no less than from the singer's, the lungs must be well inflated with air of good quality; and therefore not only should the room in which singing is practised be well ventilated so that the air inspired be pure, but the more immediate surroundings, as the clothing of the singer, must be free, so as not to impede inspiration or impair regularity and economy of expiration.

Very pertinent to this question is the hygienic aspect of respirators, which, though doubtless of service to some persons, particularly females, and in some circumstances, are by no means without practical drawbacks. In the first place they encourage mouth-breathing to the neglect of respiration through the nostrils. Secondly, from the excessive warmth of the inhaled air they may actually induce that very delicacy of the throat and lungs, and a greater liability to take cold on removal, which is the special intention of the respirator to avert. Thirdly, they cause a constant re-inhaling of the same air mixed with much foul matter, which becomes accumulated in the instrument. Certainly if employed they should be of the cheapest kind, so that there will be less hesitation in their destruction when soiled. Better than a respirator is the veil invented by Mr. Lennox Browne, and sold by Messrs. Marshall & Snelgrove, which, having a special reduplication of the gauze as it falls over both mouth, nostrils, and ears, fulfils the purpose desired with avoidance of most of the dangers just detailed. Of course these can only be worn by ladies. Our opinion is that respirators should not be necessary for men if they did not shave and learned to breathe through the proper passages.

We have both for many years been enforcing the importance of filling the chest primarily at its base by descent of the midriff, circumferentially by rib expansion, and only to the very slightest degree and in very exceptional circumstances by any elevation whatever of the collarbone. It has been, therefore, a subject of great regret to us that quite recently, just as the importance of these rules was becoming recognised, certain teachers, some of very high attainments in other respects, have endeavoured, and really it would seem for the sake of saying something new, to prove otherwise. One writer, whose arguments are so well put as to read amazingly like sense to the uninitiated, endeavours to justify collar-bone breathing by reference to the act of inspiration as practised for a sudden and violent expiratory effort, as of blowing out a candle, forgetting that in singing the air should be expelled so gradually that the flame of a candle should not be moved, and in like manner that exaggerated in-breathing is equally undesirable. The fact may once more be briefly insisted on, that breathing by descent of the diaphragm means that method which is most natural in all positions of the body, even in that in which the lungs have the smallest capacity, that is, when lying on the back. In this method of taking in the breath there is less resistance of the muscles which govern its exit, and when the diaphragm has descended, and the floating ribs have expanded, the upper ribs follow almost as a natural sequence of the same respiratory act. If the respiration be extended to elevation of the collar-bones and shoulder-blades, not only is there very little gain in lung volume, but there ensues very considerable muscular fatigue, because there is the superincumbent weight of the shoulder-blades and arms on the small upper ribs, and because the muscles attached in this region have other functions than that of breathing. It also causes congestion of the vessels of the neck and throat. In reaction from this straining, the muscles controlling the exit of the breath do not act with regularity or steadiness; and thus we see that this fault in breathing is at the root of gasping, jerking, and fatigue in inspiration, and of unevenness, trembling, and undue vibration in the production and emission of vocal tone. To correct these faults an effort is made by the muscles in the pharynx, which in turn leads to congestion and relaxation of that part.

Some may enquire why the method of filling the lungs by elevating the collar-bones and shoulder-blades should be deprecated, if there is any power to fill them by exertion of the connecting muscles. We answer that this kind of inspiration is only employed by instinct of nature when, from disease, midriff or costal breathing is impeded, and that the fact of a patient breathing in this manner is noted by a physician as a grave symptom, because it indicates mischief of a vital nature in lungs, heart, or other important organs.

Nothing is more detrimental to free expansion of the

chest than corset-wearing of the form and material now manufactured, even if not tightly laced. All sensible people begin to admit this fact, which, as we shall relate presently, is susceptible of demonstration. But if the right method of breathing were by upward elevation, with the consequent safe submission to the slight inward movement which results from the simple drawing out or lengthening of the upper frame, confinement of the lower chest by stays would be innocuous. That corsets, as usually worn, are injurious may be seen by comparison of Pl. XVIII., in which the ribs are delineated as in an unconfined or natural chest, and in Pl. XIX., the outline of which is multiplied by the thousand in fashion plates, and again in Pls. XX. and XXI., in which the portion of the lungs and other important organs are contrasted as in the natural and in the constricted cavities.

Mr. Bernard Roth, to whom we owe the idea of the two last figures, very well explains the injurious effects of the corset, and we cannot do better than quote him at length. ('Dress: its Sanitary Aspect.' Churchill, London, 1880, pp. 8 to 11.) "The lower ribs which are least supported in front are precisely those which are influenced by anything tight about the waist; thus close-fitting, unyielding *stays*, as generally worn, gradually compress the yielding lower ribs more and more, till their anterior extremities, instead of being far apart, meet almost or quite in the middle line. (Compare Pl. XVIII. with Pl. XIX.) This deformity occurs so gradually during years of growth, that the wearer is generally quite unconscious of having disfigured herself, and I have never yet met with a lady who owned to having a tight pair of stays. 'I can put my whole hand inside,' is the usual reply when I find fault with a patient. This is generally quite true; for, by drawing in the abdominal muscles which act upon the anterior extremities of the ribs, by raising the diaphragm, and by slightly inclining the body forwards the girth of the trunk can be still further diminished. The real test is to have the stays opened, and

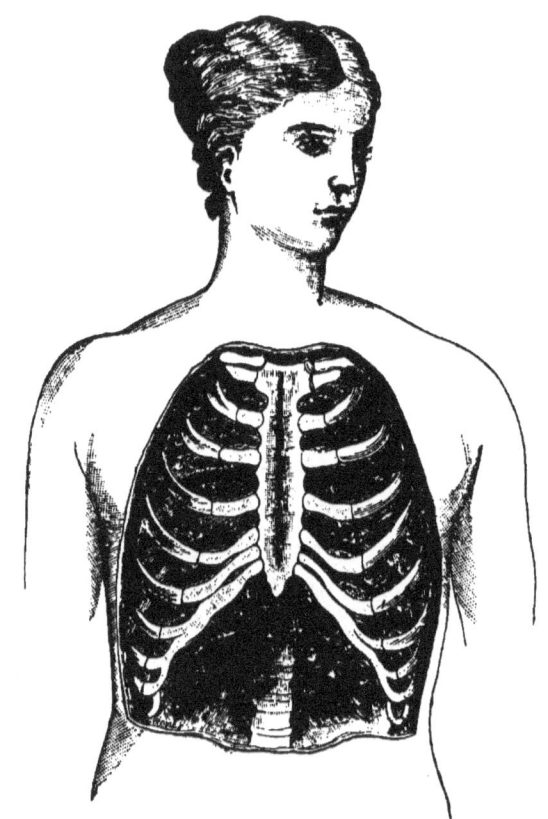

XVIII.—FRAMEWORK OF CHEST.—NATURAL WAIST. (*Adapted from Professor Flower's 'Fashion and Deformity.'*)

all other constricting bands loosened, and to request the patient to breathe deeply and slowly a few times, with the arms directed upwards if necessary, and then to ask her to fasten the *outer* dress alone while holding the body as erect as possible. It is generally impossible to bring the dress together after such an experiment, because the chest, having at last a chance of freedom, has expanded a little and refuses to be put back into its narrow prison. This pressing inward of the ribs, which become in time per-

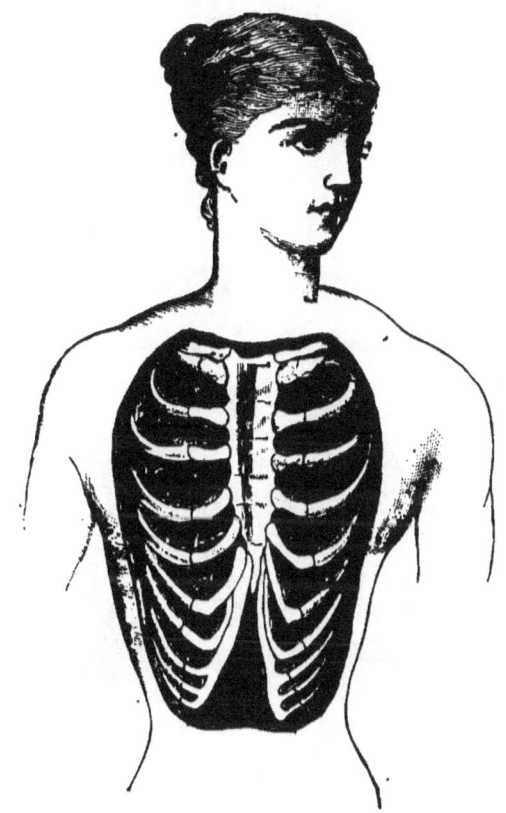

XIX.—FRAMEWORK OF CHEST.—DEFORMED WAIST. (*Adapted from Professor Flower's 'Fashion and Deformity.'*)

manently deformed, causes necessarily a very great diminution in the size of the chest and abdominal cavities. (Compare again Plates XVIII. and XIX., also XX. and XXI.) One very serious effect of this is that the bases, or lower parts of the lungs, do not perform their functions properly, for there the chest walls can hardly move at all during respiration, in addition to their volume being much diminished; the upper halves of the lungs have consequently to do more than their

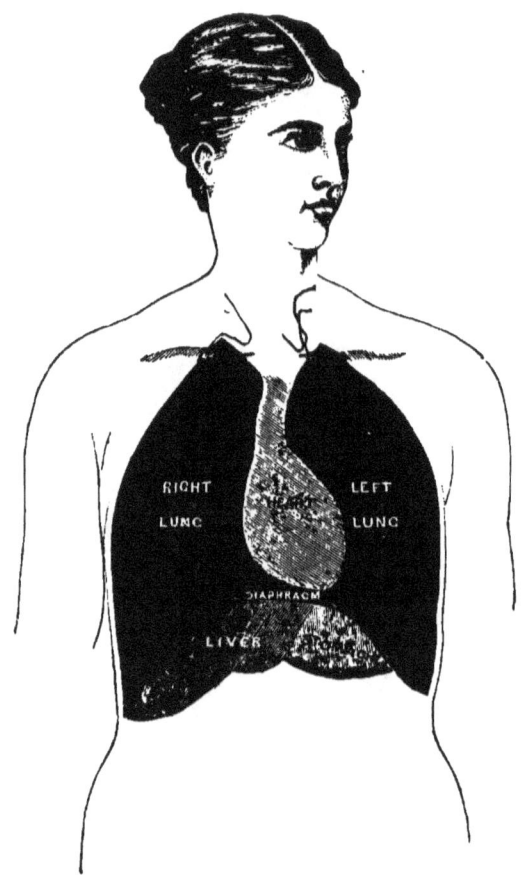

XX.—Natural Position of Organs in Unconfined Chest.
(*Adapted from Roth.*)

proper share of work." A writer in *Knowledge*, October 13, 1882, naïvely uses this fact as an argument in favour of the "well-applied corset," stating that it "leaves the upper part of the chest perfectly free, and develops the capacity of the lungs in that situation—the most important situation, by-the-bye, especially in the female sex. Tubercular consumption usually attacks the apices of the lungs, a part far removed from the pressure of a corset, however

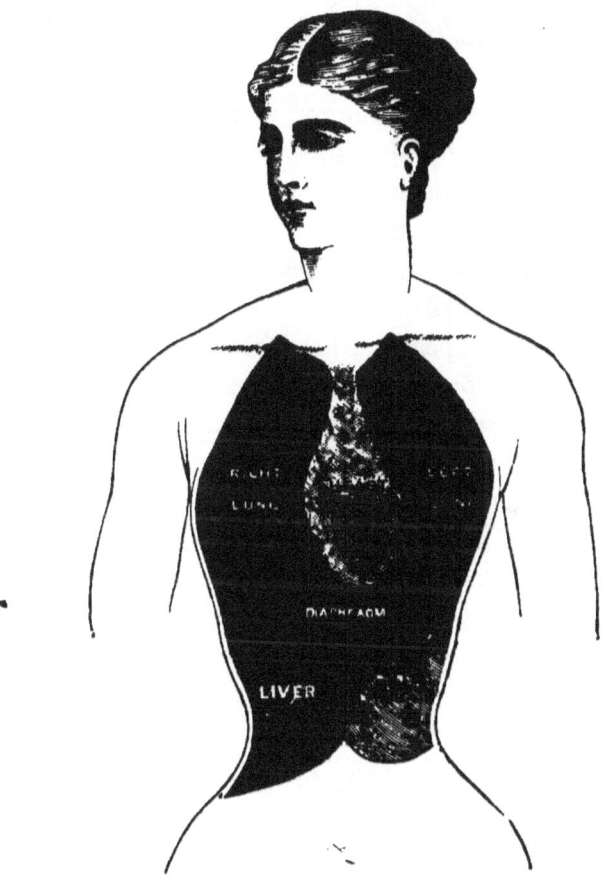

XXI.—Distorted Position of Organs in Body Deformed by Stays.
(*Adapted from Roth.*)

tight—in fact the tighter the corset in the lower part of the chest, the greater amount of work and expansion in the upper part, but this would not lead to consumption."

Such an argument will not bear a moment's consideration, since overuse of one portion of the lung and impeded action of the other must necessarily be followed by disease in both directions. Returning to Mr. Roth's argument, that writer continues: "At the same time the respiratory action of the diaphragm is obstructed not only by the reduced extent of its attachment to the ribs, but also from the compression of the abdomen. This insufficiency of respiratory power and diminution in the size of the lungs can account for many a serious illness, the way for which was prepared by deficient oxygenation of the blood; besides, all the above-mentioned abdominal organs are displaced downwards, because there is no longer any room for them at the so-called 'elegant' waist; the liver reaches down to the hips (pelvis), whereas in its natural position it should hardly project beyond the margins of the chest cavity. (Compare Pls. XX. and XXI.) This displacement of and pressure on these important organs offer a serious obstacle to the proper carrying out of their special functions, hence indigestion, congestion of the liver, and similar troubles. The deplorably large percentage of women who have some displacement or affection of the womb is due, no doubt, to this pernicious habit of tight-lacing, which is more general than may be supposed by any one who has not paid special attention to this subject.

"The *Lancet* writes, on January 10, 1880:—'The notion of "improving" nature by forcing the feet into tight boots, and the divers other devices with which fashion beguiles the love of personal embellishment are sufficiently monstrous, but the audacity of attempting to compress the trunk, which contains the central organs of life, for the sake of appearances, surpasses belief. . . . Perhaps the recent death from tight-lacing, in which the heart was found to be so impeded in its action as to render life impracticable, may have some deterrent effect, but we doubt it. Fashion will prevail, and wasp-like waists will be cultivated in defiance of nature and art.'

"In addition to the injurious effects already mentioned tight stays are a common cause of so-called 'weak' spine, due to weakness of the muscles of the back. It is well known in physiology that for a muscle to remain in a healthy condition it must be fulfilling the functions proper to it, namely, of being constantly alternately contracted and relaxed. When muscles are prevented from being thus exercised they invariably waste. Any one who has had either one of the long bones of the upper or lower extremities broken, or some local injury or disease which has necessitated complete fixation of the limb in splints for six weeks or longer, will remember how all the muscles of the quiescent limb wasted, and how it took some time to restore the previous muscular power. A tightly-laced pair of stays acts precisely as a splint to the trunk, and prevents or greatly impedes the action of the chief back muscles, which therefore become weakened. The unfortunate wearer feels her spine weaken, thinks she wants more support, so laces herself still tighter; she no doubt does get some support in this way, but at what a terrible cost? everything embraced by those tight stays is fearfully compressed; and it has always been an anatomical enigma to me to conceive how the numerous organs, which I know to be there, can possibly exist in some ladies, whose bodies are not inaptly compared to those of wasps.

"I do not say that stays should necessarily be given up altogether, although many women would enjoy far better health if they were. Stays are, no doubt, of some use in supporting the bust of the adult woman"—provided they have been educated to their use, but not by any means

necessarily if they have never been worn in childhood—
" but this can be easily effected without pressing upon the
lower ribs, and without obstructing the respiratory movements. Rational stays should be made of some yielding
material with narrow strips of elastic webbing let in from
above down on the sides; and the fewer the pieces of
whalebone, and the smaller they are, the better."

Ladies inclined to *embonpoint* who have always worn
stays will find the material called "single coutil," or sateen,
a very suitable one from which to make hygienic corsets.
The form should be that of a "slip-bodice" cut low,
with or without the addition of broad straps or bands
over the shoulders. This corset or bodice should fasten
in front only with buttons, or with the usual fastenings,
but there should be no laces; it should come well down
over the hips, about as low as ordinary stays. Strips of
thin elastic webbing, two inches wide, should be inserted
at each side under the arm. We particularly emphasize
that the webbing should be *thin*. Some descriptions are
so stout as to require considerable muscular effort to
expand them, and would render the corset harmful to the
wearer by impeding the circulation. One piece of whalebone, or of the lightest-made flexible steel, should be placed
on each side of the spinal ridge—that is, along the middle
of the back—*not over it*, there being an interval of an
inch and a half between the two pieces—while another
similar piece on either side of the fastenings will be
sufficient to keep the corset from creasing. But there
should be no stiffening material inserted which would press
against the curved part of the ribs, as that would, of course,
interfere with their lateral expansion; and any additional
aid to the "set" of the garment can be efficiently gained
by "cordings." On to the lower edge of the corset

should be sewed flat buttons, at equal distances, and corresponding button-holes be made in all under garments by which they may be suspended from the corset, that is from the hips, instead of being fastened above them by bands and strings around the waist. For children and well-formed girls and women "coutil" is too heavy a material, and a very light twill, as employed for summer stays, simply corded, may be substituted. For ladies of slender figure, corsets made of the shape known as "riding stays," but of the material and fashion we have detailed, will be found to answer every requisite. *Thin* whalebone or equally thin steel can, if desired, be inserted in the front of the dress on each side of the fastening itself to keep it straight, but is not necessary as a means of "support." Should support be really needed for any spinal weakness or incipient deformity the pieces already described on each side of the spinal ridge—*again not over it*—will be found sufficient. Hygienic corsets, exactly of the kind we describe, can be obtained from Mr. Pratt of Oxford Street, or of Messrs. Ward & Co. of Ilkley, both of whom have made some under our express supervision. The waist and chest measure should be taken while the lady or child to be fitted is standing with head, shoulder-blades, and heels *all touching a wall;* the body being held very erect, and the tips of the fingers of each hand placed as far on the back of the shoulders as possible. Every female should be able to fasten her under-bodices and dresses while standing erect against a wall. If once properly fitted, there is no rational excuse for tightening or for varying the calibre of a corset.

If we can succeed in persuading mothers to adopt this sort of corset for their children, the gain in beauty of figure and graceful bearing will be immense. It is impossible for the stiffly-corseted girl to be other than inelegant and ungraceful in her movements. Her imprisoned waist, with its flabby muscles, has no chance of performing beautiful undulatory movements. In the ball-room the ungraceful motions of our stiff-figured ladies are bad enough; there is no possibility for poetry of motion; but nowhere is this more ludicrously, and to the thoughtful, painfully manifest than in the tennis-court. Let any one watch the movements of ladies as compared with those of male players, and the absolute ugliness of the female figure with its stiff, unyielding, deformed, round waist will at once be seen. Ladies can only bend the body from the hip joint. All that wonderfully contrived set of hinges, with their connected muscles, in the elastic column of the spine is unable to act from the shoulders downwards; and their figures remind one of the old-fashioned, wooden Dutch doll.

Another point in favour of the abandonment of tightly-fitting corsets, and one which may perhaps have influence with our lady readers, is the fact that their use tends to produce obesity. Our opinion on this point is confirmed by others.

In a letter headed "Stays and Fat," which appeared in *Knowledge* for 6th April last, Mr. Mattieu Williams says, "There is one horror which no lady can bear to contemplate, viz., fat. What is fat? It is an accumulation of unburnt body-fuel. How can we get rid of it when accumulated in excess? Simply by burning it away —this burning being done by means of the oxygen inhaled by the lungs. If, as Mr. Lennox Browne has shewn, a lady with normal lung capacity of 125 cubic inches, reduces this to 78 inches by means of her stays, and attains 118 inches all at once on leaving them off, it is certain that her prospects of becoming fat and flabby, as she advances towards middle age, are greatly increased by tight-lacing and the consequent suppression of natural respiration."

Hygienic stays, such as we have described, allow of the "proper respiratory movements of the lower part of the chest, and yet will not produce deformity, nor favour the abnormal accumulation of fat, although fitting the waist sufficiently well to please the dressmakers. Modern taste is unfortunately so vitiated that when a woman tries to avoid deforming her body, and possesses a natural waist, unless she is very thin, remarks are at once made about her clumsy figure, and these as frequently by men as by the deformed of her own sex. Indeed, this degraded taste for acquiring deformed waists would seem to have even infected men, if the expensive advertisements of men's corsets to be seen in so many newspapers are profitable to the advertisers."

It will be seen from the foregoing remarks that the idea of "support" being necessary to the figure is absolutely unfounded. The all-wise Creator has given to the female as many muscles as to the male. No one dreams of suggesting that a man or a boy requires stays "to keep him up" as the phrase goes; why then should girls and women? From actual knowledge we can testify that no girl who has never worn corsets feels the need of a "support." On the point of warmth alone stays have an advantage; but it is of a very slight character, and one that can be easily, and even better, supplied by a less tight and rigid garment, which would also cover the upper portion of the chest and back. And here let us caution ladies against the erroneous notion that if only their chests are well protected from cold they will take no harm. Extra warmth is necessary at the back, over the situation of the chain of nerves known as the sympathetic, whose purpose it is to regulate the supply of blood to the various organs of respiration and digestion, and to keep those organs in co-ordination. It is undoubtedly by draughts on the back of the body, whether the neck, chest, or loins, that colds, and inflammations due to colds, are most frequently taken. And that such is the case is shown by the fact that the sympathetic nerves which lie along the side of the spinal column are, when attacked by cold, impaired in their power of control over the circulation.

By the spirometer it has been demonstrated as the result of experiments on thousands of individuals of the male sex in a state of health, and of various occupations, that the lungs are capable of containing a varying amount of air in proportion to the height of the subject, the ratio being a difference of about 10 cubic inches for every inch of height between 5 and 6 feet. Above that limit the additional capacity diminishes with increased stature. This measurement holds good in subjects between the ages of 15 and 55, the vital capacity being at its maximum between the ages of 30 and 35 years, and is only further affected by the weight of the individual, and that not unless the corpulence be really excessive. A man in health, of the height of 5 feet 7 to 5 feet 8 inches, should breathe an average of 250 cubic inches of air. Such a man should weigh about 156 pounds; but he may weigh 10 or 12 pounds more without affecting his breathing powers. This and other allowances may be made which would account for variations to the extent of 16 per cent., or a diminution of about 38 to 40 cubic inches; below this standard the physician will suspect disease. As a matter of daily experience, however, we find many who cannot breathe even this minimum health-volume, because they have not understood how to fill their lungs for any sustained muscular effort, such as voice-use implies and demands.

We also find that, by practice, the average mean vital volume can be very considerably increased, even to half as much again. Thus it can be demonstrated that breathing practice, in other words, education on a right method of the motor power of voice-users, is beneficial to the general health.

Until quite recently no experiments have been made in any large numbers on females, and a deduction of 33 per cent. has been made for the "weaker sex." We have for many years been in the habit of making an allowance of only 25 per cent. for females; and more recent experience leads us to believe that even this difference is greater than would be justified by fact in normal subjects undeformed by fashion.* That the heavy clothing of ladies makes a great difference in their respiratory power may be proved by trying it first when the subject has on her shoulders the heavy velvet bugle-covered or seal-skin mantle, and then without it. There will always be a gain in the latter case of ten or fifteen inches; but if the experiment be made, even where to the male eye the charge of *tight* lacing cannot be made, but when the corset is of unyielding material, there will be almost uniformly a difference of one-third, and an immediate regain of power almost to the full average standard when the corset is removed. This we have tried repeatedly, and we have each published a case in *Knowledge* confirmatory of our opinion. In the one a young lady who, by her height, should, according to Hutchinson's Tables ('Medico-Chirurgical Transactions,' vol. xxix. London, 1846), breathe 145 cubic inches, was able with difficulty to exhale 100; but on removal of her stays at once and with ease blew 140 cubic inches into the

* See Table kindly prepared specially for this work by Mr. Charles Roberts, F.R.C.S., on page 123.

spirometer. Another lady, less than five feet high, should have breathed about 120 cubic inches. Before the removal of her corsets she managed, after several violent efforts, to breathe 75 inches only, but afterwards, at the first attempt, she breathed 118 inches. She discontinued the use of these stays, and took to others without whalebone or steel, and continued to maintain this gain in her chest expansion.

We now add two other cases illustrative of the fuller lung capacity in young ladies who do not wear corsets.

The first lady should, by her height and age (26), have a mean breathing capacity of 148 cubic inches. Her actual breathing power is 156, or 8 cubic inches *above* her mean. She was forced, when a child, to wear closely fitting corsets, but discontinued them when about thirteen or fourteen years of age, and has never since resumed them.

The second case is that of a child between twelve and thirteen, having a constitutional predisposition to consumption. Her parents, recognising the necessity for hygienic care, have scrupulously avoided any form of dress which would impede the full and healthy development of the vital organs. Her mean breathing power, if she were over fifteen years of age instead of being under thirteen, should be 118 cubic inches, but her actual lung capacity is even now 130, or 12 cubic inches above her mean. Humanly speaking, her parents have, by their care in rearing this delicate girl, preserved her from that dire scourge of two-thirds of our race—" consumption."

Let any speaker or singer ask himself whether the acquisition of such an amount of breath power over that which he is now habitually able to control is not worth trying for. So surely as a locomotive will come to a standstill if there be not a sufficient supply of fuel to generate the motive power—" steam," so surely will a singer

TABLE SHEWING THE AVERAGE HEIGHT, WEIGHT, BREATHING CAPACITY, CHEST-GIRTH, AND STRENGTH, OF ADULT MALES AND FEMALES IN ENGLAND.—Drawn up by Charles Roberts, Esq., F.R.C.S., From data collected by the Anthropometric Committee of the British Association for the Advancement of Science.

MALES.				Height without shoes.	FEMALES.			
Strength of arm as in drawing a bow.*	Chest girth after expiration.†	Weight, including clothes.‡	Breathing capacity.§		Breathing capacity.§	Weight, including clothes.‡	Chest girth below breasts.	Strength of arm as in drawing a bow.
lbs.	inches.	lbs.	Cubic inches.	inches.	Cubic inches.	lbs.	inches.	lbs.
85·1	38·9	165·6	290	72	238	141·1	32·7	51·1
83·9	38·4	163·3	280	71	230	139·1	32·2	50·4
82·7	37·8	161·0	270	70	221	137·2	31·7	49·7
81·5	37·3	158·7	260	69	213	135·2	31·2	49·0
80·3	36·7	156·4	250	68	204	133·3	30·8	48·3
79·2	36·2	154·1	240	67	196	131·3	30·4	47·6
78·0	35·7	151·8	230	66	187	129·4	30·0	46·8
76·8	35·1	149·5	220	65	179	127·4	29·5	46·1
75·6	34·6	147·2	210	64	170	125·4	29·0	45·4
74·4	34·0	144·9	200	63	162	123·5	28·5	44·7
73·3	33·5	142·6	190	62	153	121·5	28·1	44·0
72·1	33·0	140·3	180	61	145	119·6	27·6	43·3
70·9	32·4	138·0	170	60	136	117·6	27·2	42·6
69·7	31·9	135·7	160	59	128	115·6	26·6	41·9
68·5	31·3	133·4	150	58	119	113·7	26·1	41·2

* Taken by Herbert and Son's spring balance arm-testing machine.
† Military measurement. Tape round chest at nipples; arms hanging loosely by the side: let the patient count from one to ten and then read off the measurement.
‡ The average weight of indoor clothes, including the shoes, is for the professional class 8 lbs.
„ „ „ „ „ „ „ working „ 10 lbs.
Average for men .. .. 9 lbs.
The average weight of a woman's dress has not been accurately ascertained, but it is among female shop assistants and school teachers about 7 lbs. We are very much in want of information as to the weight of ladies' dresses. The average is probably nearly equal to that of the male working class.
§ Breathing Capacity of Males.—Hutchinson's table, published in 1846, gives a difference of only 8 cubic inches for each inch of height. The above table gives a difference of 10 inches for each inch of height, and a relative increase of upwards of 20 cubic inches as compared with Hutchinson. These differences are very probably the result of the greater accuracy of the instruments now employed.
Breathing Capacity of Females gives in this table an average decrease of power, as compared with males, of only 20 per cent., instead of 33 per cent. as estimated by Hutchinson. Thus, having made allowance for the relative increase granted by us for men, a female at 66 inches, who would have breathed 142 cubic inches according to the old table, is now found to have a vital capacity of 187 cubic inches.

or speaker ultimately break down in voice, and perhaps in health, if he be unable to command a sufficient supply of, and control over, his motor power—breath.

There are many other questions connected with costume affecting the respiration; as, for instance, the wearing of constricting collars around the neck, a fault very fashionable in the present day. There is no doubt also that the heavy and multiplied articles of clothing worn around the waist by females, tightly fitting abdominal belts and unduly braced suspenders in men, all act as weights impeding the power of chest expansion.

Posture has a remarkable influence on the respiration. The spirometer shows the vital volume to be greatest in the erect, less in the sitting, and least in the recumbent positions. Since, however, many are required to use the voice in the sitting posture, as when accompanying themselves at the piano, and that the prone or semi-prone position is also necessary on occasion in opera, we advise practice in all these attitudes. Exercise in the recumbent posture can with advantage be practised at early morning before rising from bed when the body is unencumbered with clothing, and again on rising, with arms bent at right angles to the body so as to fix the shoulder-blades well back. Practice in the sitting posture should be made with the arms brought back over the chair rail, which also ensures fixture of the collar-bones and shoulder-blades.

In regard to posture, allusion may be made to the habit of short-sighted persons of stooping down to their music on a piano to read their part, instead of wearing glasses and holding their music well before them; or, again, to the clergyman, who pursues a similar plan at the desk, or if he does hold his book up, presses it against the lower part of the chest to the very serious diminution of its expansive power, and a considerable addition to its resistance.

It is not out of place here to mention that respiratory exercises, and subsequently lessons in reading, reciting, and singing are oftentimes of the greatest use in strengthening a weak chest; and indeed, it is not too much to say, in arresting consumption. We have no doubt, from our experience of the improvement to be gained in respiratory power by means of such exercises, as demonstrated with the spirometer, that it would be very desirable and often highly beneficial to pursue a regular course of lung gymnastics, modified according to each patient's individual need, at various health resorts, such as Davos-am-Platz, &c. The subject is one which is receiving a considerable share of attention in Germany, and but little at present in this country. It has been well said, and without exaggeration, that "the condition of the air which we breathe becomes only significant through the breathing gymnastics. We send the sick to healthy localities, but what use is it when the fresh air is not permitted to penetrate sufficiently in and through the lungs. Air alone does not expand the lungs, and the benefit derived from mechanical expansion may outweigh even the advantages of a healthy locality."

Thus even in our own country, by means of properly directed respiratory gymnastics in well-ventilated rooms, much may be done towards the cure of lung complaints, especially in the early stages; and those in whom there is a consumptive or asthmatic diathesis would benefit greatly by such practice. Especially should the heads of families in whom such predisposition exists see that their children are trained from an early age to the use of these lung gymnastics.

Next in importance to the method of inflation and freedom from constriction of clothing comes the question of digestion as affecting free lung play. While on the one hand singing on an actually empty stomach will be imperfect on account of enfeebled muscular action due to want of nutrition; equally, on the other hand, the food must have been at least partially digested so that the stomach may not be distended by the food taken and the gases generated during the digestive process, but may have resumed its normal size. This subject will be treated more at length when we consider the rules for a voice-user's daily living.

II.—THE HYGIENIC ASPECT OF THE VIBRATING ELEMENT—THE LARYNX AND THE VOCAL LIGAMENTS.

Having enforced at some length our belief that control of the motor element is at the foundation of all good voice production, we go further and say that, from the medical point of view, if respiration be properly practised and controlled, trouble in producing pure vocal tone in the voice-box, or, as it might well be called, the "sound-box," is very rare: in other words, and paraphrasing an old proverb, "Take care of the lungs and the voice will take care of itself." Our experience, lasting for many years from the double point of view of doctor and teacher, and equally of patients and pupils, has led us to an independent but similar conclusion on this point, and of its correctness we are both most firmly convinced. Many defects complained of by patients or pupils are, by doctors and teachers unacquainted with, or unpractised in the use of, the laryngoscope, ascribed to trouble or disease in the larynx, which on inspection will be found perfectly healthy. The so-called straining of the vocal cords only exists in an ignorant imagination which fixes the seat of disease where the trouble is most frequently felt, and not at its source of origin. Of course there may be an inflammation or congestion of the vocal ligaments as of other parts, but it is astonishing in how large a majority of cases of loss of the speaking or singing voice the larynx escapes unless there be some serious constitutional mischief.

Action of the vocal ligaments is at least semi-automatic, and provided only that the registers be not extended beyond their normal limits, or the act of singing be pursued under unfavourable circumstances, or for too lengthened a period, it is very difficult to injure them. We have seen hundreds of cases in which the vocal ligaments supposed to be at fault have been healthy and in which vocal defects have been cured solely by attention to breathing, to digestion, or to some portion of the mechanism above the voice-box, that is to say in the resonating cavities.

Nervo-muscular affections giving rise to impaired mobility of the vocal ligaments are rare, and are generally due to constitutional or cerebral causes, or to pressure of some morbid growth, as an aneurism or other tumour on the motor nerve. As far, then, as we are here concerned with the vibrating element in its medical aspect, it is sufficient to give the reader the following directions if he desires to avoid laryngeal fatigue:—

1. Never endeavour to produce a vocal tone without having plenty of breath, and that thoroughly under control.

2 Hold the breath when *in*spired and commence to

*ex*pire only on commencing to speak or sing, that is, at the moment it is required to set the ligaments in vibration.

3. Do not think that loudness is essential to force or beauty; shouting is always injurious. The telling quality of *laryngeal* tone depends solely on the amplitude of the vibrations, and this is controlled solely and entirely by the *will* which directs the due proportion of air to set the vocal ligaments into more or less full vibration. For all purposes of practice it is especially advisable for the pupil to sing *piano*, which term does not imply diminished vigour, but simply reduced amplitude of the vibrations.

4. Never use the voice when functional failure gives warning that the organ or the general health is disordered.

5. Do not attempt to use the voice in unfavourable circumstances, as in the open air, especially if the weather be cold or raw, nor in a room impregnated with tobacco smoke, foul air, or dust. Above all do not use the voice, even for conversation, in trains or vehicles, or in any circumstances of noise which will require undue functional exertion. In this connection it will be important to keep quiet and avoid chattering and laughing between songs or the acts of a drama or opera.

6. Do not use the voice for too long a period at a time, but always cease before fatigue is experienced. Especially avoid *encores* of songs which have required much exertion or production of a telling high note in the final *cadenza*. It is but rarely that a song is sung as well on a re-demand as at first.

7. After continued singing or speaking be careful to prevent exposure of the throat either externally or internally to the impressions of cold air. The same remark applies as to the necessity of guarding against sudden

changes from hot to cold air even when the voice has not been used.

A few practical hints as to the symptoms and treatment of the milder forms of laryngeal disease will be found in the chapter " The Ailments of the Voice-User."

III.—THE HYGIENIC ASPECT OF MANAGEMENT OF THE RESONATING PORTION OF THE VOICE.

Questions of alterations of form as the result of constitutional disease, and disorders of secretion, oftentimes the result of indigestion, are here involved. These also will be elsewhere considered, and it is sufficient here to remark that in a vast number of instances of vocal impairment in which there is actual visible disease in this region, the first cause may often be found in defective respiration. In such a case an effort has been made in the pharynx or fauces to correct or strengthen a tone imperfectly formed in the vibrating portion due to an improperly impelled or insufficient volume of air. Mandl ('Hygiene de la Voix.' Paris, 1876. p. 17) has drawn attention to the fact that " during the effort which accompanies collar-bone respiration, it almost constantly occurs that the tongue is retracted, and as a result there is a diminution in the dimensions of the resonant cavities of the pharynx, the shape of which is now no longer capable of adapting itself to the exigencies of various tones on account of this forced position of the tongue. One can consequently and very readily understand the baneful influence which collar-bone breathing exercises on the *timbre*."

With regard to the hygienic management of the articulating cavity, it is essential that the pupil should thoroughly understand the various alterations of the shape of the lips and position of the tongue in enunciation of the various consonants, and it is from ignorance of or inattention to this physiological information that many songs musically beautiful are unintelligible or disagreeable in their effect on the hearer. It stands to reason as a result of this statement that it is absurd for a master to endeavour to teach songs in a language not his own, or with the pronunciation of which he is not fully acquainted; and it may be added that it would be well for the same reason if singers would confine delivery of songs to the same limits, or at least master the pronunciation of a language which they oftentimes only learn as a parrot for the actual lesson of each individual composition.

Before closing this chapter it may be worth while once more to insist that almost all faults of singing or speaking resolve themselves under one large heading of *fatigue;* and the cause of this fatigue, whether felt in chest, voice-box, or upper throat, is almost always to be found in irregular muscular action, causing undue struggle with the opposing muscles. The particular muscles most frequently at fault are the respiratory; and only by correct action of these muscles of respiration can fatigue of the voice be ensured against, or if experienced can it be remedied. It is astonishing how many and various are the defects which can be explained from this one standpoint. In the chest are induced shortness of inspiration, with labour, oppression, and hurry in expiration. These give rise to prickings, spasms, cramps, and even continuous muscular pains. The lungs imperfectly aërated are liable to congestions and over-distention, and the action of the heart is impaired, and even seriously disturbed. One very characteristic pain is a sensation of sinking in the neighbourhood of the diaphragm, or midriff, which might be well described in the words of Shakespeare as "an undergoing pain." It is due entirely to fatigue and consequent collapse of this normally firm supporting medium between chest and abdomen.

In the larynx, fatigue, due to the same cause, is felt as a contraction of the closing muscles, which leads to jerky and noisy breathing. Purity of vocal tone is painfully impaired, and the voice becomes weak in intensity, unequal in power, veiled in quality, quavering and shaky in utterance. All the refinements of vocalization are also lost or rendered uncertain. The singer or speaker oftentimes, as before stated, endeavours to overcome these laryngeal defects by use of the muscles of the pharynx, and almost all troubles in this region, not only of sensation, but as actually seen to be morbid to the medical eye, may be accounted for on the basis of this argument.

To the late Dr. Mandl, of Paris, we owe our thanks for having insisted on the importance of this very great hygienic question. His first articles in the *Gazette Médicale*, 1855, attracted much attention and opposition in both medical and musical journals. That they were required was proved by the fact that the following precept, to which we were the first to draw attention of English readers nearly ten years ago, as to breathing, was given in *La Méthode de Chant du Conservatoire de Musique*: "Quand on respire pour parler ou pour renouveler simplement l'air des poumons, le premier mouvement est celui de l'aspiration, alors le ventre se gonfle et sa partie postérieure s'avance un peu. . . . Au contraire, dans l'action de respirer pour chanter, en aspirant il faut aplatir le ventre et le faire remonter avec promptitude en gonflant et avançant la poitrine."

Mandl believed that to this faulty respiration was due

the modern degeneration of singing voices, which "were in themselves better, and were longer conserved in the old Italian school, directed by the Rubinis, Porporas, &c., than in our modern schools, which teach, or at least which permit, clavicular respiration." It is now some years since we took up the subject in this country, and we are gratified to feel that the result has not been unfruitful. Much, however, remains to be done, for the question is by no means understood, even by many who most loudly acknowledge the justice of the charge, and profess to teach on the principles herein inculcated. We feel, therefore, that no apology is necessary for the very large amount of space we have given to these considerations, and the detail with which we have pointed out the principles of correct respiration, the faults arising from incorrect, and the exact manner in which proper breathing is to be pursued by the pupil and tested by the teacher.

In illustration of the arguments in favour of scientific training, we append an account of a few of the numerous cases which have come under our attention recently. They demonstrate first, the injurious effects of wrong method, and secondly, the absolute importance of lessons in breathing and delivery for the complete re-establishment of vocal strength.

Rev. H. G. had completely broken down in voice, and for three months was entirely unable to take part in the church service. After medical treatment beneficially directed to his physical symptoms, which were all attributable to wrong vocal method, he received a course of vocal training, including lung gymnastics. At the commencement of treatment his breathing capacity, which should have had a normal average of about 275 cubic inches, was under 200; at the end of one week's breathing practice, it was 254; at the end of the second week, 272. He quite recovered his voice in twelve lessons, and, in the absence of his vicar, conducted the whole service without inconvenience.

Rev. Canon G. broke down in voice, and was unable to take duty for six months. Sang with very "woolly" tone and without power. Breathing entirely clavicular in the production of short tones. The effect of his faulty method was such that it was necessary to excise his tonsils, and to reduce the length of his uvula; and further to destroy several enlarged and varicose veins at the back of his throat. As he exhibited a strong disposition to vocal relapses on each occasion of attempting church duty or preaching he was directed to take elocutionary lessons. The result of abdominal breathing as applied to phonation was in this case little short of marvellous. At the end of three months' training he writes: "To measure the value of your help I have only to remember that after being for eight months absolutely unable to use my voice, and this in spite of all that medical treatment could do, I have now, after so few lessons, just completed a fortnight's duty in the choral services of the cathedral, and am actually the better in voice for the practice. It causes me neither strain nor fatigue now to take a service. You will see what this means for me, my duties being what they are."

Rev. H. H. suffered from spasm of the glottis to such an extent that speaking in ordinary voice was almost impossible to himself, while his efforts were painful both to hear and to see. Had been for years under treatment, and had by advice resided for five years in Spain, without beneficial result. On his return he consulted us. Medical attention, galvanism, and every form of nerve tonic having proved unavailing, he was earnestly urged to undergo a course of lung gymnastics. After a very short course he writes: "I am sure you will be pleased to hear that last Sunday evening I preached in —— Cathedral, in the nave, and was heard perfectly throughout the whole building, both in the choir and down to the end of the nave. People have remarked what a strong voice I have! With God's blessing I owe this to your skill."

A. B., Esq., M.P., suffered from impediment in speech and weak voice. Had been for years in the House of Commons and frequently spoken, but was unable to make himself heard sufficiently to obtain a report of his speeches. After two courses of instruction he is able to speak with fluency and ease, and is now well heard in the gallery, as proved by the frequent reports of his speeches in the papers.

C. W. P., Esq., Mus. Bac., spoke in a child's treble, and thought his voice had never broken. After twelve lessons has acquired a full sonorous man's voice, which has since developed into a bass of excellent quality.

Miss M. E. C. suffered from severe throat affection and loss of voice consequent upon over-straining and forcing of the registers with clavicular breathing. Received medical treatment and subsequently vocal gymnastics. Her mother writes: "In addition to the improvement in her voice I can perceive benefit to general health under the method of breathing which you suggested."

Miss D. M. was rapidly losing the upper and middle notes of her voice from faulty production. The quality of tone was very impure. After six months' training her voice has become clear and bell-like, and the registers are perfectly blended. The compass has greatly increased, she being able to sing with ease F in alt.

Mr. R. A., a precentor in a Scotch church, suffered so

severely with chest symptoms, the result of wrong delivery, that one doctor recommended him to relinquish singing altogether, another to go to the country to live, although no actual organic change in his lungs could be detected. He received some few lessons in the right method of respiration, and shortly after wrote : " I have neither given up my Precentorship nor changed my residence, and I am at present enjoying excellent health. I attribute all that human means can claim to careful and proper breathing exercises. Your instructions were listened to by me with eager attention and practised most religiously."

THE RELATIONS OF THE THROAT AND EAR IN REGARD TO VOICE.

THIS question is a somewhat complicated one. We have seen, in the section on the "Resonator," that the throat is directly connected with the ears by means of the Eustachian tubes. (Pl. III. E., p. 39). These tubes are, in a state of health, slightly open, and they are still more widely opened during each act of swallowing. By these means the air outside and inside the drumheads of the ear is kept in the same state of density, thus allowing the membranes to vibrate regularly and freely, a condition which is indispensable to good hearing.

If, on the other hand, the Eustachian tubes are closed by a swelling of their mucous membrane caused by a cold in the head or by a sore throat, &c., then the hearing is impaired, and speakers and singers are particularly inconvenienced by not being able accurately to judge the sound of their own voices. Accumulations of wax in the external passages of the ear by exerting too great a pressure on the drum cavity from without may have the same effect on the character of the voice and impairment of hearing, and in both conditions very annoying noises in the head may occasion a further complication.

One striking case of this nature occurred to us in which a very well-known actor, formerly under our care, came later blaming us for not having recognised some serious diseased condition of his larynx, which he had been informed by another doctor was at the root of all his vocal disability. But he was not aware until his hearing was tested that the auditory function had simultaneously deteriorated. On syringing the ears very large plugs of impacted wax were removed from each passage, with the immediate result of complete and permanent vocal improvement and restoration to the sufferer, not only of perfect hearing, but of a satisfactory sensation to himself of the sound of his own voice.

When the defect is due to extension of disease of the mucous membrane in the throat or nasal passages, the trouble is often remedied by inflating the Eustachian tubes, an act easily accomplished by the simple expedient of shutting the mouth, closing the nostrils, and then forcing the air into the Eustachian tubes by blowing. When this experiment has not the desired effect, medical assistance should be procured at once, and the more accurate method of inflation with the Politzer air syringe will probably be effectual where mere inflation by blowing was of no avail; or it may even be necessary to pass a delicate hollow cannula or catheter into the nostrils directly to the orifice of this tube, and thus project air or medicated vapours, so as to overcome the obstruction and to reduce the thickening of the tissues causing it. It is on account of this connection of the throat and ear that scarlet fever, which, as is well known, almost always attacks the throat, is followed by inflammation and discharges from the ear, and the continuance of some of the muscles of the palate into the walls of the orifice of the Eustachian tubes accounts for pain in the ears felt in many acute diseases of the throat—as quinsy—these pains being experienced more especially during the act of swallowing.

So much for the direct relation between throat and ear. Now for the indirect relation: this implies that, voice and hearing being under immediate and absolute control of the brain, the voice should be capable of producing with unfailing accuracy any tone which the ear has mentally heard in advance, and the ear should be able to recognise with equal certainty any tone produced by the voice.

A failure of this process is sometimes caused by want of control over the laryngeal muscles governing the pitch of the voice, and this is a source of great trouble to singers. They perfectly hear that they are out of tune, but they are, nevertheless, unable to put matters right. This is, however, comparatively speaking, a rare occurrence, due in most cases to relaxation or other indisposition, and will generally quickly pass away, and the same may be said when it is caused as a reflex of an impaired digestion. Where it is constitutional there is probably no cure for it, and certainly no one so afflicted could ever hope to have the slightest chance as a singer.

Or the ear is at fault and fails to appreciate the tone of the voice. One person may be very short-sighted and yet have an exquisitely delicate eye for colour. Another's vision may be as keen as possible, but he cannot distinguish black from red or blue from green, &c. The person in the latter case is said to be colour-blind.

Things are very similar with regard to the ear. One

person's hearing may be very dull, so far as discerning faint sounds or sounds at a distance is concerned, and yet he will have the power of recognising and of classifying sounds, so that he can correctly name any tone struck, behind his back, on the piano, or write down a tune played or sung to him. Such a person is said to have a musical ear.

Another person will have the acutest hearing imaginable, and yet be unable to distinguish a high tone from a low one, or one tune from another. We know a clergyman who cannot tell "God save the Queen" from "Yankee Doodle," and who only becomes aware of the fact that the National Anthem is being played when he sees the people rising from their seats or uncovering their heads. Such a person is said to have no musical ear. Cases of this kind are not amenable to medical treatment except when the loss of the power to recognise different musical sounds is the result of disease.

But the musical ear may be *trained*, and the results to be obtained in this manner are frequently most astonishing. It is quite a common experience that people who could not at first distinguish one tone from another eventually obtained that power in a very high degree, and distanced many others who originally appeared to be much more gifted. The points here to be attended to are as follows :—

1. Take the pupil in hand early in life.

2. Do not attempt to cultivate a sense of *absolute* pitch. There are very few people naturally endowed with it, but to create such a power by training is perfectly hopeless. To cultivate a sense of *relative* pitch is comparatively easy.

3. Do not rely upon tempered instruments for exercises and illustrations, but make pure intonation the basis of

all teaching. In other words, avoid the piano and the harmonium, and use a string instrument or the voice.

4. Try to awaken in the pupil a perception of the characteristics by which every tone in key is distinguished from its neighbours.

We should not endeavour to recognise a tone by the fact of its standing a semitone or a tone above or below its predecessor, but rather by the general impression it makes upon the mind.

It must be admitted, finally, that although in many instances the ear can be trained to a wonderful extent, there are also cases in which little or no improvement is obtainable. Under such circumstances a speaker will always be more or less a failure, and a singer an impossibility.

EXPERIMENTS BEFORE THE INVENTION OF THE LARYNGOSCOPE.

WE think it unprofitable to give an account of the more or less erroneous theories about the production of the human voice entertained by the ancients. Anatomy and physiology made considerable progress during the 16th and 17th centuries, but it was not till four decades of the 18th century had passed away that investigations were made with voice-boxes of animals and of men; and, although even these appear antiquated in the present state of our knowledge, yet they are still relied upon by some old-fashioned people who do not "believe" in the laryngoscope. A short survey of these experiments may therefore be interesting, and they will be mentioned in the order in which they were published.

Ferrein (1741) was the first who succeeded in producing tones upon an exsected voice-box—that of a dog. He blew into it after having approximated the vocal ligaments, when he says it appeared to become animated, and it produced tones which were pleasanter to him than the most charming concerts. We have already seen on page 88 the conclusions at which he arrived, and although they are now known to be incorrect in the most essential particular, they were generally accepted for a long time afterwards.

Kempelen (1791) made considerable advance upon the above theory by maintaining that a greater tension of the vocal ligaments went hand in hand with a diminution of the slit between them, and *vice versâ.*

Dutrochet (1806) compared the action of the vocal ligaments with that of the human lips in playing upon the horn.

Liskovius (1814) objected to Ferrein's string theory, but he arrived at the equally wrong conclusion that the human voice is the result of the air being forced through a slit formed by the vocal ligaments, and that the pitch of the voice depended upon the size of this slit.

Savart (1825) strayed still farther from the truth by comparing the mechanism of the voice with a bird-catcher's call. This theory, in which the pockets of the larynx (the ventricles of Morgagni) play an important part, would seem to be sufficiently disproved by the fact that many animals with very powerful voices are not endowed with laryngeal pockets at all. Nevertheless, this theory is, even at the present time, upheld by some authors although in a somewhat modified form.

Malgaigne (1831) proved by experiment that the voice was produced by the vibrations of the vocal ligaments, and pointed out the great importance of the movements of the soft palate, though going too far by asserting that the formation of the "falsetto" depended upon this.

Lehfeldt (1835) was the first to observe that the "chest voice" is formed by the vibrations of the vocal ligaments through their entire thickness including the shield-pyramid muscles which constitute the bulk of them, and that in "falsetto" the vibrations are limited to the thin inner edges of the ligaments.

Magendie (1838) made experiments upon living dogs whose vocal ligaments he laid bare. In this way he ascertained that the first and indispensable condition of tone production is the approximation of the pyramids, and that there can be no tone while the glottis is open. He also saw the vibrations of the vocal ligaments in the production of tone, and asserted that the pitch was higher or lower according to the ligaments vibrating only partly or in their entirety.

This brings us to the important investigations of Joh. Mueller ('Ueber die Compensation der physischen Kraefte am menschlichen Stimmapparat.' Berlin, 1839). Mueller made, like Ferrein, the fundamental mistake of supposing that the vocal ligaments were the *sounding* element, and that they were made to produce tone by the force of the expiratory air, just as the wind plays upon the strings of an Æolian harp without producing any sound itself. His experiments are, moreover, now in a great measure superseded by the observations with the laryngoscope. Nevertheless, his researches are so exhaustive that they are still most valuable in considering questions of theory concerning the voice.

Having prepared a detached larynx and connected it with a bellows, Mueller approximated the pyramids; after which, by blowing into the voice-box, he could produce tones somewhat resembling those of the human voice. This was the easier the closer the vocal ligaments were together, and a bubbling noise was the result if a space remained between the pyramids. It was further necessary to allow the air to pass over tepid water, as otherwise the ligaments soon became dry and were then incapable of producing any tone at all.

The pitch of the tones depended upon the weights by means of which the shield cartilage was pulled forward and downward, thereby stretching the vocal ligaments; although the laws here ascertained were not those relating to strings, which is not surprising considering that the vocal ligaments are made longer by being stretched, which is not the case with strings upon musical instruments. By pushing the shield cartilage backward and upward the vocal ligaments were relaxed, and produced the lowest tones of a bass voice. If the ligaments were allowed to vibrate through their whole dimensions it was possible by thus stretching and relaxing them to get a serviceable compass of about two octaves. It was possible to raise the pitch even beyond this limit, but the tones so produced were shrill and hissing.

Mueller also ascertained that in order to vary the pitch by adding tubes to the larynx a much greater length was required than could be supplied by the corresponding cavities of the human body, and he consequently came to the conclusion that the pitch of the voice in the living subject is independent of the length of the vocal passages. He also discovered, however, that pitch *was* raised very considerably by the introduction of a hollow plug into the pipe just below the vibrating element, and when this action is imitated by compressing the plates of the shield cartilage while singing it has the same effect upon the voice.

Another factor greatly affecting the pitch was found to consist in the power of blast, and it was possible by this means to raise the pitch with the same amount of stretching as much as a fifth. This shows that it is necessary to compensate the raising influence of an increased power of blast by a corresponding relaxation of the vocal ligaments, without which the tone cannot be maintained upon the same height. Of the difficulty thus created we have painful practical experience in the sharp singing of unskilful performers when they produce *fortissimo* tones.

We have just called attention to Lehfeldt's original

observations with regard to the mechanism of the "chest voice" and of "falsetto." These were confirmed by Mueller, who further showed that the dimensions of the space immediately below the vocal ligaments is of great consequence in this matter, and we have already described his experiments with a hollow plug, and how this action may be imitated in singing. A similar effect may be produced by contraction of the inner portion of the shield - pyramid muscles, which diminishes the space below the vocal ligaments. This is one of the factors in the production of the upper series of tones in "chest voice."

It will now be necessary, in order to estimate the experiments upon exsected larynges at their proper value, to say a few words about the way of conducting them. The voice-box, with a piece of the windpipe attached to it, is put with the back part upon a little board, to which the ring cartilage is fastened with a piece of string. A needle is pushed through the bases of the pyramids and they are pulled together by applying to the points of the needle a thread in the form of an 8; or, dispensing with the needle, the pyramids are simply sewn together. After this they are, like the ring cartilage, fastened to the board just mentioned, thus making them a fixed point for the purpose of stretching the vocal ligaments, which are, of course, brought close together by the above-described process. Another thread is now inserted in the front edge of the shield cartilage, and passed over a pulley, after which the larynx is ready for stretching the vocal ligaments to almost any extent by attaching weights to the thread.

It is a point of the greatest practical importance to observe that by these means the pocket ligaments are *not* approximated, but that they remain widely separated. In order to bring them together two needles are pushed through the shield cartilage into the pyramids in such a manner that they are contained within the free edges of the pocket ligaments. Only by separating the needles in front and by pressing them together behind and along the whole length of the pocket ligaments can these finally be made to come into contact with each other.

It will thus be seen that it is necessary to take great liberties with the dead larynx in order to produce tone. But, what is worse, it is admittedly impossible to imitate the action of the shield pyramid or vocal muscles upon which, as we have learnt, the voice chiefly depends. Experiments of this kind can therefore not be received as evidence except in so far as they are corroborated by investigations upon living persons.

THE INVENTION OF THE LARYNGOSCOPE.

The claimants for the honour of having invented this beautiful little instrument are many, as may be seen from the following brief historical account:—

Bozzini (Frankfort-on-the-Maine, 1807) invented an apparatus for illuminating the internal cavities of the human body, and among these the throat. This instrument, although clumsy and difficult of application, certainly embodied the principle of the laryngoscope. However, it never came into use, and was soon again forgotten.

Senn (Geneva, 1827) had a mirror constructed with which he endeavoured to explore the larynx of a little girl. In this he failed, and although he suggested that a larger mirror might be employed upon adults, yet he never made any further attempts to use it.

Babington (1827) exhibited before the Hunterian Society, under the name of "glottiscope," a combination of two mirrors exactly upon the plan of our present "laryngoscope." Here, then, we have undoubtedly the *instrument*, but, unfortunately for the claims made on behalf of Dr. Babington, he does not appear to have produced any results with it, and there are certainly no cases on record in which it has been of service.

Beaumés (Lyons, 1838) used a mirror attached to a piece of whalebone.

Liston (London, 1840) employed "such a glass as is used by dentists, on a long stalk, previously dipped in hot water," and seems to have been the first who really *saw* anything with it. But even he merely looked upon it as an aid to diagnosis, and never dreamt of the enormous importance which the process was destined to acquire in the hands of a later observer.

Avery (London, 1840) not only used a mirror attached to a stem, but also artificial light in the shape of a candle with a metal reflector attached to it. But he has left no description of his instrument on record, and it is clear that he had no more idea of its immense value than Liston.

Warden (Edinburgh, 1844) used prisms of glass in a similar manner, and is reported to have caught sight of the glottis in two instances. The prisms, however, were too thick and occupied too much space to make really successful experiments possible.

It will be seen from the above notes that the principle of laryngoscopy had been known to several men of science, yet the results obtained with the instruments formerly employed were almost *nil*, and it was reserved for Manuel

Garcia, the famous professor of singing, to show the world the real value of the little laryngeal mirror; to make original additions to vocal physiology; to settle, beyond the shadow of a doubt, the true theory of voice production; to disprove many absurd notions still entertained upon this subject, and to revolutionise the whole treatment of diseases of the throat.

Garcia brilliantly succeeded where all his predecessors had more or less failed, and he was certainly the first to conceive the idea of making observations upon his own larynx in the act of singing. These he carried out in the most marvellous manner, giving a detailed description of even the minutest movements of the vocal ligaments, which is still recognised as being substantially accurate, and which is the more wonderful as Garcia had practically to create the whole process of investigation for himself, and was neither an anatomist nor a physiologist. Garcia is, therefore, to all intents and purposes the real inventor of the laryngoscope, and he is now also universally recognised as such.

Here is the description which he himself gives of his *modus operandi* :—

"The method which I have adopted is very simple. It consists in placing a little mirror, fixed on a long handle suitably bent, in the throat of the person experimented on against the soft palate and the uvula. The party ought to turn himself towards the sun, so that the luminous rays falling on the little mirror may be reflected on the larynx. If the observer experiment on himself he ought, by means of a second mirror, to receive the rays of the sun, and direct them on the mirror which is placed against the uvula." ('Observations on the Human Voice,' by Manuel Garcia, read before the Royal Society by Professor Sharpey on May 24th, 1855. *See* 'Proceedings,' vol. vii., No. 13, p. 399.)

It is a remarkable circumstance that although Garcia's statements were never actually disputed by any one, yet they were received coldly and with distrust. Of this discreditable feeling we see an instance in the following passage by no less a person than Professor Merkel, of Leipzig, which, in the present state of our knowledge, it is impossible to read without a smile:—" I have not yet, it is true, been able to obtain Garcia's original observations, and do not know, therefore, how he proceeded in these alleged experiments, what he has seen and what he has not seen, but I have just grounds to doubt the reality of his observations until I am informed in what manner Garcia has prevented the mirror from becoming dimmed, and how he draws forward the lid which to a great extent hides the glottis from the eye even though it be by means of the mirror placed near the uvula, etc." ('Anthropophonik.' Leipzig, 1857, p. 608.)

It is to be feared that Garcia's laryngoscope would eventually have been neglected as all its predecessors had been but for Türck and Czermak, two physicians in Vienna, who saw the practical importance of the process, and who introduced it to the medical profession in general. There is a squabble of priority between these two gentlemen into which we do not propose to enter; but it is certain that Czermak laboured enthusiastically in the new cause, and that, by his demonstrations and lectures in almost all the chief cities of Europe, he did more than any other man to disarm prejudice, and to popularise the laryngoscope among his professional brethren. On the other hand, Türck has left a clinical volume full of the most interesting cases and with superb illustrations, which it is unlikely will ever be surpassed: it will always stand as the classic practical work, *par excellence*, of the specialty.

Czermak has also improved upon Garcia's process by substituting artificial light for that of the sun, thereby enabling investigators to carry on their work in any place and at any time. His services in connection with this matter are therefore very considerable, and by many he is even regarded as the true inventor of the laryngoscope, which distinction, however, clearly belongs to Garcia, and to no one else.

THE LARYNGOSCOPE AND HOW TO USE IT.

The laryngoscope in its simplest form is nothing but a little mirror about the size of a shilling, set in a metal frame, and fastened at an angle of 120° to a piece of wire from three to four inches long, which is put into a small handle of ebony or ivory not much thicker than a pencil. We have already seen how Garcia, with the aid of sunlight, worked with it upon others; add to this that the little looking-glass, which is called the laryngeal mirror, must be warmed before being introduced into the throat in order to prevent its becoming dimmed by the moisture of the breath, and the description is complete.

In auto-laryngoscopy—that is to say, in the process of making laryngoscopic observations upon oneself—the observer sits with his back towards the sun, and with a hand looking-glass reflects the light falling upon the laryngeal mirror at the back of the throat. The laryngeal image will then be seen in the hand looking-glass by which the light is reflected.

The light of the sun is, of course, vastly superior to even the most brilliant artificial light, but it is not so easily managed, and, unfortunately, in this country it is not often available; therefore, for laryngoscopy to become of any practical importance it was necessary to improve upon Garcia's simple method, and to contrive instruments enabling observers to work with ease in any place and at

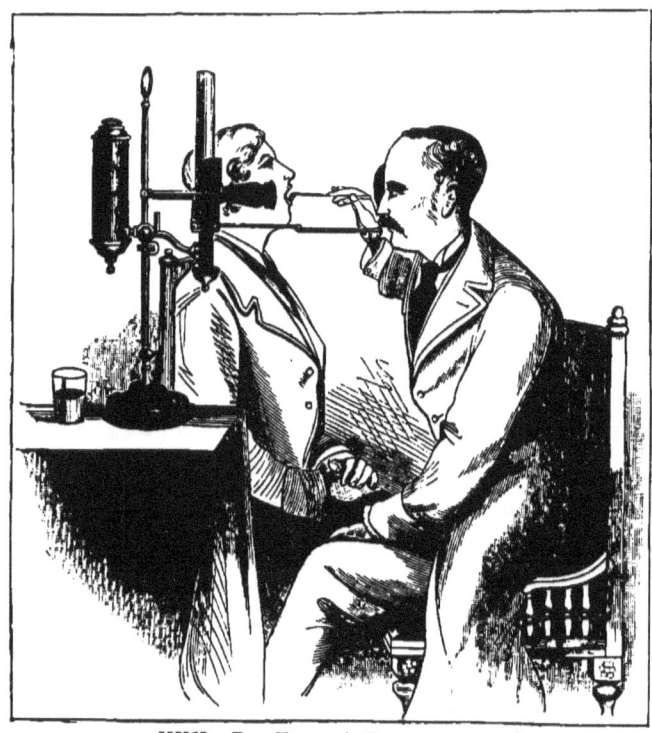

XXII.—Dr. Tobold's Laryngoscope.

The right hand of the observer is represented as introducing the mirror into the mouth for the purpose of examining the larynx.

any time. For the practical purposes of observing other persons' throats, as is done by the doctor, gas or oil lamps on the principle of the "Queen's reading lamp" are equally serviceable. To those in constant practice the limelight is recommended as giving the best illumination—the electric light being not, as yet, available for this purpose.

A handy, inexpensive, and thoroughly useful apparatus (Pl. XXII.), designed by Dr. Tobold, of Berlin, which answers the double purpose of making observations upon others as well as upon oneself, is shown in the annexed cut, and may be had, complete in case, at a moderate cost, from Messrs. Krohne and Sesemann, Duke Street, Manchester Square, who have, at our desire, provided a supply of them.

The illustration, in a large measure, speaks for itself, but the following directions may be of service to the intending laryngoscopist.

1. Direct the person whose throat is to be examined, and of whom for convenience' sake we will here speak as the singer, to sit erect, with the knees together, and the head slightly thrown back.

2. Arrange the lamp so that it is distant about nine inches to the right of his head and in a line with his ear.

3. Sit opposite him and adjust the reflector, which is attached to the light-condenser by a metal arm, so that your right eye looks through the hole in the centre.

4. Direct the singer to open the mouth widely.

5. Throw the reflected light on to the back of his throat.

6. Take the laryngeal mirror in the right hand, and slightly warm it over the lamp. The glass will be covered with a film of moisture, and the instant this has disappeared and the mirror becomes clear it is of the right temperature. Its warmth should, however, always be tested by placing the back of it against your hand or cheek.

7. Hold the mirror like a pen in the right hand, and introduce it into the mouth of the singer with the reflecting surface directed downwards.

8. Be careful not to touch the tongue with the mirror in introducing it.

9. Rest the back of the mirror against the uvula, so as to press it gently upwards and backwards, but do not force it against the back of the pharynx, or retching and gagging will be the result.

10. Turn your hand slightly to the right, so as to keep it out of the line of view.

11. Direct the singer to take a deep inspiration, and then to produce tone on the vowel *a*, as in the word *sad*.

12. Let each examination be short; the mirror may then be introduced six or eight times without inconvenience, whereas if the mirror be too long retained spasms or nausea may be produced and put a stop to further examination.

A view of the larynx should thus be obtained, and the vocal ligaments, easily recognisable by their pearly-white colour, should be plainly seen, and their movements observed. But if the operator does not, at first, see more than the back of the tongue or the upper rim of the lid, he must not hastily conclude that this is all that *can* be seen in the case before him. He should, on the contrary, repeat the experiment upon the same person day after day until at last he succeeds, for it must be borne in mind that the proportion of cases in which a fairly skilled laryngoscopist is unable to get a satisfactory view of the interior of the larynx is very small indeed.

It is generally supposed that it is necessary to cause the singer to put out his tongue, and then to hold it with a cloth in order to get a good laryngeal image; but this is a great mistake. The tongue and the larynx being intimately connected, any movement of the former cannot fail to affect the latter; if, therefore, the investigations with the laryngoscope are to be of any value with regard to the hidden configurations of the voice-box in the production of tone, the formation of the "registers," &c., it is clear that no contortions of any sort must be indulged in. They might help to show the larynx in making some noise, but it would be pointed out, and with great force, that such revelations are of no use. The tongue must remain in its natural place, and if the singer has the power, which he ought to have, of keeping it flat, it will not interfere in the least with the proposed observations. This is shown very plainly in the photograph printed as the frontispiece of this book, with the mirror at the back of the throat, in which a complete image of the larynx in singing is reflected, while the tongue lies so flat as to be practically not visible.

We have thus demonstrated the utter groundlessness of the objection urged in some quarters with so much persistency, that all observations with the laryngoscope are untrustworthy on account of the contortions they involve. In medical practice, it is true, patients are generally directed to put out the tongue and to hold the tip of it between the index finger and thumb. But patients are not always singers, and the object in their case is to observe disease, and not a physiological process. The practitioner consequently avails himself of every help to remove difficulties, though even in medical examinations it is now found that the protruding of the tongue is by no means indispensable, and that in some instances it even defeats its own object.

Beginners in laryngoscopy will do well to practise upon a model of some sort and then upon themselves before asking another to submit to the operation. A great deal is said about the sensitiveness of persons' throats, and that they cannot endure the touch of the mirror; but we have no hesitation in asserting that inexperience and consequent clumsiness on the part of the operator are the chief cause of failure, and that his difficulties will diminish in proportion as his dexterity increases.

A "Laryngo-Phantom" by Dr. Isenschmid, of Munich, will greatly facilitate preliminary practice, and may also be had from Messrs. Krohne and Sesemann. It consists of an imitation of the throat, and "is intended to familiarise students with as many of the details connected with the use of the laryngoscope as it is possible to learn before the application of the instrument to the living subject." A number of little paintings, representing different laryngoscopic appearances, may be slipped into this phantom unknown to the student, who has to inspect them by the ordinary process. This phantom may be put in place of the singer, as represented on Plate XXII., and will be found to afford excellent practice.

For auto-laryngoscopy—that is to say, making laryngoscopic investigations upon oneself—the student takes the place of the phantom just indicated. He proceeds in every particular with himself as on p. 151 he was advised to proceed upon others. A little square mirror, supplied for this purpose with the laryngoscope, must be attached to the reflector, and in this square mirror the student will see a reproduction of the image in the laryngeal mirror in his own throat. This image may also be seen quite distinctly by another person taking the place of the observer, and looking through the space between the reflector and the square mirror.

It will thus be noticed that the laryngoscope here recommended is a very complete little instrument, and may be used for three purposes, namely—1, for observations upon a second person; 2, for observations upon oneself; and, 3, for demonstrating results to others.

Where the object is only self-observation and demonstration another instrument may be used which was designed by the late Dr. Foulis, of Glasgow. It is simple, useful, and cheap; but it is not, as already hinted, available for examining another person's throat. It consists of a plain stand on which is placed a glass globe filled with water, the whole being surmounted by a small square mirror. The rays from a lamp or candle placed behind

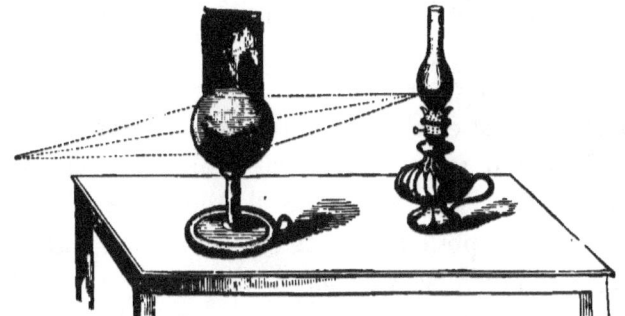

XXIII.—Dr. Foulis's Auto-Laryngoscope.

the globe are concentrated into the open mouth of the student, who sits in front of it, holding the laryngeal mirror at the back of his throat in the manner already described, and he himself seeing the resulting image in the larger mirror fixed to the globe. This apparatus, as shown in Plate XXIII., including a throat-mirror, and safely packed for transmission, may be had from Messrs. W. B. Hilliard and Sons of Glasgow, at an almost nominal price.

THE TEACHINGS OF THE LARYNGOSCOPE.

THE first thing we see after having introduced the mirror into the throat is the back of the tongue, which presents a more or less uneven appearance and is covered with gray, and sometimes elevated, spots. We then notice the lid or *epiglottis* which greatly varies in shape and position, and which is connected with the tongue by an elastic band forming a sort of bridge, on either side of which there is a little hollow. The lid in many instances hangs over the larynx, thus hiding a great part of it from view; in which case nothing more than, perhaps, the pyramids will be visible.

The result is often the same although the lid is not pendant; in that case the position of the laryngeal mirror is at fault and must be altered until a perfect view is obtained. But even when the lid does overshadow the voice-box in a position of rest we soon find that it rises during respiration as also in phonation, particularly in singing the vowel *a* as in the word *sad*, which puts the whole of the vocal apparatus in the most favourable position for observation. In addition to this in auto-laryngoscopy we soon get a great deal of command over the lid and indeed over most parts of the voice-box, and the process of investigation becomes easier in every way. It may be added that soft, veiled tones afford the best opportunity for investigation, as with these the lid is almost perpendicular and the vestibule widely open;

while in louder and more brilliant tone the lid falls and the vestibule is more constricted.

When no longer hampered by difficulties arising from want of skill and experience we are in a position to extend our observations, and to notice the following particulars.

The colour of the upper surface of the lid is of a warm pinkish yellow, resembling that of the inner surface of the eyelids, and upon it may frequently be observed a delicate network of fine red blood-vessels which in some cases looks exceedingly pretty. The under surface of the lid is always of a deeper colour than the upper surface; and the cushion (Pl. XV., p. 72), which shows itself at the lower extremity, is of a bright red.

Immediately below the free part of the lid there are the two folds of mucous membrane connecting it with the pyramids, which we know (Pl. XV.) under the name of the *ary-epiglottic* folds. They are thick when relaxed and thin when tense. In the hinder ends of these folds there are four little elevations, caused by the cartilages of Wrisberg and those of Santorini (the "buffers") which are embedded here. Connecting the pyramids behind there is another fold of mucous membrane completing the upper rim of that tube described on p. 73 as the vestibule of the larynx.

A little below this there are the pocket ligaments, formerly called false vocal cords, and nowadays, in medical phraseology, ventricular bands (Pl. XV.). The colour of the ary-epiglottic folds, as well as of the pocket ligaments, is that of the mucous membrane lining the cheeks, while the portion covering the cartilages has a colour resembling that of the gums.

Beneath the pocket ligaments there are the entrances to the pockets or ventricles of the larynx. At first sight they show only as dark lines between the pocket ligaments and the vocal ligaments; but on turning the mirror so as to get a lateral view these spaces will be seen to be much larger than they appear when looking directly down the centre of the larynx.

Below the entrances of the laryngeal pockets, and in fact forming the floor of them, we see the vocal ligaments, which glisten like mother-of-pearl, thus forming so strong a contrast with the more or less pinkish colour of all the surrounding parts as to make it impossible to mistake them.

XXIV.—Laryngeal Mirror, showing the Reversion of the Reflected Image.

When the vocal ligaments are separated in the act of breathing we can, with a strong, well-directed light, look below them, and see a portion of the ring cartilage and some rings of the windpipe. In a few rare and exceptionally favourable cases we can see right to the bottom of the windpipe, where we notice its division into the two branches entering the lungs.

It must be borne in mind that the laryngeal image is a reflection in a mirror, and is, therefore, in some respects reversed. What this means will be best understood from Plate XXIV., showing the letter V, which corresponds with the glottis as it is placed in the body (see

Pl. XIII., p. 66), and the reflection of it in a mirror where it appears reversed. The thick stroke of the original letter is on the left of the observer, and so it is in the reflection; the thin stroke of the original letter is on the right of the observer, and so it is in the reflection. But apart from this the reflection is the exact opposite of the original.

It is the same with the laryngeal image. The singer's right vocal ligament, which, of course, is on the observer's left, is also on the left in the mirror, and the singer's left vocal ligament, which is on the observer's right, is also on the right in the mirror. It is plain that this equally applies to the pocket ligaments, to the ary-epiglottic folds, and to everything else which exists on both sides of the larynx. But with regard to front and back, the image in the mirror is reversed in exactly the same manner as the letter V in Pl. XXIV.

It is necessary to be perfectly clear on this point, in order to understand why the pointed part of the glottis on Pl. XIII. is below, while, in the laryngeal pictures which follow, the same pointed part is above. This is a matter which, to our knowledge, has created great confusion in the minds of several readers of Mr. Behnke's 'Mechanism of the Human Voice,' and we are anxious, therefore, to avoid this difficulty in the present instance.

The reader who has given us his attention so far is sufficiently familiar with details to conceive a true picture of the process of voice formation which we are now going to describe.

Plate XXV. gives a laryngeal image with the glottis open in a state of rest. T represents the back part of the tongue; L the lid; W, W, the cartilages of Wrisberg; and S, S, the cartilages of Santorini. The lid somewhat covers the larynx, so that we get but a partial view of the vocal ligaments, V, V, and between these we notice some rings of the windpipe. While the vocal ligaments are thus separated the air passes between them silently in respiration, and the chink of the glottis is the more enlarged the more deeply we breathe, or *vice versâ*.

Plate XXVI. shows the laryngeal image in a deep and vigorous inspiration. The glottis is here very widely

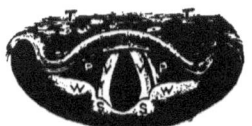

XXV.—Gentle Breathing.

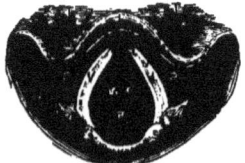 

XXVI.—Deep Breathing.   XXVII.—Tone Production.

LARYNGEAL IMAGES.

T. Tongue.
V, V. Vocal ligaments.
W, W. Cartilages of Wrisberg.
L. Lid.

P, P. Pocket ligaments.
B. Bifurcation of the windpipe.
C. Cushion of the lid.
S, S. Cartilages of Santorini.

opened, and we are enabled even to see the opening of the bronchial tubes B at the bottom of the windpipe.

If we sing a tone, we see the pyramids, with the vocal ligaments attached to them, close with great rapidity, and the pocket ligaments also move towards the centre. But these, in a state of health, *never* meet in phonation, so that we always see the broad white vocal ligaments forming, as it were, the floor of the cavity revealed to us. The vocal ligaments are then thrown in vibrations by the air forced against them from below, as described on page 59.

The result is tone. As soon as we cease singing and take an inspiration, the pyramids, with the vocal ligaments, fly asunder again, and we see once more the triangular space between them, as before. From these movements we learn, as a first lesson, that the approximation of the vocal ligaments is an indispensable condition of tone production.

But upon studying these movements carefully we further observe that the glottis may close under different conditions, each of which is followed by a different result.

1. The vocal ligaments meet *after* the air has commenced to pass between them; this constitutes an aspirate, or in other words the sound of the letter *h*. The mechanism by which it is produced is called the "glide of the glottis," and a further attribute of it is this, that the vocal ligaments are often not held together sufficiently tightly, thus allowing more air to pass than is necessary for the process of phonation. The tone consequently not only lacks a prompt, decisive beginning, but it also suffers from an admixture of "wild" air which makes it breathy or "woolly." This kind of tone production is, unfortunately, very common.

2. The vocal ligaments meet *before* the air has had time to reach them, the pyramids come into close contact with their inner surfaces and the vocal ligaments are held firmly together. The gate is securely shut, the air accumulates below, until the pressure becomes great enough to overcome the resistance above. Then the gate is forced open, and the action is accompanied by a distinct click. The mechanism by which this is accomplished is called the "check of the glottis." It is generally followed by a continued tight closure of the vocal ligaments, so that the air has, from the beginning to the end, an unnecessary

amount of opposition to overcome. This also interferes with the tone, and tends to make it hard and metallic.

3. The vocal ligaments meet just at the very moment when the air strikes against them; they are, moreover, not pressed together more tightly than is necessary. No preliminary escape takes place as in No. 1, and no obstacle has to be overcome as in No. 2; but the attack is clear and decisive, and the tone consequently gets a proper start. The mechanism by which this is done is the "coup de glotte" or "shock of the glottis." The closure of the vocal ligaments being maintained at the most suitable degree, the tone production is carried on, so far as the glottis is concerned, under the most favourable conditions, and the result is the best which can be obtained.

There are four ways of ending a tone:—

1. The glottis opens suddenly, and before the expiratory effort quite ceases. In this case the tone is followed by a slight wind-rush, which is frequently distinctly audible.

2. The larynx closes as in the act of pressing; this causes a snap which is the louder and the uglier the more abruptly it is made, and the popular description of it is that the tone has "stuck in the throat."

3. The expiratory effort ceases while the vocal ligaments remain approximated.

4. The expiratory effort ceases while the glottis opens exactly at the same moment.

We will now study the movements of the larynx in the production of different pitches as revealed in the laryngoscope, and this brings us to a consideration of the various "registers." We shall have to refer to this subject again in the chapter on teaching, and we here propose, therefore, to confine ourselves simply to a description of the physiological alterations involved in the matter, without entering into any arguments.

We start with our definition, according to which "*a register consists of a series of tones which are produced by the same mechanism*" (Behnke, op. cit., p. 86), and we will endeavour to show the variations which take place in the voice-box by passing in review the different classes of voice, commencing with the bass, and leaving off with the soprano. When a bass sings his lowest tones, very little is to be seen of the glottis except its back part, because the lid hangs over the larynx, and hides the front part of it

XXVIII.—LARYNGEAL IMAGE—LOWER THICK REGISTER.

T, T. Tongue.
P, P. Pocket ligaments.
L. Lid.
S, S. Cartilages of Santorini.
V, V. Vocal ligaments.
W, W. Cartilages of Wrisberg.

from view. This difficulty may, to a large extent, be overcome by practice, which enables us to get control over the lid and to raise it. We have also had the opportunity of observing instances in which, even in the lowest tones, a large portion of the vocal ligaments was always visible, and we remember particularly the case of a gentleman in Scotland as the most favourable one which has ever come under our notice. Under such exceptional circumstances we see that in the lowest tones, commencing, we will say, at 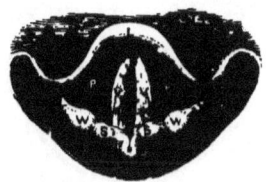, the hindermost points of the pyramids are closely approximated, and that there is a slit of an elliptical shape between the vocal ligaments.

We have already more than once called attention to the fact that the pocket ligaments never meet in phonation, and they are here seen so widely apart that the vocal ligaments appear as two very broad white strips which are agitated through their whole length, breadth, and thickness by full loose vibrations which in the production of these deep tones are sufficiently slow to be most clearly and distinctly visible. The elliptical shape of the vocal chink, in this state of complete relaxation of the vocal ligaments, is in exact accordance with the curve of the shield-pyramid muscle, as shown in Pl. X., p. 60. After the singer has

XXIX.—LARYNGEAL IMAGE—UPPER THICK REGISTER.

T, T. Tongue.
P, P. Pocket ligaments.
L. Lid.
S, S. Cartilages of Santorini.
V, V. Vocal ligaments.
W, W. Cartilages of Wrisberg.

gone a few tones up the scale, the vocal processes of the pyramids commence to be visible by pointing more and more inwards, until at last they meet. By this time the elliptical shape of the vocal chink has gradually disappeared and become linear, while between the pyramids there is a little triangular space, with its points towards the front, which gets smaller by degrees as the singer continues to go up the scale, until it quite disappears upon his reaching . It is, however, worthy of notice that this triangular space, in many bass voices, closes very much earlier, and that in baritone and tenor voices it is frequently never visible at all. Meanwhile we observe that the lid rises with the pitch of the voice, so that we see more and more the higher the singer ascends the scale. It now becomes obvious that the vocal ligaments are being considerably stretched, a fact which is corroborated by the diminution and eventual total disappearance of the aperture between the ring and the shield (Pl. VII., p. 52), which was widely open in the production of low tones.

The bass having by this time reached the end of his compass, we proceed to study those of his tones which belong also to other voices; let us say in a tenor the range upwards from [♪] ; in a contralto upwards from [♪] ; and in a soprano upwards from [♪] ;*
and we find that *they are in all voices produced by precisely the same mechanism,* namely, by vibrations of the vocal ligaments through their whole length, breadth, and thickness. The vibrations being much quicker than in the lowest tones of the bass voice it follows, of course, that they are not so full and loose; but they are nevertheless plainly discernible. We must also bear in mind that the vocal ligaments in the production of these tones, as we shall more fully discuss presently, are of great bulk and thickness. We will, therefore, adopting the terms of the late Mr. John Curwen, and leaving a further justification of our choice for a future occasion, speak of this series of tone as the "thick register." If then, for the present, we leave subdivisions out of consideration we find that *all tones of the human voice up to* [♪] , *whether sung by a*

---

* Tenor music is now generally written in the treble clef *an octave higher than really sung.* We have, therefore, in order to prevent misunderstandings about the actual pitch of the tones here referred to, so far noted them all in the bass clef.

bass, tenor, contralto, or soprano, are produced *in the thick register.*"

As the various voices went up the scale we noticed that the vocal ligaments became more and more stretched. When we now watch the tenor, contralto, and soprano as they approach the [musical notation], which we have just indicated as the average limit of the thick register, we perceive that the tension, not only of the vocal ligaments, but also of all surrounding parts, is getting very great, and if this mechanism is carried higher still the strain upon the vocal organ increases to such an extent that it looks as though it were going to burst, and its pinkish colour changes more and more into red. These appearances are not so marked in the soprano as in contralto and tenor; the bass we leave out of the question, because its average limit is below the point just indicated.

If tenor, contralto, and soprano wish to sing without straining beyond [musical notation] (remember that this tone for the tenor voice is generally written an octave higher), they have to change the mechanism, or in other words they must sing in a different register.

When this occurs the following alterations take place: the lid is more raised than before, and we consequently get a complete view of the larynx, so much so that we even see the cushion of the lid described on p. 72, and the insertions of the vocal ligaments in the shield cartilage. The vestibule seems longer and narrower, and the ary-epiglottic folds (Pl. XV., page 72) thinner; the pocket ligaments are closer together, and the entrances to the pockets less marked than before. The vocal ligaments seem quite still, and their tone-producing vibrations appear to be confined to the thin, inner edges. But more: the vocal ligaments, by the process explained on p. 64, are made much thinner than they were in the thick register.

This is almost equal to the insertion of a new set of tonguelets, and fully accounts for the remarkable diminution of volume which here takes place in all natural and uncultivated voices. The alteration in the bulk of the vocal ligaments can be demonstrated to the eye by illuminating the voice-box, not, as usual in laryngoscopy, by throwing the light into it from above, but by allowing a

XXX.—LARYNGEAL IMAGE—LOWER THIN REGISTER.

T, T. Tongue.
P, P. Pocket ligaments.
L. Lid.
S, S. Cartilages of Santorini.
V, V. Vocal ligaments.
W, W. Cartilages of Wrisberg.

strong light to shine through its lower part from the outside, and then making observations with the laryngeal mirror in the ordinary manner. This process is particularly successful in the case of very lean individuals, and it shows the vocal ligaments to be almost transparent, while in the thick register they are much more opaque.

Mr. Curwen, therefore, in calling this the "thin register," hit upon a singularly appropriate name, though at the time he decided upon it he had no idea of the new and great significance it has since acquired by the experiment just detailed.

The foregoing change is accompanied by a great feeling

of relief, for the strain the voices experienced in carrying the thick register beyond its natural limit is removed, and they now sing with the greatest ease. The change is further indicated by a re-opening of the ring-shield aperture which had quite disappeared in the upper tones of the thick register.

If the voices continue to sing in the thin register we observe that the slit between the vocal ligaments is linear, and that the pitch is evidently raised by the ligaments being stretched. This fact is corroborated by the state of the ring-shield aperture, which again commences to become smaller and smaller, until at last it once more quite

XXXI.—LARYNGEAL IMAGE.—UPPER THIN REGISTER. (*Female Larynx.*)

disappears. In this manner the voice is carried to about [music notation], where a new change is found compulsory if straining and forcing is to be avoided, and we now see an elliptical slit between the vocal ligaments, as in the accompanying diagram, which slit is gradually reduced in size as contralto and soprano sing up from [music notation] to [music notation].
It is, however, worthy of notice that this mechanism may be resorted to almost from the beginning of the thin register, and that even tenors may use it, and do use it, in the production of the few tones just above the thick register, which form the highest part of their compass as applied to modern music. But tones so produced are

very poor and unsatisfactory, and they constitute what is commonly called "the falsetto voice," of which more will be said in the chapter on teaching.

We now come to a last change, which brings us to the highest part of the soprano voice commencing with , which Mr. Curwen has called the "small register," because the action of the vocal ligaments is confined to a small part of them, and this mechanism consists in the formation of an oval orifice in the front

XXXII.—LARYNGEAL IMAGE—SMALL REGISTER. (*Female Larynx.*)

part of the glottis which contracts the more the higher the voice ascends, the vocal ligaments being, in the hinder part, pressed together so tightly that scarcely any trace of a slit remains. No vibrations are here noticeable, while they are, on the contrary, so very marked in the anterior portion as sometimes to blur the outlines of the orifice to a considerable extent.

The supposed mechanism of the small register has been explained on p. 76, but it must be confessed that the evidence in support of it is of the slenderest kind. Nor is this mechanism at all indispensable, and enough is now known of the power of the shield-pyramid muscles to contract in a great variety of ways to justify the conclusion that their action is quite sufficient in itself to cause the formation of the orifice described. We can, at any rate, vouch for the existence of it, as we have repeatedly, and independently of each other, had opportunities of observing it in women as well as in boys.

We have thus seen that there are, broadly speaking, three registers in the human voice, namely, the *thick*, the *thin*, and the *small*. We have also found certain indications, more or less vague, of alterations in some degree accounting for subdivision, called the *lower thick*, the *upper thick*, the *lower thin*, and the *upper thin*. These registers are plainly shown in Plate XXXIII., and so far as our present chapter is concerned there is no more to be said about them.

We have also noticed the visible straining which takes place when an attempt is made to carry the thick register beyond its natural limit; and we must add that similar signs make their appearance, though not always so clearly marked, when any of the other registers are forced up too high.

Lastly, we are anxious to account for the differences in the description, by various observers, of the laryngoscopic appearances in the process of voice production, and we cannot do this better than by making the subjoined extract from a most admirable treatise on the voice by Dr. Gruetzner, of Breslau. ('Physiology of Voice and Speech,' by Dr. P. Gruetzner, in Dr. L. Hermann's 'Handbook of Physiology.' Leipzig: F. C. W. Vogel, 1879. Vol. I., Part II., p. 112.)

"About the manner in which these small laryngeal muscles take part in the production of high and low tones there are different, and to some extent contradictory, opinions. It is certain from all these statements, and from my own observations, that there are indeed individual differences which are the greater the more one has to deal either with trained singers or with non-singers, or with

XXXIII.—THE REGISTERS OF THE HUMAN VOICE.

From Behnke's 'Mechanism of the Human Voice.' By permission of Messrs. J. Curwen & Sons.

'nature-singers,' and the more the voice-boxes under investigation originally differ in size and shape.

"There are at our disposal the following entirely different means for changing the pitch of our voice:—

" 1. The altered *longitudinal tension* of the vocal ligaments brought about by the different actions of the stretching muscles, and of their antagonists.

" 2. The *shortening* of the vibrating portions of the vocal ligaments, produced by the pyramids coming more and more in contact with their inner surfaces, thereby reducing the parts of the vocal ligaments which are capable of vibrating, just as the violin player shortens the string by putting his finger nearer and nearer to the bridge.

"3. The *alteration of the shape*, particularly the sharpening or blunting of the vibrating edges, brought about by the different actions of certain portions of the shield-pyramid muscles.

" 4. The *narrowing or broadening of the vibrating edges* which frequently goes hand in hand with this.

" 5. Lastly, the different *pressure of the air* under which the chest muscles put it in the windpipe.

"Now in accordance with the way in which a singer gives preference to one mechanism or another for altering the pitch of his voice, or in which he employs different mechanisms at the same time for this purpose, the image of the larynx will, of course, be different in the production of either high or low tones."

LARYNGEAL PHOTOGRAPHS AND THEIR LESSONS.

We conclude this section by appending on page 178 first on one side (Pl. XXXIV.) the five engravings representing the various registers of the human voice, and on the opposite page four photographs of Mr. Behnke's larynx in the act of singing. These last differ from the laryngeal images which we are accustomed to see in books on vocal physiology, and indeed from our first three engraved figures of the registers, which were drawn before the photographs were taken, in that, on the one hand, they do not show the cushion of the lid which is generally depicted in engravings; and, further, that they give not only distinct indications of the cartilages of Santorini and of Wrisberg on the summit of the pyramids, but also a sharp outline of the bases of the pyramids.

These apparently double outlines in the photographs for a long while greatly perplexed us, and we did not know what to make of them. We first conceived the idea that they were due to double reflection in the laryngeal mirror, one on the surface and the other on the silvered back; and to overcome this difficulty we had mirrors silvered on the surface; indeed one of the pictures in the group is taken with such a mirror. But the result was the same as before, and we now tried to account for it by a shifting of the laryngeal mirror, or as the result of the strong vibrations into which the parts were thrown, though in either case, if this had been so, the lid, the vocal ligaments, and other parts ought also to have been doubled.

In fact, we tried in every conceivable way to account for what we considered a blemish, and it was only after much needless trouble and great mutual waste of time that the thought struck Mr. Lennox Browne to compare one of the photographs with Mr. Behnke's own larynx as seen in the ordinary way, and he then discovered that the photograph (as we might have been sure at first) was right, and the conventional image wrong, because when the larynx is, as in most cases, looked into from in front, there *must* be double outlines, due to the perspective view of the interior surface of the pyramids. The extent of the portion which is visible will largely depend upon circumstances. If we see the whole under surface of the lid—that is, of the front wall of the funnel of the voice-box—we shall obviously expect to see less of the opposite side, and *vice versâ*. In our photographs the cushion of the lid and the front insertion of the vocal ligaments are not seen. Hence we get a full view in perspective of the back wall.

Our whole experience is one more proof of the way in which the judgment is allowed to be warped and the vision to be distorted by things, however false, which happen to be customary or which have been accepted on the fiat of another, until at last even truth itself is disbelieved when it is accidentally revealed to us.

Two of our photographs—namely, the frontispiece and the lower of the two "falsetto" images—are absolutely untouched, and we have not even interfered with some spots on the teeth and on the back of the throat caused by moisture. The other three images are not quite in their original state, because the glare of illumination in photography with the electric light interferes with clear definition of the contrast between the vocal ligaments and the pocket ligaments. The fact that the photographs are pictures of reflections in a glass mirror also accounts to some extent for this defect.

Mr. Lennox Browne has done what little touching there was necessary from nature, Mr. Behnke singing the same tones he sang when the photos were taken, and we do not think, looking at the untouched photographs, that any one will consider our supplementary work to be worth mentioning further than as an answer to possible objections from such few as prefer to remain in error rather than to be convinced against their will.

The images show plainly the lid, the pocket ligaments, the cartilages of Santorini and of Wrisberg, the bases or inferior borders of the pyramids, the hollows between the pyramids and the tongue-bone, and, in two instances, even the prominence of the tongue-bone itself. When it is now borne in mind that in the majority of cases the throat surgeon only gets a partial view of the voice-box, and that he has to move the laryngeal mirror to and fro in order to make a complete inspection, it will surely be granted that it would be difficult, if not impossible, to obtain more perfect laryngeal photographs than those here appended; for in them are seen, in one picture, not only a complete image of the voice-box itself, but positively some parts outside of it.

We have already, in another place, insisted on the completeness with which these photographs dispose of the objection, urged *ad nauseam* against all observations with the laryngoscope, that it is impossible to make them except by holding the protruding tongue of the singer with a napkin, thereby pulling the laryngeal image out of shape and distorting the image. We admit that this objection, if true, would have weight, and we had quite recently under our joint observation a case in point:—A lady, a talented public singer, showed, with her tongue in its natural position, the upper thin and the small register so clearly that we asked her permission to publish them in this volume, and they are now depicted as Figs. XXXI. and XXXII., and repeated as D. and E. on p. 178. As soon, however, as we attempted to hold her tongue while making our investigations, we certainly saw the vocal ligaments and their surroundings, but every trace of the mechanism of the two registers just mentioned had *totally disappeared*. We repeat, then, that the objection, founded upon the supposition that no laryngeal observations can be made except when the singer's protruding tongue is held with a napkin, is completely silenced by our photographs, which represent the tongue as lying in the floor of the mouth.

Again, they show, what is known to all who are in the least familiar with the larynx, that there always exists a large space between the two pocket ligaments in the production of tone, and that the vocal ligaments alone meet. This appearance is the same from the beginning of the tone to the end, and clearly disproves the ignorant notion of a very limited but loud-crying faction, that the pocket ligaments, as well as the vocal ligaments, meet in phonation; and also the assertion that the "shock of the glottis" is not what Garcia declares it to be, and as we have described it on p. 162; but that it is an actual explosion of the air compressed in the cavity between the pocket ligaments and the vocal ligaments. The exposure of this fallacy, then, is the second lesson taught by the photographs.

And, lastly, the photographs show the difference between the upper thick and the falsetto registers, and they absolutely confirm not only the delineations of our own engraved images, but also those given now exactly ten years ago by Professor Merkel, of Leipzig, in that latest book of his on the larynx which we have repeatedly referred to in these pages.

Tenors will be specially interested in the mechanism of the "falsetto." The shape of the vocal chink clearly accounts for the waste of air and for the want of power by which this register is characterised, but we desire to repeat here that the "falsetto" and the "lower thin" are produced by different mechanisms—a fact which is of the greatest consequence in the actual process of voice training.

It now only remains to meet one more objection of the enemies of the laryngoscope, viz. that a person may make all sorts of noises with the mirror at the back of his throat, but that it is impossible under such circumstances to produce a pure vocal tone. To this we simply reply that Mr. Behnke has repeatedly of late demonstrated his larynx to musicians of eminence for the express purpose of settling this point, and it is the opinion of all who have been thus appealed to that no fault could possibly be found with the quality of his voice while under laryngoscopic observation. We wish to add that we have found people whose case was exactly the same from the very first, and that others acquire the same facility so soon as they become accustomed to the touch of the mirror.

A. Lower Thick.   B. Upper Thick.

C. Lower Thin.

D. Upper Thin.   E. Small.

LARYNGEAL IMAGES IN THE VARIOUS REGISTERS.

⁎ The first three (A., B., and C.) were drawn before the laryngeal photographs were taken, and well represent the conventional laryngoscopic drawing. D. and E., on the other hand, illustrate the perspective view of the larynx, seen in the photographs, and to be observed in all laryngeal images, as explained in the text, p. 173.

    T, T. Tongue.   S, S. Cartilages of Santorini.
    P, P. Pocket ligaments.   V, V. Vocal ligaments.
    L. Lid.   W, W. Cartilages of Wrisberg.

PHOTOGRAPHS OF THE LARYNX.

    L. Lid or Epiglottis.   H, H. Hyoid Fossœ.
    T, T. Tongue.   C. C. Pyramid Cartilages.
    V, V. Vocal Ligaments.   B, B. Interior border of the same
    P, P. Pocket Ligaments.   seen in perspective.

No. II. shows the larynx and position of the vocal ligaments in singing the note  in the upper chest or upper thick register. In No. I. the tone produced was higher than in II., and the vocal ligaments are consequently more closely approximated. The image is also lower in the mirror, and therefore more of the base of the tongue is seen.

Nos. III. and IV. illustrate the position of the vocal ligaments, and the appearance of the larynx in production of "falsetto"—the note sung being

The reader will observe the great alteration in the shape of the glottic chink, and the generally loose condition of all the muscles.

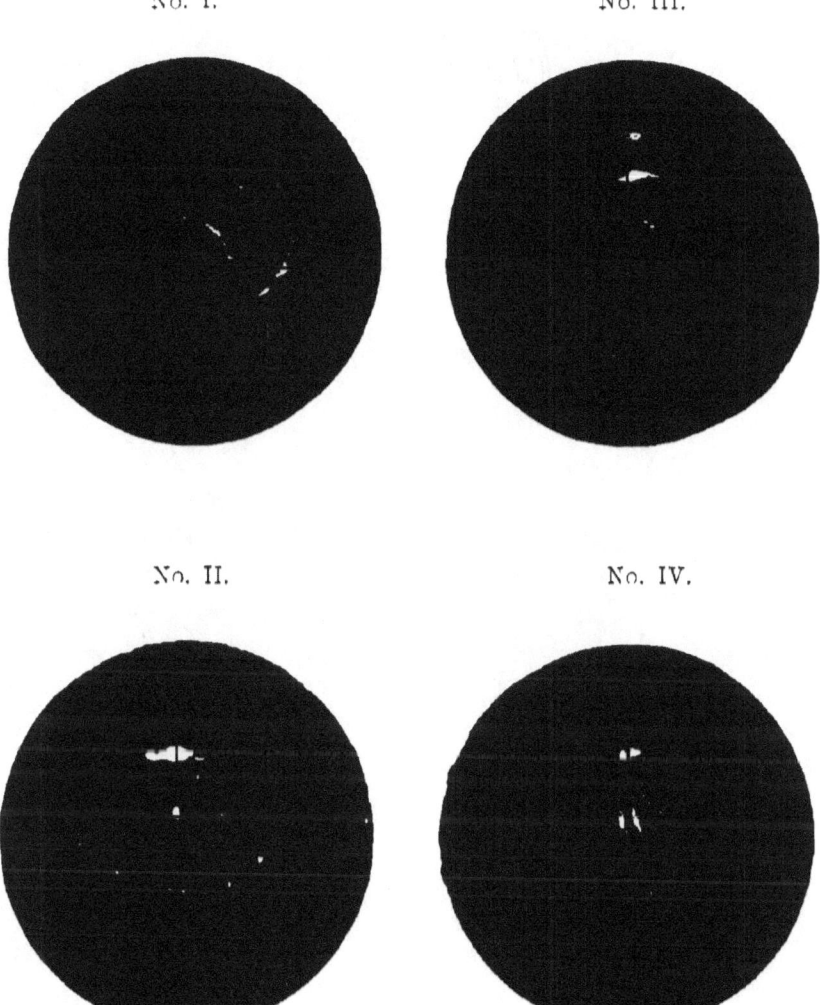

PHOTOGRAPHS OF THE LARYNX
IN THE PRODUCTION OF DIFFERENT MECHANISMS.
(Copyright.)

[*To face page* 178.

ON VOICE CULTIVATION.

THE cultivation of the voice from a scientific point of view, with which alone we are here concerned, may be divided into five parts, viz., (1) Breathing, (2) Attack, (3) Resonance, (4) Flexibility, and (5) Registers.

BREATHING.

We know from the description of the mechanism of breathing on p. 49, that there are three ways of carrying on the process of respiration, namely, midriff breathing, rib breathing, and collar-bone breathing. These three ways are not indeed wholly independent of each other; they overlap, or partly extend into each other. Nevertheless they are sufficiently distinct, and it is a general and convenient practice to give each a separate name according to the means by which it is chiefly called into existence.

The combined forms of midriff and of rib breathing constitute the right way, and collar-bone breathing is totally wrong and vicious, and should not, in a state of health, be made use of under any circumstances. Let us, even at the risk of being accused of repetition, once more consider this matter in its bearing upon the production and cultivation of the voice.

When enlarging our chests by the descent of the midriff, and by sideways extension of the ribs, we inflate the lungs where they are largest, and where consequently we can get the largest amount of air into them. When expanding our chests by raising the shoulders and collar-bones, &c., we inflate the lungs where they are smallest, and where, consequently, we get the smallest amount of air into them. It will be observed that we are here speaking of collar-bone breathing, not as an extension of the two other ways of breathing, but as a separate act; and there can be no question whatever that the result of it is much smaller than that obtained by the combined forms of midriff and of rib breathing. This may easily be demonstrated by means of the spirometer, an instrument which accurately tests the breathing power of man by indicating on a little dial the exact number of cubic inches of air blown into it; and experiments, repeated over and over again, have proved our case most clearly. Here, then, we have a fact which cannot be disputed away by any amount of argument, and which is quite sufficient in itself to turn the balance against collar-bone breathing.

But so far as the voice is concerned, there is a still more powerful reason why midriff and rib breathing should always be made use of, and why collar-bone breathing should never be resorted to.

The lungs, at their bases, are surrounded by soft and yielding parts. We can contract and relax the midriff to the greatest possible extent, and for any length of time; this will never fatigue us because nature has not here placed any obstacle in our way. Only one exception occurs, that is the occasional interference caused by too full a meal. Most people know from experience that they cannot breathe so well after a good dinner as they could before; and most public singers and speakers are so well aware of this fact, that they allow a considerable interval to elapse between food and voice use, while others even prefer to postpone their meals until after they have finished their work, when it is generally found that the proper use of their bellows has resulted in giving them a fine healthy appetite. They have certainly this additional reason for the course just indicated, that the process of digesting their food would even exercise direct interference with their voices; but that is a point with which we have not to deal in this chapter, and which will be discussed in its proper place.

Again, we can expand and contract our lower ribs to the greatest possible extent, and for any length of time, without incurring any fatigue, because here also nature has not placed any obstacle in our way. We thus see that the process of inflating our lungs at their bases is so perfectly easy, as not to require the slightest effort, while at the same time it supplies us with an abundance of air.

At the top of the lungs the very opposite is the case. The ribs are here not nearly so free as at the base, and they are much shorter. They are attached not only to the spine as are the lower ribs, but also to the breast-bone in front, and their cartilages or elastic portions are, equally with the ribs, much shorter. They are also greatly impeded in their movement by the shoulder-blades and collar-bones which carry the arms, and all this weight has to be lifted if inspiration be commenced in that region.

In addition the chest walls are forced upwards towards the root of the neck, where are situated the food-passage, windpipe, and large arterial and venous vessels carrying blood to and from the brain. It is most important that these parts should be left free as they are placed by nature, but collar-bone breathing necessarily presses against them and leads to fulness and congestion. We thus see that to expand and contract all these hard and unyielding parts, involves an enormous amount of labour, which must necessarily fatigue, and eventually, have an evil effect upon the voice, while at the same time the resulting amount of air inhaled by this mode of breathing is but very small.

It will be remembered that we have so far spoken of collar-bone breathing only as a separate act, in which case the respiration is laboured, fatiguing, gaspy, and insufficient. But it can also be made use of as an extension of midriff and of rib breathing, when it becomes excessive and choking. It may be mentioned as an extreme instance, that "Rubini broke his collar-bone in a violent but successful effort to deliver B flat in a recitative in Pacini's 'Talismano.'" (Walshe, op. cit., p. 15.)

It is from the foregoing easy to understand that collar-bone breathing, whether as a separate act, or as an extension of midriff and of rib breathing, must lead to forcing and inequality of voice, and to congestion of the vessels and tissues of the throat; and we here repeat that, in other words, it is at the root of most of the troubles to which speakers and singers are exposed. As voices are ruined, and as disease is set up by false breathing, so also voices may be restored and disease may be cured by lung gymnastics on proper principles, and we have quoted elsewhere cases of this kind which have come under our care which are so many living proofs of our assertion.

In order to explain this subject more clearly in this connection of voice cultivation, we refer the reader to the accompanying diagrams, which are intended to show the varying capacity of the chest according to the method in which the lungs are inflated.

Plates XXXVI A. and XXXVII A. show the chest after full expiration; M, D. being the line representing the midriff or diaphragm.

Plates XXXVI B. and XXXVII B. show the figure in

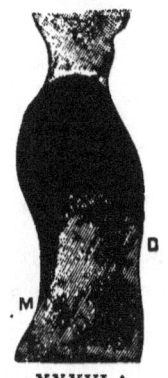  

| XXXVI A. | XXXVI B. | XXXVI C. |

MALE BODY.

 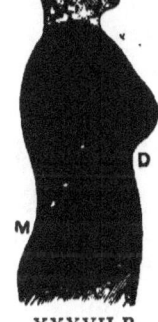 

| XXXVII A. | XXXVII B. | XXXVII C. |

FEMALE BODY.

A, A. After full expiration.
B, B. Forced collar-bone breathing.
C, C. Full abdominal breathing.
M, D. Midriff or diaphragm.

DIAGRAMS ILLUSTRATING THE VARYING CAPACITY OF THE CHEST ACCORDING TO THE METHOD IN WHICH THE LUNGS ARE INFLATED.

(*Adapted from Lennox Browne's ' Medical Hints on the Singing Voice.*)

collar-bone inspiration. The chest is bulged out and raised, the midriff remains as high as after expiration, and the abdomen is drawn in. These two diagrams illustrate *false* breathing.

Plates XXXVI C. and XXXVII C. show the figure in full abdominal inspiration. The chest is pushed forward, but not raised; the midriff is pulled down and the abdomen enlarged. The capacity of the chest is here clearly increased at the expense of the abdomen. These two diagrams illustrate *correct* breathing.

The chief lesson which the above diagrams are intended to bring home to the reader is this: *The criterion of correct inspiration is an increase of size of the abdomen and of the lower part of the chest. Whoever draws in the abdomen and raises the upper part of the chest breathes wrongly.* In making this statement we do not forget the difference between the breathing of men and that of women, to which we called attention on p. 49. The increase in size of the abdomen of a woman is certainly less than that of a man, but there is an increase nevertheless, or rather there would be if the corset did not prevent it.

This brings us to a consideration of artificial hindrances to proper breathing. We have said that the lungs at their bases are surrounded by soft and yielding parts which can be worked with the utmost ease, because nature has not placed any obstacle in their way; but unfortunately many people are continually doing this themselves.

Men and boys often think that it is injurious to wear braces, and they consequently suspend their lower garments by means of belts. But this is a great mistake; for everything interfering with the freedom of the waist is a serious hindrance to respiration and should be strictly avoided. Properly constructed braces ought to be worn, while belts fastened to anything like the extent necessary for upholding garments must be pronounced utterly objectionable.

The question of corsets has been sufficiently discussed in the chapter on Hygiene, and we need here do no more than remind ladies who imagine that they can improve their figures by imprisoning themselves in close-fitting corsets that such a practice exercises an injurious influence upon respiration varying in degree not only in accordance with the amount of constriction, but also with the degree of rigidity of construction. The spirometer, which is the most trustworthy and impartial referee it is possible to find, has already informed us that *stays deprive ladies of nearly one-third of their breathing power;* nor does this refer to exceptionally tightly-laced stays, but to such as are worn in the majority of cases.

It may be further observed, however, that bands or strings are often as great a hindrance to proper breathing as stays, and that no experiment is of any value in which impediments *of every kind* are not absolutely removed.

Our readers are asked to again refer to the diagrams, Pl. XVIII. and XIX., and also XX. and XXI., pp. 110–11, which illustrate, on comparison with the natural figure, the deformity in the chest walls, and the consequent displacement of the contained vital organs which the use of stays is capable of inducing.

The air is the motive power upon which the voice depends; without air no tone can be produced. It is therefore of the utmost importance for singers and speakers to be trained to breathe properly. We must know how to inflate our lungs in order to fill them abundantly without overcrowding them, and without any efforts causing fatigue and injuring the voice; and we must know how to regulate the exit of the air so that it may take place in a steady, even, and uninterrupted stream, enabling us eventually to hold out a long tone, to sing a long passage, or to execute a fine "*messa di voce*," i.e. the gradual swelling out and diminishing of a sustained tone.

We may say in passing that we hold the very general practice of commencing the education of a vocalist by teaching him the *messa di voce* to be wrong. This ornament is far too difficult for a beginner, and the earliest moment for attempting it is when the student has fully mastered his respiration.

The singer's and speaker's breathing corresponds to the violin player's bowing and requires as much practising.

We will now describe some exercises which will increase the student's vital capacity and give him complete control over his breathing, and consequently over his voice.

The first experiments with regard to this matter should be made lying flat on the back, because then the raising of the upper part of the chest and of the collar-bones is difficult; so that in this position nature is almost sure to have her own, that is the right, way. It will be safer still if we watch our breathing in bed, as we shall not then be hampered by corsets or tight-fitting clothes of any description. If we now place the hands upon the abdomen we shall find it rising very considerably as we commence the process of inspiration. Continuing to inhale while we slip our hands a little higher up, the ribs will be noticed to move, thus expanding the lower part of the chest. The upper part of the chest is necessarily also enlarged (see p. 41), but the collar-bones are certainly *not* raised. In expiration the ribs recede and the abdomen sinks in, until inspiration recommences. This is the way in which nature carries on the work of respiration, and we invite our readers to make themselves thoroughly acquainted with it.

This will put them in a position to understand the following description of exercises intended to improve the power of breathing.

Divest yourself of any article of clothing which at all interferes with the freedom of the waist. Lie down flat on your back. Place one hand lightly on the abdomen and the other upon the lower ribs. Inhale, through the nostrils, slowly, deeply, and evenly, without interruption or jerking. If this is done properly, the abdomen will gradually, and without any trembling movement, increase in size, the lower ribs will expand sideways, and the upper part of the chest will be pushed forward, while the collar-bones remain undisturbed. Now hold the breath, *not* by shutting the glottis, but by keeping the midriff down and the chest walls extended, and count four mentally, at the rate of sixty per minute. Then let the breath go *suddenly*. The result of this will be a flying up of the midriff, and a falling down of the ribs; in other words, there will be a collapse of the lower part of the body. This collapse may not at first be very distinct, as the extension has probably been insufficient; but both will become more and more perfect as the result of continued practice.

Let it be clearly understood—the *in*spiration is to be slow and deep, the *ex*piration sudden and complete. In *in*spiration the abdomen and the lower part of the chest expand, and in *ex*piration they collapse.

The time of holding the breath is not, at the outset, to exceed four seconds, and the student must never, on any account, fatigue himself with these exercises; they may, however, be frequently repeated at intervals. It will be found by occasional trials upon the spirometer that the breathing capacity increases with these exercises. The process of abdominal respiration becomes easy and no longer requires constant watchfulness, and the student will now be able to abandon the lying down position, and to continue his practice in sitting, and finally in standing and in walking, until the process becomes so perfectly natural to him that it would really require an effort to breathe by raising the upper part of the chest.

The criterion of correct inspiration is, as before stated, an increase of size of the abdomen and of the lower part of the chest. Whoever draws in the abdomen and raises the upper part of the chest in the act of filling his lungs breathes wrongly.

Meanwhile, in continuing the breathing exercises, the time of holding the breath may be increased at the rate of two seconds per week; so that the student who, during the first fortnight, limited himself to four seconds will, at the end of six weeks, hold his breath during twelve seconds. In some instances students have gone as far as twenty seconds; but very earnestly must the reader be warned to be cautious, and not to go to extremes. Nothing will be gained, but infinite harm may be done by over-doing these lung gymnastics, and persons who are delicate in health should not undertake the exercises at all, except with the sanction of their medical adviser, who will limit the practice according to circumstances. Nevertheless, as stated elsewhere, singing on a right method of breathing will often really strengthen lungs formerly weak.

It must also be borne in mind that unflinching regularity in this matter is of the greatest importance. Exercise in moderation, regularly and conscientiously repeated, will increase the breathing capacity, improve the voice, make speaking and singing easy, and will cure the *tremolo*. It may change, and has changed, the falsetto of a grown man into a full sonorous man's voice. It may restore, and has restored, a lost voice, as it also may cure, and often has cured, clergyman's sore throat.* It will certainly turn a greater quantity of dark-blue blood into bright-red blood; the appetite will increase; sounder sleep will be enjoyed, flesh will be gained, and the flabby, pallid skin will fill out and get a healthy, rosy colour. All this, and more, may be, and often has been, the result of lung gymnastics carried on in moderation and with perseverance. It is needless to add that a man will no more improve his breathing by fitful and exaggerated exercises than he could hope to become a proficient upon the violin by practising once or twice a month for six hours at a stretch.

The second breathing exercise is the exact opposite of the first, and consists in taking a rapid *in*spiration and making the *ex*piration slow, even, uninterrupted, and without jerking or trembling. Musical readers will at once see the importance of this exercise for the

* That there may be no mistake concerning this statement, it should be understood that the word "cure" is here used, not in the sense sometimes employed—namely, that symptoms of a diseased condition have been relieved—but to mean that instruction in *right* voice production ensures against relapse into the diseased state originally caused by *wrong* voice production. In justice to my co-author, I venture to quote from my paper delivered on two consecutive days to several hundred members of the British Medical Association, at Liverpool, last August, and since printed in the Association Journal : "A permanent cure, or indeed any effectual relief, can only be brought about by hygienic and elocutionary treatment on scientific and physiological principles. During the past three years I have been much more successful than formerly in all such cases, because I have insisted on the absolute necessity of a course under my friend Mr. Behnke after the diseased condition was relieved, and I desire here to testify my gratitude to him for the greatly increased power to help speech sufferers that I have enjoyed since I have been able to avail myself of his collaboration."— L. B.

purpose of singing sustained tones and florid passages; but it would be quite useless to attempt it before No. 1 has been sufficiently practised.

A little consideration will show that it is wrong to try to control the exit of the breath, as some would have us do, by a contraction of the glottis, because the comparatively tiny muscles of the larynx are too weak to resist with impunity so tremendous a strain; while the large and powerful muscles of the chest are clearly made to regulate expiration as well as inspiration. It is absurd on the face of it to suppose that they are only intended for inflating the lungs, while the exit of the air is to be governed by another set of small muscles, situated at a great distance, and having their full share of work in the marvellous and ever-varied combinations which are necessary in the production and gradation of tone.

In phonation the glottis is closed, and of course retards expiration in proportion to the tightness with which the pyramids and the vocal ligaments are held together. In this sense, therefore, the glottis assists in regulating the expiration, but this function is only secondary, and must not be relied upon for *controlling* the air. *Ex*piration exercises must consequently be practised in silence, i.e. with the glottis *open*, so that the breathing muscles may be exclusively called into play.

This second exercise is much more difficult than the first, and requires the greatest watchfulness and attention to conduct it properly. But even with the greatest care the air is frequently found to escape much more quickly than the student imagines, and it is still more difficult to ensure steadiness of *ex*piration by merely relying upon one's sensations. It is therefore advisable to use some kind of a tell-tale, such for instance as a light feather or a burning candle. The flame is certainly the most sensitive indicator, and the student who has learnt to exhale through his gently opened lips close to a light without to any great extent blowing the flame to and fro may take it that he is on the high road to success.

It is easy enough to perform this experiment with the first part of the out-going breath, but the difficulty commences as soon as the expiration ceases to be passive and begins to be active (see p. 48). No voice-user has therefore mastered this exercise who cannot, without causing the flame to flicker, expel from his lungs *all* the air previously inhaled.

Let it be observed that the above exercise is quite distinct from the well-known practice of *singing* before a lighted candle, which is, comparatively speaking, an easy matter.

The third and last breathing exercise consists in taking the *in*spiration as in No. 1, and the *ex*piration as in No. 2.

After the two preceding ones have been fully mastered this last is readily accomplished; and the student who has persevered so far will now have overcome one of the greatest difficulties of speakers and singers, namely the proper management of the breath, an accomplishment which seems to become more and more rare in our go-ahead times of electricity, in which every one appears impatient to attain the end without using the tardy means.

It may be added that in lung gymnastics, as well as while using the voice, the process of breathing must be carried on in perfect silence. This applies more particularly to *in*spiration, which is frequently accompanied by more or less noise. Not only is such accompaniment, certain dramatic exigencies apart, ugly in the extreme, but it also shows that the air-passage is obstructed instead of being perfectly open, and such a way of inflating the lungs is therefore on all grounds strongly to be condemned.

A great deal has now been said about these breathing exercises; nevertheless, the description is far from complete, and, what is worse, may even lead to misunderstandings, the results of which will hereafter be laid to our charge. For writing, however lucid and careful, can never take the place of *vivâ voce* instruction; and it must be distinctly understood that the explanations here given are not by any means intended to supersede the aid of a competent and painstaking teacher.

Before taking leave of this part of the subject it is necessary to warn the reader against the mistake, which may be caused by a superficial perusal of these pages, that it is the chief aim of the above breathing exercises to enable the singer or speaker to cram as much air as possible into the lungs. It is true that some of the evils which are likely to arise from exaggerated breathing efforts have been pointed out; but it must be most emphatically repeated that it is quite possible to *overcrowd* the lungs with air. This is a matter of every-day occurrence, which is not, however, on that account any the less reprehensible; for, as already mentioned, it is sure to lead, sooner or later, to forcing and inequality of voice, and to congestion of the vessels and tissues of the throat and of the lungs.

The above breathing exercises might be amplified in a variety of ways, but it is a question whether any service would be rendered to the reader by multiplying them. As they are here given they are simple and easily carried into practice. Students may therefore be induced to give them a trial, which will soon prove their great value; whereas over-elaboration would probably rather serve to bewilder and to discourage, thus defeating the purpose for which they are devised.

We would take this opportunity of warning the reader against the objectionable practice of completely exhausting the supply of air just taken in before commencing another inspiration. In this respect speakers are much greater sinners than are singers, and we know of many who habitually try how long a passage they can get through in one breath. One clergyman of our acquaintance even makes it a boast that he is able to say the whole of the Lord's Prayer with one inflation of the lungs. Independently of any question as to the irreverence of such a proceeding, we wish to urge most emphatically that all such attempts are radically wrong, and that immense mischief to vocal health is the result of persistence in them.

The golden rule for all voice-users is, on the contrary, to breathe whenever it is possible conveniently to do so, whether a new supply of air is immediately required or not. Nothing so much enfeebles the voice and eventually leads to complete exhaustion as phonation with the fag end of the breath; while, on the other hand, the habit of keeping the lungs well stocked with air helps to make the voice strong and resonant, and enables speakers and singers to preserve freshness and vigour to the end of their task.

The next question to consider is whether we are to breathe through the mouth or through the nostrils. Mouth-breathing is a pernicious and dangerous practice which frequently leads to diseases of the respiratory and of the vocal organs, and which ought to be discarded as much as possible. In singing as well as in speaking it is, unfortunately, sometimes unavoidable, but not by any means so often as is generally supposed. The fact may be new to many people that it is not necessary to shut the mouth in order to inhale through the nostrils; nor even, as advised by some professors of elocution, to raise the tongue until it touches the roof of the mouth. The air has simply to be drawn through the nostrils. This causes the soft palate to fall, thereby uniting the nasal passages with the throat, which is all that is necessary, and the process is easily carried out in practice.

Many teachers of singing, for the reason just explained, object to breathing through the nose while the mouth is open, because, they say, the soft palate has not time to recover itself and to resume the raised position necessary for the production of pure vocal tone. This objection is, to some extent, well founded, and we have expressly guarded against the assumption that a singer can *always* breathe through the nostrils. We distinctly say he can *not*.-

But the objectors to nose breathing clearly do not know that the soft palate of a singer or a speaker is just as capable of being trained as the fingers of an instrumentalist. An exercise for this purpose will be described in another section, and the student who takes the trouble to practise it regularly will obtain marvellous control over his soft palate. It will, certainly, in many instances enable him to inhale through his nostrils though he may not have time to shut his mouth, and without in the least interfering with the quality of his tone.

In any case, by mouth-breathing, unavoidable as it may *sometimes* be, an irritation is continually set up; and every possible opportunity of counteracting it by again breathing through the nostrils should be seized. In accordance with this consideration breathing *exercises* ought always to be carried on with closed lips, and it is very much to be regretted that, in some otherwise excellent singing manuals, the opposite practice is recommended.

ATTACK.

VOCAL tone is produced by the vibrations of the vocal ligaments; and we have seen on p. 160, on looking down a person's throat, that the chink of the glottis is open in breathing, and that it is closed by the approximation of the pyramids and of the vocal ligaments as soon as phonation commences. This is the "attack of tone." We have also learnt, on pp. 161 and 162, that this attack may be accomplished in three different ways, each affecting the tone in a distinct manner, either for good or for evil.

The movements of the pyramids, with the vocal ligaments attached to them, upon which all this depends, are governed by two sets of muscles, the one set pulling the ligaments together, and the other pulling them apart. These are fully described on p. 67, under the name of the "Closing muscles" and the "Opening muscles;" and the reader who has carefully given his attention so far will at once see the importance of devising a set of exercises which shall call these opening and closing muscles into play, thereby making them powerful, and bringing them under the control of the will.

This is, fortunately, a very simple matter; for it is only necessary to sing a series of short tones, each tone to be followed by a short inspiration. It has been shown that every time a tone is struck, the vocal ligaments are made to approximate; by so doing, therefore, the closing muscles are exercised. Every time an inspiration is taken the vocal ligaments are separated; by so doing, therefore, the opening muscles are exercised.

It is clear from the above explanations, that by practising in the manner just indicated, these muscles, which play so important a part in the production of the voice, will be exercised at least ten times as much as would be the case by singing sustained tones after the usual method of teaching. They are, in fact, trained just as by suitable gymnastics the muscles of the hands and fingers are trained for the purpose of performing upon the piano or the violin.

Here is a description of the exercise: Find the pitch of your speaking voice, which we will say is F. Then sing the following :—

oo oo oo oo
oh oh oh oh
ah ah ah ah
ai ai ai ai
ee ee ee ee

Attack the tone firmly and clearly, avoiding alike the *check* of the glottis and the *glide* of the glottis. This is often a matter of great difficulty, requiring much patience and perseverance on the part of the teacher as well as on that of the student. The *glide* of the glottis is particularly hard to eradicate, and in many instances the case seems to be hopeless. Do not, however, despair, but try this: Pronounce vigorously the word "Up." Then *whisper*, but still very vigorously and distinctly, three times the vowel *u*, as you just had it in the word "up." Immediately afterwards *sing* "Ah." Thus—

Up!   u, u, u,   Ah!
(spoken).   (whispered).   (sung).

Another point of importance in practising the exercise for strengthening the opening and the closing muscles is the breathing after every tone; and this must be done gently, and without effort, the only perception of it to the singer being a slight movement of the midriff. When the exercise can be sung in this manner on F, your supposed speaking tone, then go, semitone by semitone, up and down the scale, but strictly confining yourself to the easiest compass of your voice.

There is a difficulty connected with this exercise which may lead to injurious consequences and against which the reader must be on his guard. By inhaling with each inspiration more air than is consumed in producing the corresponding tones, however slight the excess may be, the lungs will, after a little while, get too full of air, until finally a sensation of being choked is experienced. This is a danger which invariably arises before the student has learned so to balance his inspiration with the amount of air consumed in striking the tone as to make both absolutely equal.

Great care must be taken to avoid it, for we have shown in former explanations the evil results arising from overcrowding the lungs with air. As soon as the student commences to feel the least sensation of fulness, he must sing a few tones without intermediate inspirations until he has sufficiently reduced his stock of air; or, better still, he must leave off singing and empty his lungs by a complete expiration, and then commence again with greater watchfulness than before.

It will thus be seen that the correct "attack" of a tone corresponds with those prompt and simultaneous actions of the breath and of the vocal ligaments described on p. 162 as the "shock of the glottis." This the late Orlando Steed very properly calls the "central point" of Garcia's system of practice. ('On Beauty of Touch and Tone':

Proceedings of the Musical Association, 1879–80, p. 47.)

But what shall we say when the same writer goes on to observe that "what Garcia calls the 'shock of the glottis' is really a shock of the *upper* glottis (the pocket ligaments) which he (Garcia) thought was never closed"?

And again: "Energetic vocalisation, while the ventricles (the pockets of the larynx) are not inflated, must therefore involve either the forcing of the vocal cords from their right position for singing towards that which they assume in a state of rest, thus producing a bad quality of tone, or an actual injury to the throat, through their being subjected to a greater amount of tension than they are intended to bear." (Op. cit., p. 52.)

This, of course, amounts to saying that the distinguished inventor of the laryngoscope has never in his life seen a tone properly struck in the larynx, and it may be added that all laryngoscopists, without a single exception, are exactly in the same position. They all agree in giving the same description of the process of striking a laryngeal tone; but if we are to believe Mr. Steed *they are all wrong*, and not one of them has ever correctly observed, or they were all observing the production of tones of "bad quality." Thus not even Garcia himself, the trainer of some of the greatest singers of modern times, is capable of distinguishing a good tone from a bad one!

It would not be worth while seriously to consider statements so obviously incorrect, were it not for the fact that people are actually trained to sing with this "shock of the *upper glottis*;" that is to say, they are instructed to attack a tone by approximation of the pocket ligaments, by inflation of the pockets of the larynx and by a subsequent sudden escape of the imprisoned air, which, according to our author, causes "an explosive noise similar to an unvoiced consonant."

We have described on p. 144 the extraordinary liberties which it is necessary to take with exsected larynges in order to cause the pocket ligaments to meet, and we have no hesitation in asserting that such an act can never, in a state of health, take place in phonation, whatever may be the case in pressing and swallowing, &c., when the constrictors of the vestibule come into play. Even then there can be no *inflation* of the pockets of the voice-box, because the vocal ligaments are inserted in the pyramids much closer together than the pocket ligaments. The lower gate will, therefore, under any circumstances be shut earlier and much more firmly than the upper one, thereby effectually preventing an accumulation of air between the two.

But the mere endeavour to bring about the result desired by his teacher causes the student to make wrong efforts, which must sooner or later have evil consequences. So far as singing on such a plan is concerned, it may be readily imagined that each tone is ushered in by a loud snapping noise which is exceedingly ugly and at times positively ludicrous.

The above theory of voice production is avowedly founded upon 'Observations on the Physiology of the Larynx,' by Dr. John Wyllie, published in the *Edinburgh Medical Journal*, September, 1866. We have read this very interesting paper most carefully, and it is only fair to Dr. Wyllie to say that his experiments as to the approximation of the pocket ligaments and inflation of the pockets were made in relation to the valvular action of the larynx, by which complete closure of the air-passage occurs—(1) in the act of swallowing, and (2) in voluntary effort as in holding a breath for certain muscular acts, or in involuntary effort, as before each act of coughing.

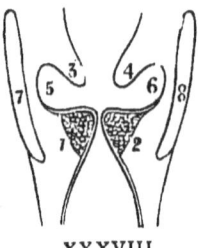 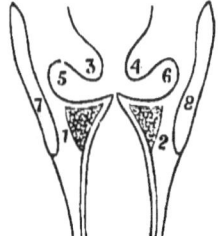

XXXVIII.   XXXIX.

SECTION OF THE VOICE-BOX OR LARYNX. (*From Merkel.*)

1 & 2. Vocal ligaments.
3 & 4. Pocket ligaments.
5 & 6. Pockets of the larynx (ventricles of Morgagni).
7 & 8. Shield cartilage.

XXXVIII. shows the shape of the vocal ligaments in the formation of the thick, and XXXIX. the shape of the vocal ligaments in the thin register. These sections, while they clearly illustrate the possibility of the valvular action of the pocket ligaments, also show most plainly that there remains a large chink between them in the middle line, and that the vocal ligaments alone are closely approximated in the production of tone.

Dr. Wyllie specially confines his remarks on this valvular action to these two conditions of deglutition and breath-holding, to the exclusion of consideration of that practical closure of the vocal ligaments which takes place during phonation. When he does consider this last question he in no instance alludes to closure of the pocket ligaments as essential to the production of tone, nor even as an accidental condition of it. There is consequently not a vestige of foundation for the theory advocated by Mr. Steed and others, and we hope we shall hear no more of the "shock of the *upper* glottis."*

We have quoted as the basis of our refutation the remarks of Mr. Steed, solely because he is the only one of the very few advocates of this fantastic doctrine whose writings are sufficiently intelligible to admit of criticism.

* See letter from Dr. Wyllie, Appendix II., page 307.

RESONANCE.

"The resonance of caves and of rocky enclosures is well known. Bunsen notices the thunder-like sound produced when one of the steam jets of Iceland breaks out near the mouth of a cavern. Most travellers in Switzerland have noticed the deafening sound produced by the fall of the Reuss at Devil's Bridge. The noise of the fall is raised by resonance to the intensity of thunder. The sound heard when a hollow shell is placed close to the ear is a case of resonance. Children think they hear in it the sound of the sea. The noise is really due to the reinforcement of the feeble sounds with which even the stillest air is pervaded, and also in part to the noise produced by the pressure of the shell against the ear itself. By using tubes of different lengths the variation of the resonance with the length of the tube may be studied. The channel of the ear itself is also a resonant cavity. When a poker is held by two strings, and when the fingers of the hands holding the poker are thrust into the ears, on striking the poker against a piece of wood, a sound is heard as deep and sonorous as that of a cathedral bell." (Tyndall, op. cit., p. 210.)

The above-quoted instances show to what a marvellous extent sounds, though feeble in themselves, may be reinforced by resonance. But experiments more clearly illustrating this matter have been described on pp. 32 and 33, and the student is advised to make himself thoroughly familiar with them as they are of the greatest consequence with regard to the present part of our subject. The experiment with a tuning-fork and an ordinary tumbler is perhaps the most instructive one, and the reader should certainly try it himself.

The lesson it teaches is that the amount of reinforcement depends upon the shape of the resonator, which, in order to produce the best result, must be exactly tuned to the tone of the tuning-fork. Now in voice production the tuning-fork is represented by the vocal ligaments, and the resonator by the cavities above the glottis, viz.: (1) the pockets of the larynx, (2) the vestibule of the larynx, (3) the upper throat (pharynx), (4) the mouth, and (5) the nose.

It will be seen, therefore, that the case of the voice is infinitely more complex than that of the tuning-fork experiment, because in the former the resonator consists of five cavities, and in the latter only of one. The means of altering the resonance cavities of the voice are also endless, while that of the glass is altered by the one simple device of partly covering its aperture with a piece of cardboard. But in tone production matters are made still more complicated, to a degree difficult to conceive, by the ever-varying pitch of the primary tones of the voice to which the resonance cavities have to be continually adjusted.

Even this, however, is not all; for not only is the primary tone reinforced in the resonator, but the quality of the voice and the formation of the different vowels also depend upon it. It is thus clear that it is highly necessary to be fully acquainted with the nature of the resonator, and to acquire the greatest possible amount of control over its component parts.

A full description of the pouches and of the vestibule of the larynx with the lid attached to it, has been given on pp. 70 and 73, and their appearance in the laryngeal mirror at p. 157; there is the less cause to refer to these parts again, as we have little, if any, direct control over them. The case is different with the throat, the mouth, and the nose. The dimensions of the throat chiefly depend upon the position of the larynx; for when the voice-box stands high the throat is short and narrow, and when it stands low the throat is long and wide. The former condition favours the formation of brilliant " open " tones, while the latter increases power and fulness, at the same time favouring the formation of " closed " tones. Both these qualities have their uses, and singers as well as speakers should be able to employ either of them at pleasure.

With regard to the general position of the larynx the most contradictory opinions are entertained by different teachers. Some say that it should be kept rigidly fixed quite low in the throat. This is a mistaken idea; for it is impossible to hold the voice-box *absolutely* in the same position. But even continually to depress the larynx *as far as possible* is an unwise proceeding, involving an unnatural strain upon the vocal organ which must, in the long run, be injurious Kofler, who is a competent judge, emphatically confirms our opinion in these words: " I have had opportunities, during the past four years, of examining a number of tenors and basses who had been trained by teachers who force them to keep the larynx in a firm and closely-confined position. Without one exception their tones sound unmusical, dry, and harsh, lacking all sympathy, no matter how good their natural voice might be." (Op. cit., p. 23.)

Other teachers maintain, on the contrary, that the larynx must have free play, and that its movements must not on any account be interfered with. The result is that the voice-boxes of their pupils fly up and down like shuttlecocks, which not only looks very ridiculous, but certainly impoverishes the tone, though it is not fraught with the injurious effects upon the voice, arising from the attempt to keep the larynx permanently fixed as low as possible.

The proper thing is to avoid both extremes and to give the larynx just that amount of fixity which enables it to offer the necessary resistance to the pressure of the air from below, thus giving the muscles governing the pitch of the voice the best chance of acting with ease and certainty.

The student will do well to test before a looking-glass the movements of the larynx described on p. 86; and to repeat them at various times until he obtains sufficient control over the elevators and depressors to raise and to lower the larynx independently of breathing, of opening and shutting the mouth, of swallowing, of yawning, and of phonation, &c. This is excellent practice, and will be of great service to him hereafter.

The mouth is undoubtedly the most important cavity of our resonator, and the shape of it may be altered by the action of the lower jaw, the lips, the tongue, and the soft palate.

We are not here concerned with the formation of the vowel sounds. "A vowel is a modification, due to resonance in the cavities above the larynx, of an original quality of tone produced by the vibrations of the vocal cords in the larynx." (Ellis, op. cit., p. 10.) But it must be borne in mind at the same time, that "vowels are quite a different affection of sound from both pitch and quality. Thus we say a man has a clear voice, a nasal voice, a thick voice, and yet his vowels are quite distinct from each other. Even a parrot, or Mr. Punch, in speaking, will produce *a's*, and *o's*, and *e's* which are quite different in their *quality* from human vowels, but which are nevertheless distinctly *a's*, and *o's*, and *e's*." (From a paper on "Vowel Sounds," by Professor Willis, in 'Cambridge Philosophical Transactions.')

We have here merely to deal with the alterations of the size and shape of the resonator in so far as they influence the volume and quality of the voice in general, and with the means of bringing these alterations as much as possible under control.

All the experiments and exercises which we are going to suggest are, like those concerning the movements of the larynx, to be made before a mirror; and for our present purpose the light should be allowed to fall into the student's mouth in such a manner as to illuminate even the back of his throat while standing in a perfectly natural position and without in the least stretching the neck, bending the head, or indulging in any other contortions. A "Queen's" reading lamp upon the piano, the light exactly on a level with the mouth, and a looking-glass attached to it, or the Tobold lamp, recommended for auto-laryngoscopy, will be found a very convenient arrangement.

Such a contrivance will enable the student to watch even his slightest movements, and those of the jaw and of the lips being so very familiar to every one it would almost seem waste of time to say anything about them. We find, however, that such is not the case, because, strange as it may seem, the majority of English people, whether singers or speakers, will not open their mouths, which is, of course, the first and most obvious thing to do if they wish the sounds they produce to be heard by others. The result is that their voices are smothered, and it is incredible how incessantly they have to be corrected before any lasting improvement takes place. In addition to this they articulate in a most negligent and careless manner, so that their utterance is anything but satisfactory, as teachers of singing and of elocution know by unpleasant experience.

Mr. H. C. Deacon, in a scholarly article on "Singing" in Grove's 'Dictionary of Music and Musicians' (Macmillan & Co.), expresses himself on this point as follows: "No nation in the civilised world speaks its language so abominably as the English. The Scotch, Irish, and Welsh, in the matter of articulation, speak much better than we do. Familiar conversation is carried on in inarticulate smudges of sound which are allowed to pass current for something, as worn-out shillings are accepted as representatives of twelve pence. Not only are we, as a rule, inarticulate, but our tone-production is wretched, and when English people begin to study singing they are astonished to find that they have never learned to speak. In singing there is scarcely a letter of our language that has not its special defect or defects amongst nearly all amateurs, and, sad to say, amongst some artists. An Italian has but to open his mouth, and if he have a voice its passage from the larynx to the outer air is prepared by his language. We, on the contrary, have to study hard before we can arrive at the Italian's starting-point."

This judgment, severe though it be, was endorsed by Dr. W. H. Stone in the course of his recent lectures on "Singing, Speaking, and Stammering," at the Royal Institution, and few persons competent to form an opinion upon the subject will be inclined to differ from it.

But to return to our exercises. The student, standing before his mirror as directed, is invited to try the following:

1. Open the mouth as widely as possible every way; look at the tongue, the soft palate, and the back of the

throat. Then shut the mouth again. Repeat this several times.

2. Open the mouth widely enough to put two fingers between the teeth; then smile so as to draw the corners of the mouth sideways until they are each bordered by a little perpendicular line. Now suddenly alter the shape of the mouth by protruding the lips as much as possible with only a small opening between them as in whistling; the change must be quick and smart. Repeat this several times. If it makes you laugh so much the better, for that will put you in a good temper, which may be useful to you in going through a few apparently still more absurd exercises.

3. Smile, with lips firmly closed, drawing the corners of the mouth as much sideways as possible; then smartly protrude the lips as in whistling but still firmly closed with no aperture whatever. Repeat this several times.

The above three exercises are intended as gymnastics for different sets of muscles which in ordinary life are called into play only to a very limited extent, and they will be found useful in enabling the student, so far as lower jaw and lips are concerned, promptly to alter the shape of the mouth in accordance with the requirements of the production of good tone, and they are also a great help to clear and distinct articulation. These gymnastics are of little value unless they are performed regularly and vigorously. Practise them for a little while three or four times a day, but never fatigue yourself with them.

Now we come to that big movable plug, the tongue, which is a most important factor in altering the shape of the cavity of the mouth. The tongue, we have it on the highest authority, is an " unruly member." It is often difficult to keep it under proper control, and we know people who have no control over it under any circumstances; it is continually running away with them altogether. As in every-day life, so in singing, instead of peacefully assuming the position necessary for the production of the various vowels, the tongue rises in rebellion, it arches up, stiffens, and defies all attempts to keep it in order. In fact the more one endeavours to control it the more it resists and impedes the vocal passage. The stiffening of the root of the tongue, accompanied by a rigidity of the surrounding parts, becomes very great, and the tone is shut in, with the result of making it "throaty."

This defect is frequently so obstinate and so difficult of cure that many teachers are driven, in despair, to recommend the use of mechanical means, such as holding the tongue down with a spatulum, or with the handle of a spoon, &c. We have known singers to be trained with a little silver instrument in their mouths which is flat at the bottom and arched up at the top like the hard palate, and which has, of course, a large opening behind and another in front. This contrivance certainly prevents the singer from closing his mouth too much, and it also presses down the tongue. It is undoubtedly the most ingenious instrument of the kind with which we are acquainted, and far in advance of either spatulum or spoon-handle.

But its use is nevertheless to be deprecated, because—

1. It limits vocalisation to those vowels which can be produced with a flat-lying tongue.

2. It rather increases than diminishes that baneful stiffening of the root of the tongue which does so much mischief.

3. It makes the singer rely upon artificial help instead of endeavouring to use his tongue rightly and naturally, and it thus really retards the cure of the evil which it seeks to remedy.

The wisest plan to pursue is to let the tongue execute a series of gymnastics which will soon reduce it to obedience and bring it under control; the gain will be great and permanent. Stand before your looking-glass and make the following experiments:—

1. Open the mouth widely. Put out the tongue straight, and as far as possible. Draw it back smartly and try to let it lie flat and low, but touching the lower teeth all round. Repeat several times. In this as well as in the remaining tongue exercises, great care must be taken to keep the lips and the lower jaw perfectly still.

2. Put the tip of the tongue against the lower front teeth, and then push it out as far as possible; this will, of course, completely roll it up. Then draw it back smartly as in exercise No. 1. Repeat several times.

3. Keep the root of the tongue as flat as you can, raise the tip and push it perpendicularly and quite slowly towards the roof of the mouth. Then lower it again as gradually, until it has once more assumed its original position. Repeat several times.

4. Raise the tip of the tongue as in exercise No. 3, and move it gradually from one side to the other so that the highest point of it describes a semi-circle. Repeat several times.

Take care not to overdo these exercises or they will be very fatiguing, but practise them regularly every day until you have quite mastered the tongue. It is, in many instances, at first found almost impossible to carry out the movements just indicated, and the tongue will perform the most curious contortions. But we can assure the reader, from extended observations, that with perseverance the tongue has to give in at last, and the result is worth trying for with all diligence, because it will not only greatly assist in the cure of throaty tone, but it will also be of the utmost value in helping the student to alter the size of the cavity of the mouth in endeavouring to adjust it to the varying pitch of the laryngeal tone, thus finding the best resonance for it.

Another device in curing throaty tone consists in singing sustained tones to *oo-oh-ah*. The *oo* is our most "forward" vowel, then follows *oh* and then *ah*. If, therefore, we sing *oo*, and then let it gradually dwindle into *oh*, without allowing it to slip back, we fix the *oh* in the same place in which we first had the *oo*. Now let us imperceptibly change the *oh* into *ah*, still taking care not to allow the latter vowel to slip back, and we shall fix the *ah* where we just had the *oh*; that is to say, right in front of the mouth. This is a very useful exercise for the purpose of improving the quality of tone and of increasing the "reach" of the voice. But it is insufficient where throatiness arises from stiffening of the root of the tongue and the surrounding parts, and in such cases the *oo-oh-ah* exercises should be preceded by rapidly singing the syllable *koo*.

The *oo*, as we have just seen, is our most forward vowel, and in pronouncing the *k* the tongue is brought into almost the identical position which is necessary for *oo*, though it comes firmly in contact with the soft palate. It requires some dexterity to *see* this, but if we manage the light well we eventually succeed, and we then perceive that the back of the tongue completely hides the arches of the soft palate and the uvula. In other words, in quickly and repeatedly uttering a syllable commencing with k, the tongue rapidly moves up and down, and the larynx being attached to the tongue-bone is compelled to execute similar movements—a fact which will be at once revealed by the mirror. By this exercise, therefore, we absolutely prevent any stiffening of the root of the tongue and of the neighbouring parts, and it will be found invaluable in getting rid of that particular kind of throatiness arising from the above cause. For reasons just enumerated it is easier, as well as more beneficial, to combine the *k* with *oo* than with any other vowel, and this is confirmed by making a few trials. A complete formula of the exercise would therefore be as follows:—

MET. 60.

Koo koo koo koo koo   oo   oh   ah

Sing this several times steadily and in strict time, breathing before *oo* and at the end of the exercise. Commence on your ordinary speaking tone, and then go higher and lower, semitone by semitone; but keep well within the easiest compass of your voice.

We have so far dealt with the lips, the jaw, and the tongue as some of the means of altering the size and the shape of the cavity of the mouth. We must now, finally, notice the movements of the soft palate, the construction of which has been described on p. 80. We can raise or lower it to such an extent as completely to shut off from the throat either the nose or the mouth. If we raise the soft palate, thereby shutting the nose off from the throat, then the tone passes through the mouth, and assuming that its exit takes place in a normal manner, it will be a pure vocal tone. If we lower the soft palate, thereby shutting the mouth off from the throat, then the tone passes through the nose, which gives it a nasal quality.

This is denied by some authors, who teach that nasal

quality is caused, on the contrary, by the tone not being able to pass through the nose; and it is amazing to see the voluminous arguments with which they endeavour to prove their case, since the matter can be settled by a very simple experiment. Take a little hand-mirror, hold it flat against your upper lip with the glass upwards, and sing a pure vocal tone; the glass will remain perfectly bright and undimmed. Now sing a nasal tone, and the glass will immediately be covered with moisture, which conclusively shows that the tone passed through the nostrils. That nasal tone implies passage of the tone through the nostrils, and is not due to obstruction of them may be proved in another way. Hold the mirror as described and pronounce the consonants *b, c, d, f,* &c., and the mirror will remain clear, but on pronouncing *m* or *n*, which are essentially and admittedly nasal consonants, the mirror is at once dimmed.

But the tone could not pass through the nostrils if the soft palate were not lowered, which is proved by the fact that it is quite possible to shut the nostrils and yet to sing without any nasal twang whatever. This matter is further illustrated by the two photographs of the mouth, facing p. 215, showing the position of the soft palate in the production of [musical notation] with a pure quality, and the position of the soft palate in the production of the *same tone* with a nasal quality. These photographs speak for themselves and do not require any further comment.

Another proof of nasal quality being caused by the tone passing through the nose is found in the circumstance that persons partly or entirely without a soft palate can, under no circumstances, produce pure vocal tone, though with *entire* absence of the soft palate the nasal twang is less marked than with *partial* absence of it. This is accounted for by the fact that in the former case the mouth, the upper pharynx, and the nose are practically converted into one great cavity.

The question may be asked how it is that by singing through the nose with the lips closed the tone has no nasal quality. The reply is that such a way of producing tone is humming and not singing. It is quite possible, however, even to hum with a strong nasal twang, but an explanation of this matter is not called for in the present volume.

Again, it may be objected that if the nasal passages are obstructed, as, for instance, by the swelling of the mucous membrane during a cold, the voice immediately partakes of a more or less nasal quality. This is perfectly true, but in that case the soft palate is sure also to be affected so as to be unable by proper contraction to prevent the tone from entering the nose. When such is the case, and the tone is afterwards arrested or impeded in its passage through the nose, then the tone will be even more nasal than it would have been otherwise; it is also, however, much less resonant.

We repeat that there can be no nasal twang while the singer or speaker has the power sufficiently to raise the soft palate in order to prevent the tone from entering the nostrils.

But there is another side to this question which often leads to misunderstandings. However tight the closure of the soft palate may be it is never sufficient to prevent the air in the nasal cavities being thrown into co-vibrations with that in the mouth. These co-vibrations are, in fact, necessary for a certain amount of the brilliancy of the voice, and if they are prevented by a stoppage of the posterior openings of the nasal passages, the voice will sound dull and muffled. This, of course, is due to an *absence* of nasal *resonance,* and must on no account be described as nasal *twang.* It is, indeed, the very opposite of it.

The action of the soft palate in two extreme cases has now been described, and the difference in the respective positions is so clearly defined that it is easily recognised. But the movements of the soft palate are, under other circumstances, far more complicated, because it not only occupies different positions for different pitches, but the closure assumes different degrees of tightness in the production of the different vowel sounds.

The soft palate rises with the ascending scale, the arch between the pillars of the fauces becomes narrower and higher, and the uvula diminishes in size, until at last it not only quite vanishes but a dimple appears in place of it. This is illustrated by the photographs of the throat which show the soft palate in the production of three different tones. The reader will now see the importance of exercising the soft palate, and we recommend for this purpose the following practice:

Stand in front of your mirror as before, open the mouth widely, and see that the back of your throat is well illuminated.

(1) Breathe through the mouth; the soft palate will be moderately raised, with the uvula in its normal shape and position. In expiration through the mouth the uvula will be thrown a little forward.

(2) Open the mouth again and inhale through the nostrils. This will cause the soft palate to fall, and the tongue to rise, which has the effect of shutting the mouth at the back just as you shut it in front by closing the lips.

No. II.   No. III.

No. I.   No. IV.

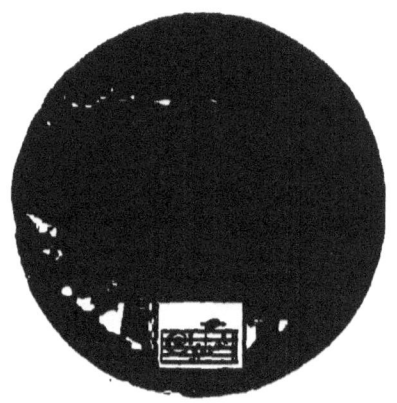

PHOTOGRAPHS OF THE SOFT PALATE
IN THE PRODUCTION OF VARIOUS TONES
(Copyright.)

[*To face page* 215.

DESCRIPTION OF PHOTOGRAPHS, ILLUSTRATING THE SOFT PALATE IN THE PRODUCTION OF VARIOUS TONES.

1, 2. Anterior pillars of the fauces.
3, 4. Posterior pillars of the fauces.
5. Uvula.

No. I. shows the soft palate in the production of the note F, as indicated in the picture. The reader's attention is called to the arch of the palate, 3, 5, 4, and he is requested to contrast it with the much greater height of that in

No. II., representing the same throat during production of the note A.

No. III. illustrates another change, and still greater elevation of the arch when singing C. The uvula in this case is seen to have almost completely disappeared. As a further contrast, No. IV. represents the soft palate in production of the same C as in No III., but with strong *nasal* quality. The whole palate and uvula are seen to have dropped on to the tongue: the space between the curtain of the palate and the back of the throat for the passage of the tone through the nostrils, is indicated by the very strong line of shadow which, as will be observed in the other pictures, had been gradually lessening in production of pure tone from the lower to the higher note.

Exhale in the same way, and the mouth will remain shut at the back. Repeat several times.

(3) Inhale through the nostrils, with the mouth wide open. Prevent the tongue from rising, keep it still and flat. You have learnt to control your tongue and will have no difficulty on that score. This will compel the soft palate to come down more smartly, which is just what is wanted. Now exhale through the mouth, when the soft palate will rise again.

By thus *in*haling through the nostrils with the mouth open, and the tongue still and flat, the soft palate is pulled vigorously down, and by *ex*haling through the mouth the soft palate is raised again. If therefore these two actions are repeated for a little while, the soft palate is continually moved up and down, which must necessarily have the effect of strengthening the muscles of which it largely consists.

This is a great gain from a mechanical point of view, because it will enable the soft palate to do its work much more satisfactorily than before, and prevent it from becoming fatigued by long talking or singing. But it will also make its limp, flabby substance tense and hard, which is, it will readily be granted, of the highest importance from an acoustical point of view. The effect of the change upon the voice is very marked, and we strongly recommend the reader to conscientiously practise these soft palate gymnastics every day, for he is sure to reap the benefit of his perseverance.

It is clear from the above that a perfectly healthy state of the soft palate is of the highest importance. If it is weighted with an elongated uvula or with enlarged tonsils it cannot act in a proper manner, and singers or speakers with such *impedimenta* are handicapped for vocal purposes.

They might just as well try to run a race with heavy weights on their shoulders as to sing or to speak with such appendages to their soft palates.

We now come to the vowel sounds. This is an exceedingly complicated subject which, together with a scientific consideration of the consonants, has been most exhaustively treated by Mr. Alexander Ellis in his 'Pronunciation for Singers,' to which we have already so frequently alluded. No man is better qualified for this task than Mr. Ellis, who has devoted half a lifetime to the study of speech sounds, and whose capacity for patient and painstaking research is unbounded. It would therefore be presumption on our part to attempt to explain here in a cursory manner what he has done so thoroughly.

We prefer to confine ourselves to a few points absolutely essential for our purpose, and we strongly advise the reader carefully to study Mr. Ellis's book and, above all things, faithfully to carry out all the experiments which he suggests. We ourselves are deeply indebted to Mr. Ellis for much valuable information, and we feel sure that our readers will have the same experience.

We know that, whatever vowel we may pronounce, the laryngeal tone is, pitch and loudness apart, exactly the same in all cases, and that it takes the form of one vowel or another solely according to the shape of the resonator, which may be described as a mould into which the tone is cast. This can easily be demonstrated by a simple and instructive experiment. Strike an ordinary C tuning-fork, put your mouth in position for the vowel *oo*, and hold the fork in front of your mouth. Although you utter no sound whatever, the tuning-fork will distinctly say *oo*. Now rapidly change the position of your mouth for *oh* and then for *ah*, again in perfect silence, when the tuning-fork will distinctly say *oh* and *ah*. The *ah*, it is true, will not be sounded very loudly, because the cavity of the mouth necessary for the production of that vowel only reinforces some of the upper partials which, in the case of tuning-forks, are exceedingly faint. Even in the production of *oo* and of *oh* much better results may be obtained by substituting for the C tuning-fork other forks which give tones exactly corresponding with the pitch of the resonator; but the experiment is sufficient to show the importance of properly shaping the mouth in uttering the various vowel sounds. For an illustration of this matter we refer the reader to the diagrams on p. 14 in Mr. Ellis's book.

This brings us to the fact, already hinted at in several places, that the various vowel sounds, *if whispered*, have each a definite pitch. If we put a tall jug under a tap, and let the water fall into it, we can tell by the sound when the jug is getting full. When the jug is empty it constitutes a long pipe, producing a low tone; as the water gradually fills the jug it shortens the pipe, and the tone is raised in proportion, until at last it becomes quite shrill. A similar alteration takes place in the resonator for the production of the various vowel sounds. Thus for *oo* the voice-box stands lowest, and it rises more and more for *oh*, *ah*, *ai*, and *ee*.

The consequence is that when a tone is produced, not by singing, but by whispering—that is to say, merely causing the air in the resonator to vibrate—it will be found that the resonator is tuned lowest for *oo* and highest for *ee*, the succession being, as before, *oo*, *oh*, *ah*, *ai*, and *ee*.

The most curious part of this arrangement is that the pitch of the cavity for each vowel is *exactly* the same, whether in the case of a man, a woman, or a child, the only condition being that the vowel be exactly of the same quality in every instance. It is, no doubt, the difficulty, or we should perhaps say, the impossibility, of getting exactly the same quality which accounts for the fact that different observers, as, for instance, Donders, Helmholtz, Koenig, and others, do not quite agree as to the pitches which they assign to the various whispered vowels.

Now it is obvious, as we know from every-day experience, that we are not, by these pitches of the resonating cavities, prevented from uttering the vowels upon every tone of our voices; but it is an undoubted fact that there are certain tones which are more favourable for the production of each vowel than others, and it may be laid down as a general rule that *oo* and *oh* are most easily sung upon the lowest, and *ai* and *ee* upon the highest, part of our voices, while *ah* lends itself most readily to be used over the whole compass.

There is consequently good reason why the *ah* should be selected by teachers of singing as the most favourable vowel for the cultivation of the voice. But considering that in singing words the vowels have to be rendered as they come, and to the best advantage, it is clearly a mistake to vocalise exclusively on *ah*, and the wise teacher will see that other vowels receive a proper share of attention as well. We have known persons who could sing a fine *ah*, but whose *oh* and *ai* were wretched, to say nothing of *oo* and *ee*.

A truly laughable, though probably very exceptional, case of cultivating one vowel at the expense of all others occurred a few years ago in a large Scotch town, and may be related here for the benefit of the reader. The conductor of a choral society being impressed with the fact that *oo* is the most "forward" vowel, and that much depends upon bringing the voice well to the front of the mouth, conceived the idea of drilling his pupils for some considerable time exclusively on *oo*, with the result that at their next appearance in public, it was almost impossible for them to sing any other vowel. Some of our leading singers were engaged for the *soli*, and they found it difficult not to join in the merriment of the public, which was caused by the extraordinary pronunciation of the words of the choruses, choir and conductor being quite unconscious of anything singular taking place. The climax was reached when, in the Hallelujah Chorus, the choir sang vigorously *Hoolooloojoo, Hoolooloojoo*, and it may be imagined that the effect was intensely comical.

If we want to get the greatest amount of resonance for our vowels, we must modify them to suit the various pitches at which we have to sing them. Mr. Ellis has a number of admirable exercises upon this subject. Their practical results are roughly as follows:—

1. *Oo* as in *pool* is a favourable vowel for the lower part of the voice; the quality of tone deteriorates as we ascend the scale, and the *oo* must now be sung as in *pull* prolonged, when the quality will at once improve materially.

2. *Oh* as in *those* is not so favourable a vowel for singing as in *on* prolonged, which yields a good tone at nearly all pitches, but the best results are obtained from the *oh* as in *door*.

3. *Ah* produces a good tone at nearly every point of the scale, although the quality of the vowel slightly alters.

4. *Ai* as in *pain* has a harsh effect at all parts of the compass of the voice, and is greatly improved by singing it as in *pen* prolonged.

5. *Ee* as in *peep* is a favourable vowel in the higher part of the voice, but singing down the scale it becomes more

and more clouded, until at last it assumes a character of gruffness. If, however, from the middle of our compass downwards we sing the *ee* as in *pip* prolonged, the quality of tone will be most materially improved.

We have in the above hints only noticed the five elementary vowels, and for any additional sounds, as well as for a complete explanation of the whole subject, we once more refer the reader to Mr. Ellis's 'Pronunciation for Singers,' which, we repeat, cannot be recommended too highly.

The "reach" or "tellingness" of a voice, as Dr. Walshe calls it, does not so much depend upon the power of blast as upon—

1. The attack of the tone;
2. The absence of superfluous breath;
3. The forward production of the tone; and,
4. Resonance.

We have all heard and admired the ringing pianissimo tones of our great singers, which so completely fill even the largest buildings that they are not only distinctly heard, but almost felt, while the voice of a mere shouter, however loudly he may sing, does not penetrate to any distance. A singer who can produce a fine piano tone will have no difficulty in increasing its power, but he who relies upon mere force will never be able to sing a true pianissimo. He may certainly sing less loudly, but he will also in the same proportion become more inaudible.

The student is recommended to give his attention to the following points :—

a. Strike the tone firmly and clearly in accordance with the explanations in the section on "Attack."

b. Use no more breath than is actually necessary, or the tone will be diluted, as milk is diluted by the addition of water.

c. Let the tone come well forward in the mouth, and *try to keep it there.* If you have a feeling as though it went away from you, and you had to run after it to catch it, it will never be a "telling" tone.

d. Sing softly but *vigorously*, and above all things sing *beautifully;* or in the words of Mr. Deacon, "Work for quality, and power will take care of itself." (Op. cit., p. 504.)

Dr. Stone says, in the syllabus of his Royal Institution lectures, "the voice excels all instruments in the power of combining sounds with significant words." With this we thoroughly agree; but what if the "significant words" are pronounced in so slovenly a way as to be quite unintelligible? We all know that singers whose articulation is so clear that every word they utter is perfectly understood are scarce, while those who leave us in doubt as to whether they sing English, or Italian, or any other language are plentiful, and the number of those who mispronounce their words in a deplorable manner is legion.

It might therefore be expected that we should, in this chapter, say something about articulation. We can, within the limits of this manual, only call attention to it in a general way; and the best advice we can offer to singers as well as to speakers, is that they should make a daily practice of reading aloud some of the tables on p. 110 of Mr. Ellis's 'Pronunciation,' and that they should also carefully work through those on pp. 128 to 143. The reader is led by easy stages from simple words, as *eel, ill; eat, it; peat, pit*, &c., to such as *incomprehensibility* and *intercommunicability*. It is needless to add that the tables are systematically arranged, and that nothing is omitted.

FLEXIBILITY.

The flexibility of the voice depends almost entirely upon the control we have over the muscles governing the pitch; that is to say, upon the readiness and exactness with which we are able to allow them to contract or to relax.

Performers upon various instruments know that certain exercises are indispensable to brilliant execution, because they strengthen the muscles of the wrist and of the fingers, and make them obedient to the will. It has even been found that simple finger gymnastics, exercising separately different sets of muscles, and making them independent of each other, are of the greatest value, and save long hours of tedious and wearisome practising. In a similar manner we may spare ourselves much trouble, and gain our end most readily, by vocal gymnastics, calculated to bring into play the stretching and slackening muscles of the larynx. There is no difficulty about it. Sing F, the same tone on which we started when exercising the opening and the closing muscles, and after it G. The alteration of the pitch is brought about by a contraction of the stretching muscles overcoming the resistance of the opposing slackening muscles, thereby *tensing* the vocal ligaments. If you again sing F, the case is reversed, and the new alteration in pitch is brought about by a contraction of the slackening muscles overcoming the resistance of the opposing stretching muscles, thereby *relaxing* the vocal ligaments.

oo	.	.	.	.	.	.	.	oo	.	.	.	.	.	.	.
oh	.	.	.	.	.	.	.	oh	.	.	.	.	.	.	.
ah	.	.	.	.	.	.	.	ah	.	.	.	.	.	.	.
ai	.	.	.	.	.	.	.	ai	.	.	.	.	.	.	.
ee	.	.	.	.	.	.	.	ee	.	.	.	.	.	.	.

The above is an example. Take care to render it perfectly. Sing every tone clearly and distinctly, but without jerking, at the same time *uniting* all the tones, but without drawling. The tones should be like a row of pearls upon a string, each one well defined and separate, yet all strung together, and forming an uninterrupted whole. Sing softly and with pure intonation. Hold the jaw, the lips, and the tongue absolutely still. Remember that the pitch is altered in the larynx and not in the mouth. *Do not try how quickly you can sing, but rather how distinctly.* Commence slowly and be in no hurry to increase the speed. Raise and lower the exercise semitone by semitone within the medium part of your voice. A variety of exercises founded upon the same principles may be introduced, and will serve to increase the flexibility of the voice in a short time.

There is nothing new in this, and it may be thought superfluous to point out a physiological basis for vocal gymnastics so universally recommended as these. But personal experience has taught us that students of singing are very apt to look upon flexibility of the voice as a natural gift, and that they are, in many instances, reluctant to submit to a discipline which every instrumentalist undergoes without questioning and as a matter of course. It is true that some voices are naturally more flexible than others, but it is also true that *all* can acquire nimbleness and agility if they proceed in a systematic manner and with the necessary perseverance.

There is, in fact, no department of vocal training in which results may be obtained with greater certainty, if students would only *work;* but this, unfortunately, many of them will not do, and the result is that even public performances are frequently disgraced by a clumsiness of execution which would make it impossible for an instrumentalist to get a hearing, and which is tolerated in the case of singers, only because she or he has a fine voice.

THE REGISTERS.

We have defined a register as "a series of tones produced by the same mechanism." The five registers of which the human voice, taken as a whole, consists are carefully described, and the means by which they are formed minutely explained on pp. 163 to 170. These registers, nevertheless, continue to be a stumbling-stone to many, and the fact of the existence in the throat of different actions for the production of different series of tones has led some teachers into the deplorable mistake of developing and exaggerating them, instead of, on the contrary, smoothing them over and equalising them. The result is, that we often hear singers who seem to have two or three different *voices.* They growl in the one, moan in the second, and shriek in the third; while it should have been their aim so to blend and to unite the registers as to make it difficult even for a practised ear to distinguish the one from the other. Such singing is outrageous, and we protest against the opinion, expressed in some quarters, that it is the natural outcome of the teachings of the laryngoscope.

We will review the whole subject, putting it into a new

light, and hope to succeed in removing doubts and in destroying errors.

Let us imagine we are listening to a bass, commencing with his lowest tones, and singing up to [♪]. In so doing he is playing, we will say, upon the *double bass*. This is the "lower thick register." A tenor joining in as soon as the bass has gone high enough for him to do so, would produce his tones in exactly the same way—that is to say, he also would be playing upon a *double bass*. Both our singers now sing up the scale from [♪], the bass to the end of his compass, and the tenor to [♪]. In so doing, they have both changed instruments; they do not play these tones upon a *double bass*, but upon a *violoncello*. This is the "upper thick register." Many of the tones that have just been sung by a bass and by a tenor can also be produced by female voices, the compass of a contralto going down to, say [♪]. Her lowest tones she sings, like the bass and the tenor, in the "lower thick;" that is to say, like the men, she plays upon the *double bass*; the only difference, so far, between her voice and that of the male singer's being this, that the contralto continues a third higher in the "lower thick" than the bass and the tenor; or, referring to the instruments, the men exchange the *double bass* for the violoncello at [♪], and the woman makes the change at  .

At this point a soprano joins in, and going from [music] to [music] she sings like bass, tenor, and contralto in the "upper thick," or, to keep up our comparison, she plays upon the *violoncello*. Observe the important fact that the series of tones last mentioned, from [music] to [music], is played by bass, tenor, contralto, and soprano upon the same instrument, the *violoncello;* that is to say, *they all sing in the same register*, the "*upper thick.*" Here we must part company with our bass (who has probably not sung the last tone or two), while tenor, contralto, and soprano continue to sing up the scale, the tenor as high as he can, and contralto and soprano to [music]. In so doing they have all three exchanged the *violoncello* for the *viola*, or, in other words, they have been singing from [music] to [music] in the "lower thin."

Contralto and soprano from this point continue by themselves, laying aside the *viola*, and playing upon the *violin*, singing, that is to say, in the "upper thin." The tenor, it is true, could perform in the same way, and so be still with them; even the bass might make use of the same means, and has to do so when taking the part of a male alto. But we will not needlessly complicate matters, and prefer to confine ourselves to the voices as generally employed in modern music. Let us, therefore, listen to contralto and soprano, as they play upon their *violin* up the scale to [music]. Here we must also take leave of our contralto, and the soprano finishes alone; but to do so she requires again other means, and as we have exhausted the family of stringed instruments, we have no choice, if we wish to carry our illustration to the end, but to give her a *toy fiddle* which, with lighter strings, might certainly, without injury, be screwed up to a much higher pitch than an ordinary violin. Upon this *toy fiddle* she plays up to  or even to , which constitutes the highest register of the human voice, namely, the " small register."

It should be borne in mind that it is not for a moment intended to suggest by these comparisons that the human voice has any resemblance to string instruments—a matter which has already been fully discussed on p. 88.

In order to correctly understand the above explanation of the registers, it is necessary to bear in mind that the tones spoken of are represented by notes expressive of their *actual pitch*, while tenor music is, in the treble clef, generally written an octave higher than it is sung. Thus the high F of the tenor, which we are accustomed to see on the fifth line, is here put in the first space, &c.

The registers are found as here described in the vast majority of voices, though there are, of course, exceptions to the rule. But although most teachers have had more or less painful experience of the registers, there are some who either deny their existence altogether, or who admit only two, namely, " Chest and Falsetto." With these it is impossible to argue. "We can take a horse to the water, but we cannot make him drink," and we can give a man the opportunity of listening to the registers in a voice, but we cannot make him hear them. There are also those who have committed themselves publicly to theories which do not agree with the facts now put before them. And, finally, there are those who are open to conviction if only the opportunity be offered to them to form a correct opinion.

These we would advise to listen carefully and patiently to raw and untutored voices, because in such the registers will be noticeable in all their primitive distinctness and in all their glaring contrasts, while in cultivated voices the teacher, if he understands his business, has already strengthened some parts and softened down others, so that it is often difficult to detect the differences. It must also be borne in mind that the registers are not in all voices equally plain; it is therefore necessary to listen to many before a satisfactory conclusion can be arrived at. We have, in the case of young contralto singers, often had the opportunity of hearing *all the five registers* in one voice, and we also have frequently succeeded in making them clear to sceptics. There is nothing like personal experience, and we counsel our readers to try for themselves. We are certain that those who have now studied the question theoretically, and who afterwards in a candid and unprejudiced frame of mind, put the matter to a test, will agree with us that there is overwhelming evidence in support of the statements put before them.

The difference between some of the registers is very noticeable in tenors. There are few people, little though they may otherwise know about the human voice, who have never heard of a tenor's "Chest" or "Falsetto" voice; and teachers, while they know that he has another register besides, are also aware of the difficulty, in many instances, of uniting the two just mentioned. It is indeed a feat never attempted by some, who have an idea that the

"Lower Thin" (to be called "Falsetto" only when wrongly produced) is of no use whatever. They do not consider that it was in this "Lower Thin" they themselves could shout so lustily while they were children; that it is now weak partly through disuse, and that it may be again cultivated to a wonderful degree of power. They are unaware also that the lowest tones of this "Lower Thin" supply the material for the "*voce mista*" or "mixed voice," and that by judiciously blending the "Upper Thick," the "Mixed," and the "Lower Thin," a voice may be formed, at once sweet and full of power, yet easily produced and lasting.

They prefer, alas, to force the "Upper Thick" far above its natural limits, and the result is that their pupils can never produce a high tone except by a shout, and that but few voices for any length of time survive such barbarous treatment.

"There seems reason to believe that in the attempt to acquire notes unnatural to the individual, the natural portion of the voice undergoes impairment in *timbre*, if not in power. . . . . On plain physiological grounds all attempts at forcing up a voice (and from the dearth of tenors and the abundant supply of baritones, the practice is likely to become more and more common) must be injurious to the vocal organs. The effort, in truth, implies a forced change in the span of vocal cord habitually employed; a modification of natural muscular action; and a change in the amount of vocalising play, upward and downward, of the windpipe normal in the individual." (Walshe, op. cit., p. 18.)

In contraltos the break between two of their registers is as great and as difficult to deal with as in tenors, and it is a noteworthy and instructive fact that it occurs in both voices between the same registers *and at the same pitch;* that is to say, it is found in contraltos as well as in tenors between the "Upper Thick" and the "Lower Thin," at or about [musical notation] (for tenors generally written an octave higher). This break is, in many contralto voices, so marked as to be noticeable even to those who know nothing about the subject, and it requires years of patient and persevering practice to bridge it over; in some cases this end is never attained at all.

It will be readily understood that the difficulty of uniting increases in proportion as the "Upper Thick" is carried above its natural limit. We have repeatedly met with ill-trained contralto voices in which the "Lower Thin" was omitted altogether, the "Upper Thick" being extended up to [musical notation] or [musical notation] where it was followed by the "Upper Thin." These ladies really appeared to have two separate voices, the contrast between the registers being so great. It is almost superfluous to add that under such circumstances it is simply impossible to eradicate or even to conceal the break of the voice.

A great deal has now been said about tenors and contraltos, and we have seen that they are, in some respects, exactly alike. It may, in fact, be asserted, that the chief difference between them consists in this: the tenor extends a few tones *below* the contralto, and the contralto extends a few tones *above* the tenor. The greater part of their compass they have in common, and so far as this is the case they produce their voices by exactly the same mechanism. The result is, as might be expected, that when they avoid the extremes of their compass, their voices are very similar, and when the singers are not seen it is often impossible to say with any degree of certainty whether we are listening to a tenor or to a contralto.

This is a matter of common experience, and we venture to say that there are few musicians who have never been in such a state of doubt themselves. The fact once admitted of course immediately disposes of the mistaken idea that female voices are but a reproduction, an octave higher, of the corresponding male voices, a fallacy which has, however, by this time been pretty generally abandoned.

In sopranos another and rather curious difficulty is connected with the question of the registers. They have in many cases never discovered their "small" register, and the consequence is that few of these can ever go above

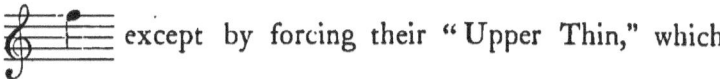 except by forcing their "Upper Thin," which

generally means shrieking, and which always, sooner or later, brings ruin to the voice. If, on the other hand, these same ladies are taught to use the top register with which Nature has provided them, they are astonished and delighted to find that they can almost at once sing much higher than before, and with such ease and grace as they had formerly thought quite impossible.

Exercises given later on for the easy management of the registers will be found to answer this particular purpose completely. Before, however, they are applied to any special case the teacher must make sure that he is dealing with a voice which has the *true* soprano character, or the experiment will fail.

In basses the registers give little or no trouble, as the difference between the "Lower Thick" and the "Upper Thick" is easily smoothed over. The only danger is that the "Upper Thick" is sometimes quite ignored, from the supposition that in this class of voices there exists but one register. We have met with basses trained on this principle, and their voices were, as a natural consequence, of very limited compass, and their upper tones had a very rough and unmusical quality. Moreover, they all complained of a feeling of tightness in their throats often amounting to pain, which ceased as soon as they had learnt to sing with the proper mechanism. But basses must also cultivate the "mixed voice" for the production of their highest tones.

The following rather amusing directions with regard to the registers are taken from Signor Randegger's otherwise excellent 'Singing Primer.' (Novello, Ewer and Co.)

LOWER THICK.—"The column of tone must be energetically pressed towards the lowest part of the chest, the whole cavity of the chest acting as a 'sounding board' to the voice."

UPPER THICK.—"The column of tone must be directed downwards, so that it may ring between the lower part of the throat and the upper part of the chest."

LOWER THIN.—"Direct the sound quickly and lightly towards the front part of the mouth. Feel as if the voice came from the lower part of the throat."

UPPER THIN.—"The sound must be directed perpendicularly towards the roof of the palate, exactly behind the upper set of teeth, so that the voice may ring in the upper part of the mouth and in front of the head."

SMALL.—"The sound must be sent in an oblique direction, so that it should ring in, and reverberate from, the highest part of the back of the head."

It is almost unnecessary to say that the tone cannot be directed in the fashion here suggested upon any given point, like a jet of water out of a fire-engine; nevertheless the physical sensations in producing the various registers are correctly described by Signor Randegger, and it is of great practical importance for the student to be thoroughly familiar with them. We therefore strongly recommend teachers to call the attention of their pupils to this matter of reverberation whenever they rightly produce a tone in any desired register, as it will be a great assistance to them in finding the register again upon other occasions.

In developing and strengthening the registers our first exercises are based upon the fact that some vowels are most easily produced upon the lowest tones of the voice, while others are most easily sung upon the highest tones, which matter has already been discussed in the chapter on "Resonance." It will, therefore, here suffice to repeat that the "vowel scale," going from low to high, is *oo, oh, ah, ai,* and *ee*, and that consequently the highest tones will be produced most readily when singing the vowels in the order just given. If any one doubts it let him reverse the order, and he will see how it increases the difficulty.

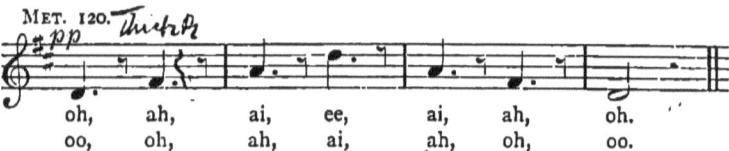

Sing this exercise pianissimo, strike each tone clearly and distinctly, and take a slight inspiration after every tone. Be careful to take a full inflation only at the beginning, and afterwards to inhale *less* air than has been consumed in each preceding tone, or you would after a while overcrowd the lungs and experience a sensation of being choked. This is a thing to be avoided in any case; but under present circumstances it should be remembered that the short inspirations are not taken for the purpose of re-filling the lungs, but simply to compel the opening and closing muscles to do their work. By so doing we give them much more exercise than by breathing only once at the beginning, and what is still more important with regard to our immediate object, we greatly facilitate the task of the vocal ligaments to arrange themselves in different ways according to the registers they are to produce.

It is self-evident that the danger of carrying the mechanism of a register beyond its proper limit is greater if the vocal ligaments are kept together, as in *legato* singing, than it would be if they were made to separate, as they are thereby more readily enabled to re-arrange themselves under different conditions. It will be seen, therefore, that the slight inspirations after every tone are an essential part of the exercise, and must on no account be omitted. The exercise is to be taken at a convenient pitch, and then to be raised semitone by semitone in accordance with the requirements of individual voices. It may, after some time, be taken right through upon the vowel *ah*, and finally *legato*, gradually increasing the speed, to the Italian word *scala*, singing the syllable *la* to the last note.

The change from one register to another should always be made a couple of tones *below* the extreme limit, so that there will be, at the juncture of every two registers, a few "optional" tones which it is possible to take with both mechanisms. The singer will be wise, however, to avail himself of the power of producing an optional tone with the mechanism of the lower register only on rare occasions. To force the register beyond its natural limit is, of course, infinitely worse, and should never be tolerated. The practice carries its own punishment, as it invariably ruins the voice, and tones so produced always betray the effort, frequently in a most painful degree, and are consequently never beautiful.

"Art goes after bread," we know, and we also know that a high A in "chest-voice" goes down with the multitude, and makes up for many shortcomings. But the singer who thus panders to the taste of a musically uneducated crowd ceases to be, for the time, an artist, and lowers himself to the status of a mountebank who astonishes the public by lifting heavy weights, or by performing other acrobatic feats.

It is evident that the last exercise given may be varied to any extent, so long as it is based upon the principle which has been explained. The beneficial results in the development of the voice will be speedily noticed, and then sustained tones may be sung through the whole compass after the orthodox fashion.

This brings us to the consideration of the "mixed voice," which is essential in bridging over the break between the "upper thick" and the "lower thin" of the tenor, and which is also frequently made use of by baritones and basses in the production of their highest tones. We have seen it stated in a book on singing, of which we do not remember the title, that the "mixed voice" is produced by the full loose vibrations of one of the vocal ligaments through its whole thickness, while in the other ligament the vibrations are confined to its fine inner edges. We might as well expect to see a horse galloping on one side and trotting on the other! The explanation is so amusing, that it might be supposed to have been intended as a joke. We believe, however, we are doing its author no injustice by asserting that he made the statement in perfect seriousness; in any case it must be uncompromisingly rejected as having no foundation whatever in fact.

The "*voce mista*" is "mixed" in the sense that it combines the *vibrating mechanism* of the "lower thin" with the position of the larynx of the " lower thick "; that is to say, while the vibrations are confined to the thin inner edges of the vocal ligaments, the larynx itself takes a much lower position in the throat than for the " lower thin," and the result is a remarkable increase of volume without any corresponding additional effort in the production of tone.

There are, apparently, many exceptions to this rule, and it must be understood that the ease of production which characterises the mixed voice is due, not so much to the lower position of the larynx in itself as to the contraction of the " depressors," by which the voice-box is pulled down towards the chest, and which has the effect of pressing together the plates of the shield cartilage below the vocal ligaments.

The depressors of the larynx, in the performance of this function, are often so effectually opposed by the "elevators" that the position in the throat of the voice-box is but little altered. But the contraction of the depressors has nevertheless the effect of pressing together the lower parts of the plates of the shield cartilage, as may be seen by the formation of a hollow in front of the throat which extends from the voice-box downwards.

According to some authorities the "mixed voice" is nothing but " chest voice " *disguised*. To this we cannot agree, for the distinguishing characteristic of the *voce mista* consists in the perfect ease with which it is produced when the singer has once hit upon the right mechanism. In the upper thick, on the other hand, the effort in producing the high tones of which we are now speaking would remain the same, no matter how and by what means they might be "disguised."

It must be borne in mind, finally, that in many tenors the upper thick is naturally so light, and the lower thin so full, that there is, from the beginning, no perceptible break, so that there is no difficulty whatever perfectly to blend the two registers without fitting in the mixed voice between them.

In short, voices differ as much as faces. Strongly as they resemble each other in general structure, there are no two exactly alike, and a teacher to be successful must carefully study the vocal organs of his pupils and treat each according to its own individuality.

A word may here be added about that mysterious register the "falsetto," of which, so far as we are aware, no satisfactory definition has as yet been given anywhere. Most persons understand by it that series of tones in the tenor voice just above the upper thick register. But these tones may be sung in two ways.

1. With the mechanism of the "*upper* thin" carried below its proper limit. The vocal chink has here an elliptical shape, the lid is completely raised, the larynx widely opened, and all parts are in a lax condition. In accordance with this there is a striking absence of tenseness in the soft palate, and the uvula is in nearly the same state as in quiet breathing. The tones so produced are feeble and unsatisfactory; no *crescendo* of any consequence can be executed upon them, and no amount of cultivation will render them more powerful.

2. With the mechanism of the "*lower* thin." The vocal chink is here linear; and although the voice-box is still more widely opened and therefore more easily inspected

than in the thick, yet the whole is tense, and in accordance with this the soft palate is raised and the uvula quite obliterated. The tones so produced are naturally stronger than those spoken of above; they may be swelled out to a considerable extent, they are capable of being made more powerful by practice, and they may, as has been pointed out before, be converted into the mixed voice.

The "*upper* thin" carried below its proper place is therefore an essentially *false* production, to which the term "falsetto" justly applies. But this is not the case with regard to the "*lower* thin," which is, on the contrary, perfectly legitimate. It is also clear from this explanation why it is undesirable, and from a physiological point of view even wrong, to apply the term "falsetto" to the medium register of the female voice.

It may be pointed out in conclusion that we play upon the same instrument in speaking and in singing. Speakers must not, therefore, imagine that this chapter on voice cultivation does not concern them. They will find that their voices will derive immense benefit from some of the exercises described in this chapter, and they are strongly recommended to give them a trial.

(Voice cultivation exercises with piano accompaniments, on the principles advocated in the foregoing chapter, have been prepared by Emil Behnke and Chas. W. Pearce, Mus. Doc. Cantab. A separate book has been devoted to each variety of voice, and the exercises are published by Messrs. Chappell & Co., of 50 New Bond Street).

POSITION.

A chapter on "Voice Cultivation" would not be complete without a few remarks with regard to the position speakers as well as singers should assume, and this subject may perhaps be best understood if a description is given of what it should *not* be. Of this we unfortunately find frequent illustration in the case of clergymen when holding the book out of which they are reading.

It is a favourite device with many to allow the lower arms to rest upon the chest, and to put the hands open one upon the other to serve as a desk for the book, which is held slantingly, the lower edge resting against the chest to prevent it from slipping down. It is clear that by this attitude the reader seriously interferes with his breathing, because he throws an obstacle in the way of his lower ribs by compelling them to move the weight of his arms, hands, and book every time they expand in inspiration.

The next consequence is that he has to bend the neck and to hang the head in order to be able to see the contents of his book, and the evil results of this are threefold:

1. It makes him stoop, thereby still further impeding his breathing;

2. His chin presses upon the larynx and prevents it from having fair play; and,

3. He throws his voice on the ground just in front of him, so that he is quite inaudible even at a very short distance.

This is about the most unfavourable position which a speaker can possibly assume, and we should find it difficult to suggest anything by which it could be made worse. It is no wonder that a clergyman habitually assuming this attitude, in his struggles to make himself heard under such adverse, though self-imposed, conditions, is quickly tired out, and that he eventually suffers in health.

Now let the reader try this: Stand straight, shoulders back, chest active, head up, spine curved inwards, but not too hollow. Raise the arms so that they do not touch the chest at all; grasp the book instead of letting it lie upon the hands, and hold it up high. Let the voice travel straight over it, directing it at the people right at the back of the church, it may be in the gallery. It will be well to practise a similar way of reading at home in the presence of a friend, capable of criticising, who should be situated at the far end of the room. We feel sure that both speaker and audience will be equally surprised and gratified at the result, and neither will wish for a return to the former method of delivery.

It is, perhaps, even more astonishing that clergymen make the same mistake of stooping and of bending over their Bibles, prayer-books, and sermons when they have a desk or lectern to hold them. The remedy is, of course, the same as before, and there is no need to repeat the instructions.

Singers are not often found to fall into similar errors because no teacher, however little qualified, would for a moment tolerate such a position as that described above. Singers, indeed, more frequently sin in the opposite direction. In their anxiety to stand *quite* upright, they not only take the shoulders back, but they slightly raise them; that is wrong, as may be seen from the section on breathing

(p. 181). Then, so far from bending the head, they are more likely to tilt it slightly backwards; that also is wrong, because it tends to fix the larynx in too high a position.

These mistakes are as much to be avoided as those described above, and the position we have recommended to clergymen, with such modifications as may be required by circumstances, will be found the most advantageous. No pains should be spared until it has become second nature.

THE DAILY LIFE OF A VOICE-USER.

Enough has been said in the chapter on Hygiene to prove the necessity of perfect bodily health for the efficient and comfortable performance of the vocation of all voice-users, from the special aspect of the parts of the human frame more directly concerned in voice production, and therefore no preface is wanted for this portion of our subject further than to say, that above all other professions that of a singer or public speaker requires the observance of a strictly physiological life—that is to say, such a life as will most certainly ensure perfect exercise of every function of the body.

A man's life may be said to be controlled—1, by residence; 2, by ablutions; 3, by clothing; 4, by diet; 5, by exercise; 6, by amusements; and lastly, by individual habits.

1. As to *residence*, it is all important that a singer should occupy a well-ventilated room and should not sleep and live in the same. If he do not occupy a house he must ensure that one room communicates with the other, so that, the windows of each being open, he may get a draught of fresh air each day right through both living and sleeping apartment. It will be preferable that he live on a hill with a south aspect, and in a house in which every regard is had to the state of the drains, for the throat of a voice-user is always more or less in a state of congestion, and therefore always more liable than that

of ordinary persons to receive the injurious impressions of any insanitary exhalations. For this same reason poisonous paints and wall papers should be avoided.

Such advice as the foregoing may appear unnecessary to many, but it would not be given did we not daily see ill-effects produced by neglect of such obvious precautions in choice of a dwelling-place. Especially is this the case with singers going to a new city, and with curates in country villages.

Naturally the climate will vary very considerably with the country in which a singer may be called to reside, but it should be his study to assimilate the temperature, &c., of his temporary or permanent residence to that of his home or that of the last country which he has inhabited. Thus he will often require fires and closed doors at seasons when the regular inhabitants may prefer open windows, and *vice versâ*.

In this matter of residence there are individualities which may require to be humoured. Some persons breathe better in a smoky city than in the country. Some whom we have known always lose their voice at the seaside; some, subject to dry catarrhs, enjoy the soft air of a valley; others, of relaxed habit, require the invigoration of mountains. To many who gain their livelihood by their voice, attention cannot be given to these peculiarities all the year round, but at least all may observe them when they take a holiday.

2. *Ablutions.* It may be thought that details on this head might be omitted and the subject dismissed in the simple advice that absolute cleanliness and frequent ablution of the whole body is good for all—singer and non-singer alike—but experience shows that many voice-users neglect bathing not from want of taste or respect for cleanliness, but because they are afraid of exciting a

disposition to take cold. Thus one will say, "I never dare take a cold bath, I should never get warm"; another, "I dare not take a hot bath, for I should be sure to take cold upon it." It is quite certain that the ordinary cold bath, so much boasted of by Englishmen, however agreeable and invigorating it may be to some, has little to recommend it on grounds of cleanliness. The following is the method we advise. In cold weather take a hot bath, rub the body freely with flesh-brush or glove and plenty of soap (a coal-tar preparation is the best for cleaning the pores and promoting action of the skin), then sponge or douche with cold water while standing in the hot, and dry the major portion of the body before taking the feet out of the warm water. If the bather is at all liable to take cold it will be well that he should lie between sheets for ten minutes before dressing until all fear of perspiration is passed over. This bath much resembles the Turkish bath in the following particulars, softening of the skin, cleansing of the skin, opening of the pores, closing them again by the cold douche and reaction of the skin afterwards before re-clothing. But it lacks one great quality of incalculable value to a singer, at least in this climate, that of the hot dry air inspired while in the *callidarium*, which is so useful in counteracting the effects of the ordinary cold damp air of an English winter, or it might be said of three-fourths of the year in a British climate, on the mucous membrane of the respiratory tract. There are, however, many who say they cannot endure a Turkish bath; it is believed by us because they neglect the following precautions which are hereby enjoined on all Turkish bathers. 1. Never to bathe at a less interval than two hours after a meal. 2. To put a wet towel on the head on entering the bath so as to prevent heat-stroke, a fruitful source of palpitations, faintings, &c. 3. To have the body slightly shampooed and to take a glass of water if perspiration is not active. 4. To always have the head as well as body washed. 5. Not to take a cold plunge or swimming-bath after, but to have a douche, at first warm and only gradually cold—a warm douche being at the same time or *immediately* after applied to the feet. 6. To take sufficient time to cool before dressing, and during the cooling process to keep the whole body and feet also covered with a wrap. 7. Not to take a bath oftener than twice a week in winter and once in summer. Those who in spite of attention to these details cannot take the Turkish bath, must be content with the warm bath already described. To both it will be agreeable and beneficial in summer to wash the body all over with soap and warm water each morning and then to take a cold sponge bath. Those whose circulation is slow to react should stand in a foot-pan containing hot water, on leaving the cold bath, and remain in it during the time they dry the body. It is a mistake to suppose that a cold bath is injurious when the body is heated, provided it be not taken too soon after a meal and that the precautions we have given to ensure thorough reaction of circulation be observed.

It may not be out of place to advise all who indulge in sea or river bathing, which involves plunging or even ducking the head, to place a plug of cotton wool in their ears before entering the water. This simple precaution may prevent an annoying, and even dangerous, deafness.

A word may also here be said as to the necessity for frequent cleansing of the teeth and washing of the mouth after food and just before use of the voice. Retention and after-putrefaction of small particles of food in the teeth is a common source of offensive breath, of excessive saliva, and of discomfort in practice of the voice. There is nothing better for hardening the mucous membrane of the gums and mouth than cold water with a small quantity of ordinary eau-de-cologne, which has also the merit of being very easily to hand. As elsewhere stated gargling, in the usual acceptance of the term, which implies irregular action of the muscles of the throat, is a useless, and sometimes a harmful process, but the holding of cold water in the mouth, the while throwing back the head, so as to thoroughly lave the whole cavity of the mouth and the back of the throat, is attended with considerable comfort and is useful in keeping the soft palate braced. The water should be held in the mouth until it becomes tepid, and then fresh should be taken, the process being continued for ten or fifteen minutes. Bathing the throat *outside* with cold water or cold salt and water may be indulged in, but is of no special benefit, as one might be inclined to think, from the frequency with which patients ask to be advised on that point.

Our remarks would not be complete did we not give a word of warning against the too frequent continuous use of face and neck powders and washes by those who, requiring them for stage purposes, are apt to indulge in them at all times, in the belief that their appearance is thereby improved. While it may be unhesitatingly stated that the pleasure to the on-looker is diminished in proportion as efforts to beautify a complexion are obvious, it may also be accepted as a fact that the skin and the bodily health are injured in proportion to the extent of surface covered, and the impermeability of the material employed. For body use especially it will be well to have a flesh powder that, being soluble, is non-obstructive to transpiration by the skin.

3. The question of *Clothing* is one treated very irrationally by singers, but one over which they have not always entire or even any satisfactory control. We commonly see persons enter our consulting-room, class-room, and the theatre, and remain with overcoat, heavy mantle and fur which had been donned as against the cold of external air on leaving their homes; or, on the other hand, a singer will often enter a hot concert-room or the stage in low dress and omit to cover the shoulders in coming into the lowered temperature and draught of waiting-room or wings. Of course it often happens on the lyric stage that a singer is forced to wear either too little or too much clothing, in accordance with the costume appropriate to the character represented, but even this difficulty may be overcome by care on the part of the artist and attention to his directions on the part of his "dresser." Oscar Guttman, in his 'Gymnastics of the Voice' (Leipzig and New York, 1882), goes so far as to say that actors who have worn heating wigs, &c., should not, on leaving the theatre, go out into the cold outer air merely with a hat on.

Those who follow professions in which a particular dress is *de rigueur*, such as clergymen and soldiers, often suffer from being obliged to wear an undue or an insufficient amount of clothing; but here again much may be done in way of correction by attention to the amount and character of the underclothing worn. Two questions are amongst the commonest asked by the singer. 1. Should flannel be worn? 2. Should the neck be covered? As to the first we are of opinion that flannel or silk of varying thickness should be worn both over trunk and limbs by all English people, and all the year round, as the warmest garment in cold and the most absorbent of perspiration in hot weather. In addition an extra piece of flannel four or five inches in depth should be worn—across the loins only, by those inclined to be stout, by others, around the whole girth of the body, in the same region—by all who are subject to take cold, who are of a rheumatic disposition, or who are liable to liver disorder; in other words by nine-tenths of residents of the British Isles. The effect of such a band is to keep circulation active to all the organs of secretion and excretion, and so to favour activity of digestion and assimilation. As to the second point, there is much diversity of opinion, and in our belief it is not of so much importance to keep a neck covered or uncovered—that is a question rather of usage from youth and individual experience—as it is that the neck of the voice-user should be unconstricted. No button should fasten above the level of the top of the sternum (breast-bone), so that all those parts left free from the bony cage of the thorax by nature should be actually unconfined. The fashionable collar of the male "masher," the dog-collar of the fast young lady, the clerical band of the ritualistic ecclesiastic, the tight, rigid stock of the soldier, are all equally unphysiological, and when carried to excess, as has been proved by Surgeon-Major Myers of the Coldstream Guards in the case of soldiers, even productive of aneurism, one of the gravest disorders arising from obstruction to free circulation at the root of the neck. Constriction of this region is a frequent cause of glandular swellings, enlarged tonsils, and congestions of the lining membranes of the throat.

We have already spoken against the habitual use of respirators, but must repeat that it is necessary to protect not the mouth only, but nose and ears by loose cloud or veil against night air, dust, fog, and cold damp atmospheres. We have also alluded at length to the detriment occasioned to free respiration and ample tone by the use of corsets, and the hanging of excess of clothing, in the case of females, from the waist. Regarding the question of change of dress to something more rational which is at present being freely agitated, there cannot be a doubt that though, like all reforms, it is by some urged with extreme zeal, the result must in the end lead to very great improvements in the health and comfort, and, when we are used to it, even the artistic appearance of the more beauteous sex. The retort that reforms are also needed in male clothing is undoubtedly true. We trust, however, we shall not see any return to belts for supporting the nether garments, as has been advocated in more than one quarter, for if worn with anything like the necessary constricting power they must inevitably interfere with the breathing capacity, and may even result in grave surgical disorders.

That there is abundant room for reform in woman's dress is readily admitted by all who give the subject due consideration; but it is not easy to determine what direction the reform shall take. Theory and practice are often at variance, and, what appears to answer all requirements in print, is not unfrequently found to possess many inconveniences and objections in actual use. The utility of a reformed dress must stand the test of actual wear over long periods of time, and the dress must present the following features: An even distribution of warmth and weight over the body, lightness and absence of constriction or pressure on the one hand and of undue fulness on the other. In addition the dress must not depart too conspicuously from the fashion of the period.

The above desiderata are, we think, fully met by the costume to be described. It has had the test of five years' constant wear, and those ladies who have adopted it are unanimous in their verdict as to its comfort and ease, several of them testifying to a great improvement in their general health.

The dress consists (1) of a special woven and shaped combination reaching from neck to ankles and wrists. This is supplied in three materials, silk-gauze, merino, and lamb's-wool; (2) stockings drawn on *over* the combination. Garters are not usually required, as the stockings cling closely to the combination, but where any difficulty is experienced the stocking-suspender can be used. Next to the combination is worn (3) a pair of knickerbockers, which reach to just below the knee, carefully cut to the figure, with no superfluous fulness. This garment can be made of almost any material according to individual taste. The knickerbockers button at the sides, thus securing complete immunity from draughts and chills from changes of temperature; the entire weight should be buttoned to a bodice; (4) an ordinary petticoat bodice completes the underclothing. If corsets are required the hygienic stays, described on page 116, are recommended.

The style of the outer garment is left to individual taste.

One great advantage which this reformed under-dress undoubtedly possesses is that its adoption does not render the wearer odd or conspicuous in the slightest degree.

With regard to its weight (which is as equally spread over the body as possible) it may be mentioned that an entire suit of under-clothing supplied to a lady weighed only 2 lbs. 8 ozs. It consisted of a special merino combination, thick blue serge knickerbockers, double warp calico linings, calico bodice, and cashmere stockings. The lady is 5 ft. 4 in. in height, bust measurement 36 in.

We are indebted for the detailed information concerning this comfortable and useful style of dress to Messrs. Ward and Co., Ilkley, who were amongst the first to introduce hygienic costumes.

4. The *diet* of a voice-user should be that most favourable to nutrition, with the minimum of ingredients likely to produce fat, and also that which is likely to be most quickly and most perfectly assimilated. In giving, then, a rule of dietary life for our readers, we are simply prescribing a system most favourable for all. To put the matter in another light we may state that in our professional life we find a large proportion of patients of a gouty or rheumatic disposition, which to the non-medical reader may be explained as a tendency to arrest and perversion of all healthy secretions, with a ready liability to fermentive digestion and the generation of acidity; a dietary rule which excludes certain articles of food injurious to the rheumatic simply forbids what would, to say the least of it, be of no special nutritive benefit to any one.

The first distinctive division of foods is that of solids and fluids, and the quantity of each kind taken by man should be in proportion to the composition of the human body, which contains twice as much fluid as solid matter. We have next to consider the purposes for which food is taken; they are primarily to repair the daily waste occasioned by the act of existence, which implies performance of certain functions necessary to actual life, and, as has been explained in the remarks on respiration, is one of combustion; and next to enable proper performance of extraneous exercise of muscle and brain, so that the individual may enjoy life or may be in a condition of health to work for his living.

Food of all kinds may be further sub-divided into two great varieties—the nitrogenous and the non-nitrogenous or carbonaceous. The proportion of these two elements varies with the food; meat and fat containing most nitrogen, the flesh-forming or muscle-forming principle; vegetables, sugar, and starches, the most carbon or heat-giving principles. Nevertheless, many vegetables and fruits, as white beans, lentils, apples, and green peas, contain an abundant proportion of nitrogen, and, as has been proved by the "vegetarians," will supply all the necessary elements for life, to the exclusion of any necessity for eating meat. In no one substance are all elements of nutrition found so well combined and proportioned as in milk, the literally natural food of all mammalia.

The necessity for nutriment varies according to the extent and character of work required from the body of the consumer. Persons in full health and with moderate calls on muscular activity require twice as much nitrogenous or muscular nutriment as is necessary for mere subsistence, and about two-thirds of what would be necessary for the day-labourer who lives by the sweat of his brow. The proportion of carbon or heat-giver to be taken will vary with season of year and climate.

Considering how little exercise is taken by the singer, and how comparatively little is the muscular effort required for performance of his duties, there can be no doubt that meat should be eaten more sparingly than is the general custom, and this remark would apply to the majority of professional workers as distinguished from the actual labouring classes. As an ordinary rule we believe that it would be better that the largest meat meal should be eaten at the close of a day, except for a certain proportion of persons, such as those subject to asthma, who are obliged to allow seven or eight hours to elapse between a meat meal and the period for retirement at night, but such a plan is impossible for voice-users, and the dinner hour or time for the principal meal must be regulated by the time at which the voice is to be professionally exercised. And this is a powerful cause of the vocalist's digestive troubles—the unavoidable irregularity of meal-times. An interval of at least four hours for singers and of two hours for speakers between a full meal and use of the voice is in all cases advisable. An hour after a meal is the time at which the stomach is fullest, and consequently the lung capacity is smallest; it is also the time when the vessels of circulation are in most active work, and therefore when all the internal organs are most engorged. There is another great difficulty in regulating the dietary hours of a singer, namely, that the period of work, in operas and concerts especially, may extend over several hours, with intervals of rest between of very varying duration. After the first act of an opera or execution of the first song, the singer will, to a certain extent, have exhausted his energies, which will be still further enfeebled by the fatigue of waiting for his next call, and thus it is that many singers are said to fall off in vocal strength at the end of an evening's work. In those cases where, on account of nervousness, the digestion is slow, and in which, as a consequence, a very long interval between eating and singing is necessarily prolonged, it may be very advisable to take a little beef-tea, or some of the many excellent meat extracts now so largely sold, about an hour before the first song, and in case of an interval occurring before the next, immediately after it. Still better is a raw egg, seasoned with a few grains of salt and a few drops of vinegar, swallowed *whole* about twenty minutes or even less before call on the voice is made. This is especially serviceable and agreeable when the throat becomes unduly dry from nervousness. We have said that very exceptionally a glass of champagne may be allowed before use of the voice in cases of extreme and uncontrollable nervousness; we would strongly urge that the instance in which such indulgence may be observed is indeed very rare, and were it not that we have known instances in which this slight and quickly diffusible stimulant had really been of service, we would not mention it except in the way of caution. Like all artificial stimulation it is a remedy certain to be followed by injurious reaction. Much better, as more sure, active, and permanent in its effects, and as attended by a minimum of after reaction, is the wine known by the name of its introducer, *Mariani*, of Paris, the active medical principle of which is the coca-leaf, a plant much valued in South America and other sub-tropical regions as capable of sustaining muscular strength, and ensuring against fatigue in long journeys through regions and under circumstances in which other food is difficult to be obtained. The repeated testimonies in favour of the effect of this wine on the vocal muscles and respiration of many patients and pupils, and of many very eminent singers and actors, as well as our joint personal experience, is undoubted and most strong. But caution must again be repeated as to the advisability of extreme moderation in its use and indulgence only to the extent of necessity and not of luxury.

Supper is a meal much indulged in by the singer and actor, and is one for which there is much excuse, since proper use of the voice engenders hunger, but it may interfere with healthy and refreshing sleep, and must therefore be taken only by those whose digestive powers will allow of its observance.

Without going into elaborate discussion of the varying qualities of digestibility and nutritious power of all articles of food, a few remarks as to what should be avoided and of what may be with advantage partaken will doubtless be acceptable.

In the first place, although fat and sugar are permissible, and even necessary, as articles of diet, both these ingredients in a state of change are liable to favour flatulent dyspepsia, acidity, and consequent impairment of respiration and vocalisation. Thus, while on the one hand, butter may be taken with bread, salad oil with fresh vegetables, or sugar in tea, on the other all pastry, suet puddings, melted-butter sauces, and excess of fat meat, and jam (not marmalade), malt liquor, and sparkling wines in which the fermentive process is not completed, should be excluded. In like manner the majority of root vegetables, especially those that contain sugar, are liable to promote flatulence; and since they most of them contain but little nutritious properties, are to be debarred. Under this head will come beetroot, turnips, parsnips, carrots, and radishes. Potatoes are not to be universally or altogether excluded, but their importance in the dietary scale is exaggerated, and by some they cannot be digested. Artichokes, although containing sugar, are more nutritious and less indigestible, probably because they contain less fibrous tissue than those root vegetables previously named. Salads and all green vegetables are as a rule most wholesome. We decline to give an opinion on cucumber, although we confess to a conviction that it is a vegetable often wrongfully accused of mischief to the digestion.

Some dieticians consider all uncooked green vegetables injurious. This is not our experience. Tomatoes uncooked are both nutritious and easy of digestion. Of meats to be avoided, the fat of pork and salted provisions may be named; and of fish, salmon and eels. The sun fruits in season and all succulent, juicy fruits are generally acceptable; stone fruits, as plums and cherries, contain but little nourishment, and should be taken cooked.

Nuts of all kinds are to be avoided. Of condiments, all hot peppers, hot pickles and curries are injurious, as leading to artificial stimulation of the blood-vessels and follicles of the mucous membrane of the throat, &c., with the effect of relaxation on reaction. It is on this account that we have so urgently and consistently advised against indulgence in the use of every kind of lozenge containing cayenne pepper, pyrethrum, &c. Nervousness interferes greatly with digestion, and many singers are unable, even several hours before the hour of their duty, to eat on that account. Great aid is often rendered in such cases by the taking of a pepsine pill, pepsine wine, or one of the known and approved maltine preparations, of which Malto-Yerbine is probably the best for the purpose of our readers. It is always well, however, to seek medical advice in such cases.

The question of drinking involves three principles: 1. Quantity; 2. Temperature; and 3. The nature of the beverage. First, as to quantity. Although, as previously stated, more fluid food is required than solid, it is nevertheless true that the less fluid that is taken during a meal the quicker will be the digestion. Fluid between meals is seldom advisable and often harmful. For the same reasons as those just given regarding condiments, all fluids, as tea, coffee, and soup, which are usually drunk hot, should be taken at a tepid temperature by the singer. Cold drinks are locally beneficial to the throat.

Regarding the nature of the drink which may be permitted it is an undoubted fact that singers complain that hot tea deprives them of voice. On the contrary we have known not a few instances in which actors and singers have partaken of small quantities of cold tea as an aid to their public vocal exercise, and we have hardly

S

ever known a case in which either coffee or cocoa had been stated to be injurious. The alkaloid—that is, the essential principle of all three beverages—is very similar—in fact practically the same. It is probable, therefore, that the deleterious effect of tea-drinking does not depend on the supposed properties of its alkaloid to cause palpitation of the heart, for coffee and cocoa would act in the same way, though possibly with less intensity. The cause of its disagreement must then be ascribed to three other factors: first, that much larger quantities of tea are usually drunk with a disproportionate amount of solid food than with coffee, which, except at a full meal, is taken *en demi tasse*, or than cocoa, which contains, in the form usually sold, so large an amount of solid material. It is thus probable that tea is more liable to cause flatulence, with such a consequent enlargement of the stomach, as to greatly interfere with the capacity for midriff breathing. Dr. Ringer's remarks on this subject are so very pertinent that we quote them:—

"In flatulent dyspepsia few substances are more to be avoided than tea, for tea itself in this complaint is found to promote flatulence; and women, the chief sufferers from this disagreeable form of dyspepsia, are apt to drink large quantities of weak tea, and the excess of fluid keeps up the distension . . . . ." ('A Handbook of Therapeutics,' by Sidney Ringer, M.D. Seventh Ed., p. 551. London: Lewis.)

The second cause of its harmful effects may be due to the large amount of *hot* fluid consumed at a draught; for, as has been just pointed out, the frequent taking of hot drinks is a fruitful cause of relaxation of the throat. Being anxious to have independent confirmation of this view, we wrote to Dr. Albert Bernays, of St. Thomas's Hospital, as the most eminent authority on all questions relating to the chemistry of food, and we are glad to be able to state that his reply was in complete agreement with us. He further suggested that as the tannin of the tea is extracted in proportion to the time it stands and cools, cold tea taken in small quantities might, since it would contain more tannin, act as an astringent as well as a stimulant.

It is just, however, the large proportion of tannin contained in tea that makes the beverage less suited (when taken in quantities) to most digestions than coffee and cocoa; for the tannin in the tea, of which there is about 26 per cent., is apt to combine with the gelatine of the meat and to form a tannate of gelatine—in other words the basis of leather, and a highly indigestible compound. Coffee contains only 5 per cent. of tannin, and hence it has a less effect in that direction, while cocoa contains none at all.

Our advice, therefore, is that with meals, tea, coffee, or cocoa may be drunk according to individual taste and digestion, but that, as a beverage or stimulant taken before singing, cocoa, small quantities of coffee at moderate temperature, or very small quantities of cold tea are preferable; but that hot tea indulged in immoderately is harmful to the digestion of all, and directly injurious to voice-users. Even in moderate quantities, however, tea cannot be borne by some people.

Still another word as to effervescing drinks, which are very refreshing and agreeable to many. We are obliged to condemn all manufactured lemon and other 'ades, as also bottled preparations of lime-juice; but fresh lemon-juice with soda-water is both wholesome and palatable. Aërated mineral waters from only the best makers should be taken, since, if a potash, soda, or lithia drink is required, it is as well to have a guarantee that the proper amount of active ingredient is contained, as also that the water is of pure quality. The recently introduced " Salutaris " water, which is guaranteed to be absolutely pure distilled water aërated with carbon oxygen gas, has the double merit of purity and cheapness, and is an excellent water drink which can be obtained of all chemists in towns visited by the singer in which the water supply might not be all that was desirable. For home use, where the character of the drinking-water is known, a gasogene efficiently aërates, and any ingredient, as soda or lithia, can be added in proportion. Where the quality of the water is doubtful distilled water can be employed. Those whose digestions are weak, or who cannot take much solid food even several hours before singing, will find the milk preparations, Koumiss and Sparkling Bland, now sold by the Aylesbury Dairy Company, to be of high value.

Then as to alcohol. It will be presumed from our previous remarks that we do not advise its general or habitual use, neither do we unreservedly forbid it. But it may be simply laid down as an axiom—indeed as a truism —that whereas there are an infinite number of diseases occasioned by alcohol, there are none due to its non-indulgence, and but few states of health or disease in which it is absolutely indispensable. Further, let it be remembered that the less alcohol is indulged in as an habitual drink the less will be required, and the more efficiently will it act, when administered by the physician as a remedy for any diseased condition. One more statement: alcohol seldom, if ever, improves powers of work; it often, and indeed always, impairs its value. If it give force, *en revanche*, it diminishes accuracy, and on reaction leads to enfeeblement. It has further been abundantly proved by human example, and by experiments on animals, that alcohol has no power to temper the effects of either heat or cold; and the most healthy sailors in Arctic regions, the best soldiers in tropical climes, have been in each case abstainers.

But having conceded so much it may be allowed that a moderate indulgence once a day in some light wine—for singers preferably claret, Burgundy, or a light Hungarian red wine as Carlowitz—*at the end of the day's work* is not only harmless, but is even, as a recuperative agent and as a waste preventer, serviceable, and no good purpose can be served by a rigid or bigoted ascetism on this question. Malt liquors are injurious because difficult of digestion, except to those who are called upon for, or who indulge in, a great amount of physical labour and exercise. Ardent alcohol, whether as brandy, whisky, and gin, is bad for all persons, and we have no faith in the fashionable but dangerous prescription of many physicians, of brandy-and-water and whisky-and-water, in preference to wine as an aid to digestion. Hot spirits and water is the acme of alcoholic abomination.

5. *Exercise* has been already considered in its special aspect of singing and speaking, and sufficient directions for its regulation and performance are given in another place. It is, however, quite another question as to how much and what kind of *general* bodily exercise is beneficial and desirable for the singer. Without doubt the majority of singers, especially females and foreigners, neglect general exercise, of which walking in the open air for an hour or two daily at a moderate pace is the most rational, easily attainable, and in all respects generally applicable. On the other hand, for fear of taking cold, vocalists hesitate to go out of doors unless the weather is what they consider absolutely perfect, and the consequence is that there is developed a general enfeeblement of the muscles of the body, with a slowness of circulation, engorgement of internal

organs exercising a directly injurious influence on the organ of voice, a tendency to corpulence, in itself a cause of diminished respiratory and vocal power, and an increased liability to take cold from abnormal coddling and seclusion within the house.

This much having been admitted it remains to be said that whereas exercise of the singing voice could never injuriously affect the athlete, cricketer, runner, &c., indulgence to anything like excess or even to moderation on the part of a singer in athletic exercises may have a very direct deteriorating result on the voice: first, by undue training in diet, &c., necessary to athletic effectiveness; secondly, by fatigue of the muscles of locomotion, which acts both in a direct and reflex manner on the special muscles of respiration and vocalisation. To put it plainly and shortly, no one could sing if "out of breath" with running, and what is true for a sudden spurt would be equally true if this extra effort of exercise were performed as a matter of daily habit. While, then, we enjoin, and most strongly urge, daily out-of-door walking or riding in moderation, we with equal earnestness would caution against anything like training or exercise to the extent of excellence or emulation in any muscular pursuit.

6. What has been said with regard to exercise will with equal force apply to *amusements*. Bodily fatigue, shortened hours of rest, heated, ill-ventilated, or draughty atmospheres, as found in theatres, with the addition of dust of a more than usually irritating character, in the case of ball-rooms, are all likely to deteriorate from functional activity, ease, and purity of the singer or orator, and, hard as it may appear, must often be foregone, by him who values eminence in his profession, to an extent not necessary in the case of any other calling.

Of sports, those in which continuous movement without the risk of arresting an over-heated body temperature by sudden cooling, are the most permissible. Swimming, skating, shooting, all to the extent of moderation, come under such a classification; cricket, football, lawn tennis, and hunting have all of them a tendency to the danger indicated. We would give one word of caution regarding amusements of general application, but none the less necessary to our voice-using readers. It is that indulgence in amusements and sports of all kinds is carried, by Englishmen especially, to excess, so as to literally render pleasure toil. We have often enabled persons to enjoy the pleasures of sport and game to whom it had been forbidden because deemed injurious to health, by the simple advice to practise moderation, as, for example, to shoot only till lunch time, to follow the hounds only in one run, and to play but one or two games of lawn tennis. The rationale of such advice is obvious.

Lastly. There are certain *habits* indulged in by all which hardly come under any of the previous headings, but which are nevertheless of considerable importance in their bearing on the hygiene of the vocalist. The chief of these is that of *smoking and the use of tobacco*. We would preface our observations with repetition from our previous printed remarks often quoted by others. "It will be admitted that in no case can the health be positively improved by indulgence in the habit, although one hears much from ardent smokers of the soothing properties of tobacco. When it is considered, however, that Mario, who preserved his voice for a much longer period than most tenors, was hardly ever, except when actually singing, without a cigar in his mouth, it cannot be stated that smoking is necessarily injurious to the voice. But as rules are made for average and not exceptional cases, we would not on such a precedent advise singers to take to tobacco with an expectation of thereby becoming a *Mario*, any more than we would counsel stout drinking as a certain method of producing a *Malibran*. Our advice generally is, that if smoking be accompanied by much expectoration it should be discontinued, as an over-stimulation of the salivary glands will lead to general dyspepsia and to local dryness. In all cases the singer must be guided by his own individual experience, and should practise great moderation in the habit;" remembering that the effect of tobacco is two-fold, first, by the general effect of its active principle, *nicotine*, as a powerful depressant of the nervous centres, and, secondly, by its local effects on the mucous membrane, occasioning disorder of the secreting follicles, and of secretion. The use of cigarettes, often condemned as the worst form of smoking, is probably the least harmful if practised with proper precautions, which are very well defined in a recent letter to the *Lancet* (June 2, 1883) by Sir Henry Thompson, and here subjoined.

"SIR,—I think I might, if permitted, offer you a practical hint of some value in connection with cigarette smoking, which I think is not altogether appreciated by the author of your notes on the subject.

"First, the cigarette, without a mouthpiece, is really never smoked more than half way through in the East, where cigarettes are very cheap. It is well understood there, as it is by all practised cigarette smokers, that every inhalation from a cigarette slightly deteriorates in quality from the first. A small deposit of the very offensive oil of tobacco is deposited in the finely cut leaf, which acts as a strainer, and intercepts the deposit as it passes. Very little of this arrives in the smoker's mouth if he stops when half is consumed. I have seen many Oriental smokers who consume no more than a third. Turkish ladies, for example, as I have had personal opportunities of observing at Constantinople, will smoke fifty or upwards in a day, but, I need scarcely say, only in the manner I have described.

"Secondly, if a cigarette with a card mouthpiece is employed, the noxious matter may be intercepted by always introducing a light plug of cotton wool into the tube. If now the cigarette is nearly consumed, a considerable quantity of brown and very offensive matter will be found in the cotton wool, from the evil of which the smoker is thus preserved.

"Thirdly. Some years ago I designed a cigarette-holder or mouthpiece, which opened transversely in the middle, disclosing a small cavity, which is filled with cotton wool. It would surprise many people, perhaps, to find that the result of smoking six cigarettes only in this tube is that this plug is saturated with a brown fluid like treacle, of powerfully offensive odour, and disagreeable almost beyond belief. The wool then requires to be changed, and in this manner the evil of smoking is very greatly diminished. Several of these were constructed by a well-known tobacconist close to your office in the Strand.

"Lastly. The maximum of pernicious influence which occurs through cigarette-smoking is attained by the practice of inhaling the smoke largely direct into the lungs, where it comes into immediate contact with the circulation, and the toxic effect is so strongly perceptible after three or four consecutive inhalations, and so felt by a sensitive person to the very tips of the fingers. I have no doubt that the effect would in most cases be notably recorded by the sphygmograph" (an instrument for graphically recording the waves of the pulse, and consequently the strength and rhythm of the heart's action). "Such smoking is of course, or ought to be, exceptional. All the fragrance, with a little only of the toxic effect, is obtained by admission of the smoke into the mouth only, still more by passing it through the passages of the pharynx and nose; but it is the pulmonary inhalation referred to, often associated with cigarette smoking, and rarely with the pipe, which constitutes the chief mischief of the cigarette. I may say, in passing, that that well-known Oriental method of smoking, practised by means of the narghileh, in which the smoke, although drawn through water, passes invariably through the lungs, explains the powerful effects which sometimes unpleasantly surprise novices in its use.

"Smoked, then, simply, and with cotton wool interposed, I do not hesitate to regard the cigarette as the least potent, and therefore the least injurious, form of tobacco smoking. Without this precaution it may be made, although not necessarily, the most ready means of conveying the active principle of tobacco, by means of smoke, into the system.

"I am, Sir, yours truly,
"H. THOMPSON."

Snuff-taking is a habit fast dying out, but any time liable to be revived; it is not only uncleanly, but it is unphysiological, and to be therefore condemned on two grounds: 1st, the undue stimulation to the capillaries, and, 2ndly, because the mechanical forcing of a powder through the nostrils, whose special purpose it is to filter the air from such particles, is senseless and consequently pernicious independently of the irritant and poisonous qualities of the ingredient. That there should be found individuals who not only indulge in this filthy habit, but who defend it by argument (?), is a fact more interesting as illustrating a psychological problem than worthy of refutation by words which would be wasted in the quarters where they would be appropriate.

THE AILMENTS OF THE VOICE-USER.

CONSIDERATION of this question must be prefaced by the remark that whereas there are but few alterations of health special to a voice-user, on the one hand a certain immunity from some general diseases is experienced by the professional vocalist, while on the other, a certain colour—reflected as the direct effects of his professional vocation—is given to many maladies entirely general.

Thus a singer or speaker who breathes through his nostrils with closed mouth, and who thoroughly inflates his chest, is less liable to certain lung diseases which attack those who sit stooping with contracted chest in the close atmosphere of an office or work-room, and the constant breathing of such an atmosphere may lead to an extinction of voice in a person who, living possibly under restrictions as to conversation, does not use the vocal organ even to a normal extent. This loss of voice will depend on quite different causes, be of a different nature, and require an entirely different treatment from that which will assail a singer who is liable to loss of voice because of wrong use, over use, or a sensitiveness engendered by excessive training—in other words, from functional abuse. In the first case a weed or a common plant is killed by neglect and want of fresh air in an ill-ventilated and over-heated atmosphere; in the second a plant is wrongly cultured or so over nurtured as to be unable to withstand the influence of the ordinary external atmosphere.

To take another example, a person of sedentary occupation may suffer from indigestion because of want of exercise, an active man because of insufficient rest before moving; a singer from nervous excitement incidental to his profession, or from both and either of the before-mentioned causes. Such an ailment will affect his work more directly and immediately than it would the office clerk, the agriculturist, or the journalist. So that in considering these points regard must be had both to cause and effect, and the medical practitioner occupying himself specially with diseases of the vocal organs will be frequently obliged to view general ailments and maladies when affecting the singer, from a special—though by no means necessarily from a local point—of view.

In the chapter comprising directions as to the daily life of a voice-user attention has been given to those rules of living specially calculated to avert these general minor diseases, but it would be manifestly impossible to give consideration to them one and all in a treatise like the present unless we attempted a systematic work on domestic medicine, or a popular discussion of the whole range of throat diseases; and execution of either plan is very far from our purpose. Let the speaker or singer, however, divest from his mind the idea that derangement of his voice and disease of his vocal organ is due to special organic defect incidental to his calling, however special may be its result. The throat being actively engaged primarily in the performance from the first to the latest moment of life of two vital functions, those of respiration and of nutrition, and another hardly less vital, that of ordinary vocalisation in speech, has been so constructed by an all-wise nature that idiopathic or self-arising organic disease is rare. Where loss of voice occurs the vocal ligaments, which are the essential parts of the organ for production of vocal sound, are very seldom affected even in a common cold, and their intimate structure and continuity hardly ever impaired or destroyed except as the result of a specific disease, consumption, cancer, &c., and the cause of functional weakness or loss of voice will in the majority of cases be found to depend on disorders of digestion, fault of production, or imprudence in functional exercise, which have induced either a congestion of blood supply or an impairment of muscular power.

Should this statement lead to the retort, that if true, we prove the laryngoscope to be of little value in the treatment of throat diseases, we would reply that imputation of special disease in the larynx is, for the most part, laid by those ignorant of laryngoscopic teachings, or by those who use it in a narrow spirit. We can conceive nothing more consoling to a singer suffering from loss of voice, than to be assured by one competent to explore the larynx, that his vocal organ is free from disease, and that by correction of some fault in his general health or his professional exercise his voice will be restored. It is only by such a competent examination that a safe and definite opinion can be given, and it may be added, that in those rare cases in which there is intrinsic disease of the larynx, it is generally hopeless to expect complete restoration of vocal purity. The practitioner is fortunate if he can, in such an occurrence, succeed in saving life, restoring general physical health, and a useful speaking voice for conversational intercourse. It is only by acknowledgment and recognition of the intimate and mutual relations of nutrition, digestion, circulation, and respiration, and of the external effects of temperature and clothing, that a broad view of throat ailments can be obtained, an accurate opinion given as to their cause, or a safe way be pointed for their cure.

Let us now consider briefly some of the more common local ailments, which may for convenience be divided into those affecting alimentation, and those concerned with breathing and voice. The first function, the alimentary, has to do with the food passage—pharynx and gullet; the second, vocal and respiratory, with the nasal canals, the larynx and wind-pipe. To a certain extent there is a ground common to both these passages, namely, at the back of the throat—the fauces; and yet for general purposes it may be firmly asserted that disease in this region almost always implies disorder of the digestive, rather than of the respiratory, or of the essentially vocal, apparatus.

Prefatory to any more detailed analysis of throat ailments, a few words may be said on the meaning of what is generally assigned as first cause of all voice defects, namely, "catching cold." This term really implies not only a lowering of body temperature by cold draughts, but also very frequently the reaction from an unduly elevated body heat not necessarily due to lowered temperature or undue moisture of inhaled air or body surroundings, but rather to a fever engendered by disturbances in some portion of the digestive apparatus. Many "colds" are taken after a surfeit or an indiscretion in diet; but doubtless many of the attacks on singers are due to neglect of outdoor exercise, and the unwise habit of living in close, ill-ventilated rooms for fear of taking cold. As a consequence, the blood is deficient in oxygen, the muscles become flabby, all the tissues are unduly loaded with fat, and the individual resembles both in his habits and in his nutrition, the far-famed Strasburg goose, which furnishes the luxurious "*pâté de foie gras.*"

The ordinary *sore throat or relaxed throat* hardly requires special description. It is felt by the sufferer as occasioning inconvenience rather than pain. There is experienced sometimes no more than a sensation of tickling at the back of the throat, a difficulty in articulation, or an impediment in swallowing, and then only to an extent of rendering performance of function irksome, or in other words, of making the sufferer " conscious that he has a throat." The term, nevertheless, embraces a very large field of throat disturbance, and may range in intensity from slight discomfort to serious and even vital mischief. It may be caused by changes of weather and temperature, imprudence in diet and disorder of digestion, the inhalation of noxious insanitary emanations, or exposure to contagion of various diseases, as measles, scarlet fever, small-pox, &c. Special characters may thus be given to a "sore throat," which will each in turn require separate treatment, but it may be safe to assume that in one and all there is a disorder of assimilation and of circulation; so that a day or two's fasting, or low diet with confinement to the house, and without any medical treatment beyond the taking of a simple purge, will in the majority of cases effect a cure. Many such cases will be cured by a Turkish bath, which has doubtless an influence on the system, not only general and eliminative through transpiration by the skin, but locally by the action of hot dry air on the mucous membrane, disordered through inhalation of cold damp atmospheres; for that is the kind of weather most productive of sore throats. The warm bath, elsewhere described (page 245), will in many instances have as good an effect on the general circulation as the Turkish bath, and is more easy of general adoption; locally, the wrapping of a piece of flannel or of a stocking around the throat all night will be sufficient; in cases rather more severe the patient may suck ice, or, better still, lave his throat internally with cold water, as described at page 247, for half an hour at a time, or take an appropriate lozenge, such as the saline astringent made specially for us and sold by Roberts & Co. Or he may take the effervescing astringent of Cooper, or use an astringent gargle, though, as before said, the act of gargling is an inefficient remedy and not infrequently painful. If with these measures relief is not obtained, medical advice should be sought. When added to the condition described there is really pain, it will generally be found on examination of the throat, that in addition to the more or less increase of redness and laxity of the parts seen in ordinary sore throat, there is swelling of the uvula, pillars of the fauces or tonsils. Such a condition almost always implies the presence of a specific poison, generally the rheumatic. When there is exudation of membrane, it is an indication that the cause is insanitary, and though the presence of such a condition does not by any means imply certainty of a diphtheritic infection, it should, when detected, induce the patient to at once seek medical advice.

This slight common sore throat may assume a graver type, and have all the characters of an inflammation, acute or chronic. The back of the throat behind the soft palate is then principally affected, and this disease is known as *pharyngitis*, i.e. inflammation of the pharynx. Although we speak of this as a separate affection, it is really very seldom that in either its acute or chronic form inflammation is confined to the pharynx: on the other hand the fauces, tonsils, or uvula may be at fault without attacking the back of the throat. In its acute form it may be the result of a cold which has affected the patient locally, but has also disturbed the digestion, &c. In its chronic form the back of the throat is often seen to be granular, that is, with numerous red elevations and enlarged vessels. When still more advanced, the little glands in the mucous membrane, instead of being enlarged and granular, will be seen to have become atrophied, and the surface will be smooth and glazed. Accompanying these changes in the appearance of the glandules there will be experienced alterations in the character and quantity of the secretion, and the patient will complain of either too much mucus or of excessive dryness in the throat, each representing different stages of the same disorder. The disease is always associated with disorder of general health, which may be either cause or result. However looked at, there is no doubt that *chronic granular inflammation of the pharynx* (so-called clergyman's sore throat) is the commonest disorder of voice-users; and in our experience it is always accompanied—we would even say caused—by faulty voice production in the larynx, i.e. by forcing the registers beyond their natural limits, which has led to consequent straining, forcing, and congestion in the upper or resonant portion. The symptoms are those of altered secretion just described, irritation, with prickings and functional fatigue; later we have impaired quality and actual loss of notes; if unchecked, there arrives a period of complete suppression of, at first, singing, and then even of the speaking voice, due either to want of control over the voluntary muscles of articultion or to loss of power in the automatic laryngeal muscles: sometimes to both causes combined. Treatment of this condition is of two kinds, each equally important—first, medical, subdivided into general and local; and secondly, educational. Internal medicines and appropriate diet are useless to cure without local measures for destruction of the granulations, which in turn are only half cured or subject to relapse, unless the fault of voice production is afterwards corrected. It is essentially an ailment in which self-measures or half-measures do harm, principally because they delay the cure, and delay in cure means always a progress of the malady.

A very common advice given, even by doctors, to those suffering from "loss of voice," is " rest of the organ with change of air." Of course so long as the voice is not used the patient does not experience impediment to functional use; and change of air with rest are always more agreeable remedies than direct treatment by pharmaceutical or surgical measures. Nevertheless, we have over and over again witnessed cases in which much money has been spent in seeking change of scene and air, and much time lost by delay in treatment, simply because the patient has preferred to take imperfect advice or to go his own way, rather than in the first instance to have been assured of the cause, and so have been placed on the proper road to recovery.

As a result of more or less frequent and repeated attacks of relaxed throat, the soft palate may lose its power of contraction—its tonicity as doctors say—and this may lead to an *elongated and relaxed uvula*. This condition will have a very serious effect on the singer's health; first, by direct irritation of his larynx, leading to troublesome cough or desire to get rid of the sensation of a foreign irritable body; secondly, to consequent fatigue of the vocal organ, leading to loss of high notes and inability to sustain prolonged functional effort; and, thirdly, to impairment of digestion caused by the constant desire to swallow, and the consequent stimulation to secretion of mucous and digestive fluids, which in time leads to a catarrh. This term "catarrh" is very generally, but quite wrongly, limited to conditions caused by "cold." Although, however, catching cold is perhaps the most frequent cause of catarrh, the term rightly means any alteration of the character of the secreting surface of *any* mucous membrane, and may in our present consideration imply either an excessive or diminished flow, or an entire arrest of the normal secretion of the membranes of the throat, fauces, nostrils, pharynx, and larynx, either together or separate, with an almost innumerable train of symptoms affecting the functions of vocalisation, of hearing, and of digestion, as well as the general health of the sufferer.

Lest we might be accused of exaggerating the evils of a relaxed uvula we append the graphic description of the late Dr. Mandl, to whose work we have so often elsewhere alluded. "In the chronic state the uvula remains elongated. This state, which is also known under the form of 'fall of the uvula,' is capable of exercising injurious effects on the voice. The *timbre* loses both in brilliancy and purity. The uvula, which hangs on the base of the tongue, provokes a tickling which is repeated every second and forces the sufferer to heave and cough. At other times the cough becomes convulsive and paroxysmal, and is accompanied by attacks of suffocation; sometimes it occasions nausea, even to the length of vomiting—this occurring especially in the early morning and after a meal; even sleep is disturbed by nightmare.

"The irritation of the back of the tongue frequently extends to the larynx, the secretion of which becomes thereby augmented. There is then expectoration of little tenacious grey masses which by their presence on the vocal cords produce the symptom known under the name of 'chat' (there is no good English synonym) in the voice." (Op. cit. pp. 169, 170.)

For the cure of this condition it is necessary for both patient and doctor to recollect that a relaxed uvula, while influencing the general system, may likewise in turn be affected for better or worse by all causes which will affect the general health; and that a cure is not to be expected by purely local or purely general treatment. It is advisable, therefore, for the sufferer to examine his own way of living, and endeavour to discover what it is in his diet or his habits that appears to act as an exciting cause of this relaxation, and only to seek for relief by local measures after such an investigation and subsequent action. We nevertheless desire to speak with no uncertain voice as to the importance of reduction by surgical means in the length of a relaxed uvula so soon as it is recognised as a source of health impairment and impediment to production of pure and sustained vocal tones, for there cannot be a doubt in our minds that the success of such a measure is in direct proportion to the promptitude with which it is adopted after its necessity is recognised. If properly performed it can do no harm—its delay can lead to no end, but to confirm the symptoms and render them more obstinate of eradication. And let it be understood that "snipping" the uvula does not mean cutting away any muscular tissue or a part essential to any throat function, but simply the removal of an overgrowth or excrescence.

As we have had occasion to say elsewhere in treatises more directly professional, it may be safely asserted that while there is no throat ailment, and indeed few other diseases of so benign a character as a relaxed uvula that give rise to so many distressing and even serious symptoms, there is probably no surgical operation so slight as the one indicated for its cure, that has so marked and direct a beneficent effect. It is unfortunate, as Mandl says, " that this operation should encounter very ill-founded opposition on the part of artists, since there can be no doubt of its happy effect on the voice due to removal of a permanent cause of irritation in those cases in which it is really indicated." (Op. cit., p. 185.)

Allied to the relaxed uvula, both in its injurious effects on the voice and on the constitution, and also unhappily, in opposition to radical cure, is the condition known as *enlargement of the tonsils*. Of the primary value or use of these glands there is considerable doubt, but it is certain that at a very early age, and in the great majority of instances, they exist only to become diseased, so much so that a very eminent physician has stated that were he to play the part of a Frankenstein and endeavour to create a man, he would omit the tonsils. It is generally asserted that presence of enlarged tonsils implies a scrofulous disposition, but this is by no means universally true. In many instances there is no such delicacy, and their existence is quite as often an indication of a gouty or rheumatic constitutional state as of a strumous or scrofulous.

The tonsils are liable to acute attacks of inflammation of varying severity, and leading sometimes to gatherings of purulent matter, constituting the condition known as *quinsy*. Such attacks may occur as a recandescence—a fresh lighting up—of chronic inflammation and enlargement, or to tonsils, not abnormal in size in the intervals of acute attacks. The symptoms are unmistakable and the distress is extreme. It is, of course, necessary to seek personal medical advice on occurrence of an attack; it may, however, be stated that there is always an arrest of all normal secretions preceding an attack, and that a person subject to quinsy must be very careful to pay attention to the healthy action of bowels, kidneys, and skin by saline aperients, to observe an antacid diet, and to take regularly, frequent Turkish or other vapour or hot baths. In some cases the tonsils may be the subject of considerable disease of the follicles or crypts secreting the mucus, which will give rise to constant irritation, offensive breath, and disorder of digestion, though not necessarily to either actual vocal functional disability or to acute relapses of inflammation and enlargement. Cases doubtless arise in which the tonsils are to a certain extent enlarged, but yet give rise to no inconvenience; it is, however, hardly possible that the resonant portion of the vocal apparatus can be in perfect order when these glands are of at all abnormal dimensions.

The most prominent ill-effects of diseased tonsils in the career of the voice-user are:—

1. On the *voice*, which becomes more or less husky, toneless, and easily fatigued. Sometimes it is thick and guttural, and power of modulation is always rendered difficult.

2. *Articulation* is always impaired, the sufferer speaking as with a full mouth, and having such a difficulty in the pronunciation of certain consonants, that this condition alone may often be found sufficient to account for stuttering or other speech defect.

3. But, above all, *respiration* can never be carried on healthily, since whenever the tonsils are diseased all inspired air passes over an unhealthy surface. Where enlargement is considerable, the lungs are never fully aërated, the chest walls become narrowed, and the breastbone prominent, the patient is torpid and lethargic, and is liable to attacks of pulmonary congestion. Further evidence of obstructed respiration through the nostrils is afforded by loud snoring, not only in sleep, but in a hardly less offensive form by audible open-mouth breathing when awake. In addition to the foregoing, the senses of

hearing, of *smell*, and of *taste*, are all more or less impaired; there is a frequent desire to clear the throat of the impediment, and there is a very considerable disorder of digestion and assimilation of food. This account, by no means overdrawn or extended, of the discomforts due to enlargement or disease of the tonsils, is given somewhat in detail solely that voice teachers and voice users may learn what a variety and number of functions may be impaired if the cause is not promptly attacked. Unfortunately there is a prejudice, very ill-founded and unsupported by any authority, against the radical cure by removal of enlarged tonsils by the guillotine, but, in fact, it is the least painful (it might be said that it is almost painless), quickest, safest, and in every respect the most effectual. There is no argument whatever of any scientific value to be advanced against the measure, and there is the very direct evidence in its favour of many of our great singers. Louisa Pyne, Patti, Lucca, and others have undergone the operation, not only without injury, but with actual benefits. Our observations are in entire concord with those of Mandl," that while all applications of caustic, so frequently employed, are harmful rather than serviceable, excision of enlarged tonsils is the most sure means of cure, and is followed by no inconvenience to the voice, but is, on the contrary, always beneficial to it. One need not, therefore, give heed to the opposition to this operation which comes from those whose competence to give an opinion on the question is, to say the least of it, very doubtful." (Op. cit., p. 183.)

In many cases it is not so much the size of the tonsil that is the cause of vocal defect as extension of its inflammation and thickening to neighbouring tissues, which causes faults in the muscular action of the pharynx, leading to defects in brilliancy, *timbre*, &c., so that on all accounts the practitioner is justified in urging treatment and the sufferer encouraged to submit to it.

In conclusion we would repeat an oft-quoted statement, made many years ago by Dr. Bennati, who was both a good physician and a fine vocalist, that removal of the tonsils is often followed by an actual gain in upward range of voice. This observation we have often verified as a result of operations not only on the tonsils but also on the uvula, and its truth has received many independent confirmations.

We have thus alluded at sufficient length to some of the more prominent of the throat troubles visible to the eye of any person looking at the back of the mouth in an ordinary manner, and we have insisted that they are the result, not of constitutional disorders only, but frequently of faulty teaching or exercise. They are amongst the most easily removable of physical defects, but we desire to treat very briefly of *actual laryngeal troubles* in the singer, because in the first place they are rare, and in the second because no good service can be done by suggesting to the voice-user the possible existence of serious maladies which a laryngoscopic examination would at once dispel. In ordinary cases of *loss of voice* due to climate or other temperature causes, it is exceedingly rare that the vocal cords are seen to be inflamed. There is usually in such a case a dry catarrh of the parts below the larynx—that is, of the lining membrane of the wind-pipe and larger bronchial tubes—or of the parts above—that is, in fauces and pharynx. Even when the general mucous membrane of the larynx is congested or inflamed, the vocal ligaments escape and are seen in the mirror to be quite normal. This statement must be qualified only so far as to say that the vocal ligaments in professional users of the voice are not infrequently somewhat congested at their posterior part quite irrespective of any disease, and simply as the result of continuous increased circulation to the part. When a singer is attacked with sudden suppression or loss of voice consciously felt as result of cold, with constitutional symptoms indicating disturbance of temperature and secretion ; but unaccompanied by sensation of soreness or relaxation of the throat, and without symptoms of head cold, he will do well to take first an aperient and then a Turkish or vapour bath, so as to set forward the process of elimination and bring about reaction of circulation. He should take simple food and remain in the house. In this last circumstance he may find benefit from steam inhalation, but this form of remedy, although commonly employed and prescribed by high authorities, is not without danger if the patient is still exposing himself to the external atmosphere. It is, however, a most valuable measure when the patient is confined to the house, and the steam, either plain or medicated, may then be inhaled from one of the many apparatus sold, or the whole room may be impregnated with the warm and moist vapour from a bronchitis kettle.

A much better form of inhalation in mild cases is that of the vapour of chloride of ammonium as generated in one of the varieties of the apparatus known by the several names of Kerr, of Burroughs, or of Felton. This remedy, which is very serviceable in effecting resolution of congestion and in giving relief to catarrh, does not make the membrane more, but rather less sensitive to the changes of open-air temperature. It is, in any case, a perfectly innocuous process, and may therefore be safely recommended. The vapour in either case may be made agreeably stimulating by addition of essential oils (of which that of the *Pinus Sylvestris* is perhaps the most generally useful), so prepared as to be held in suspension in the water. It is difficult to prescribe internal remedies adapted with safety to all purposes, but there can be no harm in the use of mild expectorants as squills and ipecacuanha in the form of mixtures, lozenges, or pills. It will be always as well that the singer should be assured by a medical examination with the laryngoscope that his larnyx is free from inflammation, so as to relieve his mind and the more certainly to direct his recovery; but there is no reason why any one subject to these slight attacks, as many are, of loss of voice, should not be properly instructed to treat themselves, for it is above all important that treatment should be adopted at the outset.

It is often only the patient himself who, searching carefully into reasons, can discover what it is in his daily life or habits that brings about these attacks, and so learn how to avoid them. Hints have been given on this head in the chapter entitled " The Daily Life of the Voice-User."

We have seen some prescriptions of small doses of laudanum for the treatment of failures of voice, and we feel bound to say a word against their adoption unless in really exceptional circumstances; for though doubtless they give relief, they also generate a desire for a stimulant far more dangerous and insidious than alcohol; and the more so as we have known several cases in which singers have continued for many weeks or months the practice commenced under medical advice, of what is in point of fact opium eating, quite unconscious of the nature or danger thereof.

We make no apology for not following the practice of many authors who have of late, in attempted popular treatises on the throat and voice, written of croup, diphtheria, consumption in lungs and throat, cleft palate, harelip, &c.—subjects in our estimation on which it is not only unnecessary, but undesirable and harmful to dilate to the public. But there is one other class of ailments affecting the singer on which some few words may be acceptable—we refer to those affecting the nostrils.

Of these the *common head cold* is both the most frequent and the most annoying. It almost beggars description, for no list of its symptoms could be given that would be considered complete by the sufferer, and we should be probably thought unsympathetic if we expressed our view that they are all rather annoying than serious; nor would such a statement be by any means true, for a neglected cold or a series of colds may lead to a condition giving rise to vocal defects among the most difficult of cure. Constant attacks of cold in the head, *coryza* as it is called, with its prominent symptoms of increased flow of nasal secretion, may lead to chronic catarrhal changes impairing greatly the resonant quality of the voice. If unchecked this catarrh may proceed to inspissation and retention of the secretion, giving rise to offensive breath, and to greatly disordered digestion and health; or it may even go the length of superficial ulcerations of the coverings of the nostrils. Although, therefore, it is often the fashion to ridicule treatment of a cold in the head, it is very desirable that the singer and voice-user should not neglect first to check a head cold at the outset, and secondly to do all in his power to arrest the tendency.

There is a prevalent idea that a common head cold is incurable; that is by no means true, but it is equally a fact that there is probably no remedy of universal application for the sudden arrest of colds. Careful attention to the various methods of elimination already dwelt on will diminish the tendency, but when an acute attack occurs individual experience can alone determine the appropriate remedy. One person will be cured by taking a Turkish bath, which acts on the skin, another by a small dose of opium or belladonna, a third by camphor, a fourth by inhalation through the nostrils of anti-catarrhal smelling-salts (a capital remedy when there is constant sneezing); some are cured by taking no fluids for as long as possible, a treatment introduced by Dr. C. J. B. Williams.

A large proportion of persons unfortunately resist all attempts to arrest a head cold in the acute stage often because the treatment is not commenced sufficiently early. For the cure of a chronic cold and the eradication or diminution of the tendency to take cold, much may be done by hygienic measures, and by "cures" at Aix-les-Bains, Mont Dore, Cauterets, Salzungen in Thuringen, and other foreign mineral water establishments.

It may generally be said that while dry air is desirable, dust is to be avoided. Also, without desiring to advocate pampering and coddling of a system subject to take cold easily, we earnestly advocate those liable thereto, especially if singers, to guard against the effects of night air, and changes of temperature incidental from exits from theatres, concert-rooms, and the like, by means of covering the mouth and nostrils, and by sufficient extra covering. A small amount of Vaseline, introduced into the nostrils by means of a camel's hair brush, acts admirably as a protective of a sensitive nasal mucous membrane against the injurious effects of irritating particles.

One last ailment peculiar to a singer or speaker is that of *nervousness*, as exercising a most painful effect on his career, and on this head we have to repeat what we have said often times before, that its curability depends largely on the qualifications of the sufferer for the task he is attempting.

It is seldom that the competent artist is afflicted with nervousness which does not wear off as he warms to his work. On the other hand, the audacity of ignorance is generally dispelled on appearance before a public audience. We once knew of a sailor who had risen to the rank of admiral who was always sea-sick at commencement of a voyage. Similarly we have knowledge of a few rare cases of constitutional nervousness in really excellent artists. Such individuals are unfortunately handicapped, and have evidently mistaken their profession so far as its pursuance with comfort is concerned. If the encouragement of success fail, we may seek for an actual remedy, and we may find it necessary to allow a glass of *Mariani* wine to be taken just before singing. But this or any other kind of stimulant is permissible only under medical advice or quite exceptionally, since, as has been previously explained, all stimulants are apt to be followed by reactionary depression. Occasionally teacher and doctor must be prepared to advise abandonment of a profession for which the subject is from such a cause obviously unfitted.

In concluding this chapter we venture to express a hope that our readers will not be disappointed because we have not given any very definite prescriptions for even the commoner of the voice-user's ailments. It is with intention that we have abstained from so doing, and that we have rather endeavoured to direct attention to the disorders of general health or fault of functional exercise, which is probably at the root of most cases of vocal disability; and the moral of such advice should clearly be to discourage indulgence in patent and proprietary voice lozenges and other remedies which, when not harmful or negative in their effects, are only serviceable to allay symptoms. With a view, however, of meeting the wants of our readers, we have given sanction to the advertisement of a few remedies of general use for most of the conditions indicated in the text. We particularly, however, repeat one caution, that such remedies are never to be employed as substitutes for medical advice, but only as aids to treatment after cause of ailment has been discovered.

ON DEFECTS OF SPEECH, STAMMERING, AND STUTTERING.

ANY book which claimed to be a complete manual of the theory and practice of the human voice would be rightly judged to have very imperfectly fulfilled its functions were not some attention given to the subject that heads this chapter, and if on only those grounds we should feel it incumbent on ourselves to offer a few remarks.

The question is one which has always received a considerable share of attention, unhappily not always of the most worthy kind, nor always dictated by the highest motives. The victims of defects of speech, especially those of stuttering and stammering, are almost always of a shy, reserved disposition, whose failing has but seldom received sympathy, and has more often been treated with absolute ridicule. As a consequence they have been an easy prey to the charlatan and to practitioners of specific secret methods, which, like many other secrets, have been found worthless when revealed.

In these last few years this important social infirmity has been treated from a new standpoint, and much praise is due to Mr. Edgar S. Werner, of Albany, N.Y., who at the commencement of the year 1879 published his first number of *The Voice*, a monthly periodical, which, although intended to consider all " the various phases of vocal sound," was especially established as "a tongue to the thousands who are unmeasurably deprived of one of the noblest faculties given to man." The editor, himself a stutterer in boyhood, began and, it may be added, has continued his work with enthusiasm. He has published translations in his journal of some important German treatises, notably of Klencke and of Gunther, and has collated quite a number of separate valuable articles. While all systems as far as known are given, secret methods are in this journal opposed, and courageous exposure has been made of all those who practise swindling arts. By a "happy thought" speech sufferers have been invited to describe their own cases and difficulties, and to give their own experiences. Though naturally these communications from non-professional contributors have not been of by any means equal merit, and to the scientific pharisee might be thought unworthy of attention on account of defect in technical accuracy, the flood of light that has been let in on the question by means of this scheme cannot be exaggerated, and no words in praise of the undertaking can in our opinion be too flattering as expressive of high approval and congratulation.

That there is need of sound and accurate information as to the causes and means of cure of defects of utterance may be gathered from the fact that Hunt—one of the first writers of a scientific and systematic treatise on stammering —reckoned in 1856 that the proportion of cases of stammering and stuttering to the population of Great Britain was 3 per 1000. Zug, in the first number of *The Voice*, computed from statistics of the last official census in 1870 that half per cent.—that is, 5 per 1000—of the population of the United States suffer from the severer forms of defective articulation. In other words, taking the population of the United States to be 40,000,000 there are 200,000 stutterers, a number almost three times as great as that of the blind, deaf and dumb, and insane, which in that return numbered altogether but 73,957.

We ourselves do not expect to add anything very new as to causation, far less to advocate any original and infallible method of cure, but from our two-fold aspect of doctor and trainer to review what has been done by others and to give our opinion as the result of experience on the correctness of the views of various so-called authorities, and as a consequence to indicate what is in our mind the right point of view as to cause, and that of direction in treatment.

Acting on the same principle that has guided us throughout this manual, we think it useless to detail, simply for the sake of extending our pages, or as anecdotal curiosities, all the many ideas and methods which have from time to time been promulgated with regard to the subject of our present consideration. Indeed we expressly avoid doing so because such a plan only confuses the reader, and our aim is not to further confound a subject already full of misapprehension, but to clear it of all needless difficulties, and so render it more intelligible.

It is hardly within our province to discuss elementary questions as to the character of speech, and of its division into vowels and consonants, and it is sufficient here to remind our readers that while the vowels are formed by sounds which, coming primarily from the larynx, are modified by variations in the size of the mouth cavity and of its opening, consonants depend on interruption of the currents of air in the mouth or passages above the larynx. They can, in fact, only be made effective by junction with a vowel. Thus *k* is *k* and *a*, *r* is *a* and *r*, *b* is *b* and *e*, *n* is *e* and *n*, &c. Vowels have a varying musical pitch, but can be sounded mutely, that is, without an appreciable voice-sound or in a whisper, in diminished but still in varying musical quality; while consonants are characterised by a considerable difference in the time that may be occupied in their prolongation of delivery; thus some, *b, p,* and *d,* must be uttered quickly, and are called *explosive;* others, as *m, n, l,* and *r,* can be prolonged almost indefinitely. The former are mute, without vowel combination; the latter have a certain musical value in accordance with their inherent vowel quality. In the first case the vowel sound follows the consonant; in the second it precedes it. There are further divisions in the character of consonants according to the point of interruption, as *labial, p,* when the point is at the lips involving pressure; *dental, t,* produced by presence of the tip of the tongue against the teeth; and *guttural* as *k,* in which the back of the tongue is most actively employed. Still, again, some consonants derive their character from a variation in their resonance.

Lastly, there are the *aspirates,* of which *h* is the principal, and they are produced by an out-breathing, formed in the larynx which allows some air to escape, prior to actual vocalisation.

It has now been so satisfactorily demonstrated by various physiologists and philologists, Kemplen, Willis, Helmholtz, Ellis, Melville Bell, and others, that each letter and each combination of letters has a definite mode of origin and a definite mode of enunciation, that it has come to pass that persons born deaf, who have never heard, and never can hear sound, are capable of being taught the gift of speech, and of communicating their ideas in articulate, though naturally in unmodulated and monotonous, voice. This provided always—and it is very exceptionally otherwise—that the vocal organs are perfectly developed. More wonderful than this, the eye has been educated to take the place of the ear, and the deaf person literally reads by visual observation the words as formed at the lips by the person with whom he interchanges conversation. This fact that speech can be correctly taught to those born without the special sense associated by nature with it, has been a great encouragement to the speech sufferer, and has led more than anything to correct training of the organ and of the nervous influences of its direction. It has also been very instrumental in drawing away attention from, and belief in, mechanical and empirical remedies. Lastly, it has been of great use in gaining consideration from a new point of view of the importance of correct articulation for the more perfect conveyance of all speech and song even to those not afflicted with deafness.

The credit of this great discovery of making the dumb to speak, and the deaf to hear with the eye, must be given to Samuel Heinicke, of Germany, where this method of education has arrived at great perfection. This country is greatly indebted to Mr. Van Praagh, by whom the system was first introduced into England, and who was the first principal of the first school for the oral instruction of the deaf and dumb.

There are very many defects of speech to which it is quite impossible to more than allude here, such as over-hurry in delivery to the destruction of sense, the clipping of words, the omission of vowels, and the habit of making all double vowels to sound as diphthongs. These and many others are matters of individual or provincial faults of education or pronunciation, or they may arise from habits of affectation; or, again, may be the result of misconception of the laws which convey sound. Each and all require separate instruction for their cure when detected by the accurate ear of the voice-trainer. It is not too much to say that there is never a pupil who comes to a master who has not one or other such fault. But too often unfortunately it is never eradicated, if, indeed, it is ever detected.

There are many other defects of speech which are due to defective taste. The singer or speaker does not appreciate in his mind the special colour to be given to his voice, the difference between the delivery of a love passage or of an invective. Such faults may be explained by the physiologist as due to the want of a certain mental quality in the subject of observation, but are only to be cured by the trainer: where glaringly obvious and obstinate the pupil will require to be told plainly that however hard he may work at the mere mechanical portion of his art, he lacks a quality which it is as impossible for the singing or elocutionary professor to supply, as it would be to instil the gift of appreciation of the finer subtleties of colour and of light and shade to the art student not naturally endowed therewith.

Let us now proceed to consideration of the two most serious of speech defects, stammering and stuttering. There is much confusion of ideas as to these terms. By many they are thought to be interchangeable and to mean one and the same thing. In point of fact they define two separate and distinct impediments—shortly :—

Stammering	*Stuttering.*
may be said to imply fault of articulation of vocalised sound.	Fault of co-ordination between articulation and vocalisation.

Thus, a *stammerer* can vocalise a sound in his larynx, but is unable so to regulate his tongue, palate, and lip-opening as to form that sound into a distinct vowel, and the hearer cannot consequently distinguish whether the vocal sound which is uttered, and may be indefinitely repeated, is meant for *ah, ai, ee, oh,* or *oo.*

A *stutterer,* on the other hand, places his articulating organs in the right position for enunciation of some particular consonant, but is unable to combine with it the vocal sound giving it its vowel character, so that, as in the case of the consonant *b* for example, the hearer cannot distinguish whether the consonant which is articulated, and may be indefinitely repeated, is intended to commence a word as *bah, bai, bee, boh,* or *boo.*

We cannot wholly agree with Klencke that " the causes of *stuttering* lie in the auxiliary organs of speech—in the organs of respiration—without the articulating organs being *primarily* affected," and he only half saves his definition by that word " primarily " which we have italicised. Again, while we agree with him that the causes of *stammering* lie in the organs between the larynx and lips—in the articulating organs—we cannot think that any satisfactory distinction can be made on the basis of *articulation* alone, for that is faulty in both ; or taking the matter in another way, and in Klencke's own words, we do not consider " stuttering *simply* as a defect of vocalisation, and stammering a defect of articulation." In another portion of his work, however, he correctly states the case when he says, " stuttering is a lack of harmony between vocalisation and articulation, a relative predominance of the latter over the former." The consonant is in point of fact, as stated in our definition, continually repeated to impediment of vocalisation of its associated vowel. In opposition one might correctly say, " stammering is a lack of harmony between vocalisation and articulation, a relative predominance of the former over the latter."

We do not wish it to be understood that because we insist on the importance of fault of articulation as the cause of stammering and stuttering that we therefore ignore existence of a number of other defects of speech in which there is no actual impediment to utterance, but which are equally due to imperfect or vicious articulation. The same remarks will obtain when we come to speak of faulty respiration in relation to stammering and stuttering.

Resuming, and in continuance of our comparative distinctions, it may be stated that—

Stammering—	*Stuttering—*
1. Has relation to vowel sound or combination of vowel sounds.	Is associated with the delivery of consonants, especially the explosive and sibilants.
2. Involves defect in delivery of individual letters, and the fault is detected on attempt to repeat the separate letters of the alphabet.	Is experienced in articulation of words or syllables, but each separate letter of the alphabet can be correctly enunciated.
3. Is more frequently due to defective physical formation in the pharynx and fauces, palate, or tongue, or to enlarged tonsils, varying the shape of the articulating cavity.	Is generally due rather to spasmodic muscular contractions, and seldom to objective defects of the organs of speech and articulation.

Stammering.	*Stuttering.*
4. Is unassociated with other faulty muscular movements.	Is frequently associated with irregular and spasmodic movements of other muscles of co-ordination of the face and limbs.
5. Is much less frequently due to want of nerve control, independently of volition, as proved from the foregoing and by the absence of engorgement of the vessels of the face and neck.	Is accompanied by much engorgement of the face and neck, indicating a temporary paralysis of the nervous (vasomotor or sympathetic) control of the circulatory system, which is independent of volition. Columbat's definition here well applies: " dis-harmony between volition and organic movement."
6. Is improved in the presence of a teacher, and by care and effort of will on the part of the subject.	Is generally rendered much worse by observation, and by anything that makes the subject think of his defect: thus, hearing another person stutter will often at once induce an attack of stuttering in one who previously was speaking evenly.
7. Is betrayed in singing, declamation, and measured talking [(*Klencke*), to this we are only half inclined to agree].	Is seldom betrayed, but, on the contrary, may be cured in rhythmical delivery, as in low, measured declamation and singing.
8. Is equally noticed in	Is absent in whispering

Stammering.	*Stuttering.*
all variations of the vocal scale.	low tones, monotones, and often in continuous reading, and becomes apparent only on use of loud voice, or in conversational speech.

Some authors, notably Klencke, have endeavoured to make a distinction between stammering and stuttering in relation to respiration.

We are of opinion that it is just here that the two are allied, and that in the majority of cases of both kinds A FAULT IN RESPIRATION IS AT THE ROOT OF ALL THE MISCHIEF. Let it be granted that the fault of co-ordination in the stutterer is far more the result of a functional disorder of the brain than in the stammerer, or that the fault is of a different character; it must be borne in mind by both preceptor and pupil that the fault is (except in rare cases of brain disease occurring in adult life) only *functional*, not *organic*, a grand distinction to the physician, a most encouraging one to the patient. We are not concerned now with questions of enlarged tonsils, elongated uvula, cleft palate, hare-lip, malposition of the teeth, &c., further than to advise that in every case of stammering or of stuttering the voice-trainer should have his pupil examined by a competent surgeon, to see that such removable defects to sound modification do not exist.

In considering other causes of stammering and stuttering, attention must be given to the constitutional disposition and health. Doubtless stammerers are more excitable and vivacious, stutterers more shy and reserved, than the average, but there can be no doubt that there is a very similar constitutional weakness of a scrofulous or strumous character in each.

A scrofulous constitution is one which tends to chronic thickening, with but slight inflammation of the oral and nasal breathing passages, and this leads to weak respiration, defective oxygenation, and many other effects of enfeebled circulation. Discharges of the ear, enlarged tonsils, &c., often first arise in children of such a tendency as sequels of severe illnesses, especially fevers.

Stuttering not uncommonly takes its birth in such like manner. Fright, imitation, and other causes acting directly on the nervous system, are among the frequently ascribed factors of stuttering, and quick response to such influences is in itself an evidence of constitutional delicacy. The highly sensitive and feeble nervous state of all stutterers will be generally recognised; there are some who stutter in thought as well as in expression, others who stammer in movement and action.

We have recently heard it said by a very high authority, that the terms stammering and stuttering imply the same thing; and the statement was illustrated by the simile of a horse, who may be said to stammer or to stutter when he stumbles. The idea of comparison of the faulty actions of motion of the horse with those of a human being with defective speech utterance, is not inapt; only we would insist that the same difference exists in both cases. When a quadruped *stumbles*, it *stammers;* when it *jibs*, it *stutters*. In the one it repeats unnecessarily or performs blunderingly a normal act; in the other there is an impediment to, or hesitation in performance of, the necessary and normal act.

Prosser James has dilated (*Lancet*, Nov. 15, 1879) on "a stammering of the vocal cords" as "a hitherto undescribed laryngeal affection, in which syllablization is complete, phonation defective."

In point of fact, the condition has been long understood and very well described; it depends simply on fault of respiration, the act having been performed incorrectly in relation to economy in expiration, by which either the breath has been wasted before singing, or vocalisation has been continued after the lung has been emptied of its complement of air. Kingsley alludes to it in his 'Irrationale of Speech' as an advanced stage of ordinary stuttering.

There is one point in relation to hesitation in utterance which must not be overlooked by the physician, and it is this. If it occurs in children, it is generally due to some cause which surgeon and teacher in combination or separately can cure; but when it is noticed in an adult who has previously spoken fluently and clearly, there is reason for anxiety, for such a condition may be, and generally is, premonitory of brain disease.

In indicating—for we can do no more—the line of treatment for the stammerer and stutterer, it may be said that remedial measures can be divided into three classes: 1. Mechanical. 2. Surgical. 3. Educational.

Mechanical treatment, implying insertion of any foreign body whatever into the mouth, is only mentioned with the utmost brevity, that opportunity may be taken to condemn the practice in terms of the greatest possible severity. The *only* mechanical means which are justifiable in these cases are those to be employed by a dentist to correct imperfect narrowing of the jaw, by defective growth of the teeth, or, as is necessary in very rare cases, by insertion of a plate when there is a cleft or an unduly high and narrow arch of the palate.

Surgical measures, which imply division with the knife

of muscles spasmodically contracted, or removal of pieces of the tongue abnormally enlarged during the act of speech, also by spasm of its muscular tissues and congestion of its blood supply, are likewise only mentioned to be condemned with uncompromising severity. It is indeed well nigh inconceivable that positively in the present century operations so barbarous, because founded on such ignorant hypothesis, could have been suggested, much more performed, by surgeons who have achieved high distinction in other branches of their art. Remembering the fable of the dead lion, we forbear, in honour to their memory, to even mention names.

Where there is a cleft of the palate, a hare-lip, an enlarged tonsil, an overgrowth of tissue in the nasopharyngeal passages, a polypus in the nostrils, a cyst under the tongue, in fact, any actual disease or deformity interfering with the normal calibre of the articulating cavities, it is of course, not only reasonable, but absolutely necessary, that surgical measures should be employed, with promptitude and thoroughness. It is a mistake to suppose that any such treatment can do harm. If delayed it may not be successful in entire removal of the trouble; but this much may be said for certain, that want of success is not necessarily the fault of the operation, or a proof that it was wrong to have performed it. Where success does not follow surgical measure of the character above mentioned, rightly indicated and properly performed, it is not on account of, but in spite of, that operation. This question of operations on the throat has been already considered in the previous chapter. Constitutional treatment of any faulty health disposition, and proper hygiene as to bathing, clothing, exercise, diet, &c., will of course be the work of the medical adviser, and must by no means be overlooked.

Lastly, there is the *educational* remedy; this may be further subdivided into that of the teacher and that of the voice sufferer himself. With regard to education, very much can be done by both mental and physical training; the teacher can bring to bear the influence of his mind, and having knowledge of the cause of speech impediments, can explain them; having sympathy, can encourage the desponding; having power, can control the weaker will; and having discrimination, can not only detect the cause, but can watch and direct the cure.

A teacher to be successful must therefore not only be learned and experienced, he must be strong, patient, and persevering. These last qualities he must instil even to a larger measure into his pupil, for recognising all speech defects as faulty habits of mind and muscle, of education or imitation, at least equal effort must be made to eradicate this most painful and detrimental of vicious habits as would be employed for correction of any bad habit of action or manner reflecting more obviously, perhaps, but in point of fact not more practically, on the social status of the subject. The sufferer must never allow himself to forget his rules for cure; he must, as taught by Hunt and stated by Kingsley, "always speak *consciously* as others (not stammerers) speak unconsciously."

Beyond this mental education, come next gymnastic exercises—these are of several kinds: first and foremost, instruction in regular and efficient filling of the lungs through the natural breath passages—the nostrils—and then, above all, economy in the emptying thereof, or rather, perhaps, to put it more plainly, control of emission of the breath from the lungs during speech in such a way as to ensure that none is expired before vocalisation.

Reducing it to a diagram by which the arrow represents

an out-breath, the vowel ah, for example, and all others in turn, should be sounded so as to commence with the expiration, thus:

ah ⟶ not at the end
thus—
⟶ ah.

After this principle has been thoroughly inculcated and practised, not only for one vowel but for all, and also for combinations of vowels, the pupil may be instructed to rest on this vowel, and at a given sharp signal, as of a clap of the instructor's hands, to join the consonant. In the case of stuttering he may be told to place his lips in position for the commencing consonant, and at the same signal to give it its proper vocal sound.

Another useful aid to the cure of speech impediments may be found in the pupil reading or reciting to the accompaniment of his teacher who reads or recites the same words, and thereby gives him a "lead" over the vocal hedges and hurdles which obstruct his course.

Combined with these, respiratory gymnastics, as more completely detailed elsewhere in this essay, and the vocal exercises here shortly indicated, general use of chest expanders, dumb-bells, &c., should be enforced and regulated in moderation and proportion to the age and strength of the subject. Finally, the pupil may be taught the value of employing rhythmical movements of hands or feet synchronously with those of the organs of breathing and speech, so as to regulate these last actions by co-ordination with the others.

The foregoing are only hints of the line to be taken for rational treatment of stammering, and might be largely extended if we were writing a treatise on the subject, but not of much good purpose would that be, for there exist already a sufficiency of admirable works on the causes and treatment of these defects, embracing all that can be taught by book. Of these modern works those of the younger and elder Hunt and of Kingsley, published in this country; of Klencke, Gunther, and Chervin, translated and published in *The Voice,* are the most highly to be recommended. Much valuable information is also to be found in various treatises on elocution as to all defects of speech, and we have recently read an able synopsis of all that is known on the causation, pathology, and treatment of stammering, with much original matter, by Mr. C. C. Caleb, a medical student, in the junior medical periodical, *The Student's Journal,* vol. xi., Nos. 289, 290, and 291.

One word in conclusion. It will be observed that we have advocated no system. Why? Because there is none that is honestly applicable to all cases. The varieties and causes of defects of speech are so numerous that to pretend to apply one empirical remedy to all is as preposterous as are the claims of the many largely advertised quack nostrums; and their adoption in both cases does harm, not necessarily because of any inherent noxious principle, but because no attempt is made to discover the real cause of the malady which, uncured, is therefore allowed to proceed to more chronic aggravation.

The safest, cheapest, quickest, and indeed only way for all these cases to be cured is that they should be treated on their individual differences by persons skilled to detect their nature and qualified to correct them. Those who cry loudest their own wares are not by any means to be the most depended upon, but unfortunately there always have been, and always will be, but too many dupes who will answer to their call. Hence our brief but earnest word of warning.

APPENDIX I.

ON PHOTOGRAPHY OF THE VOCAL ORGANS IN THE ACT OF SINGING.

LARYNGEAL photography is by no means of recent date. As far back as 1860 attempts were made by Czermak, and his results laid before the Academy of Sciences in Vienna. A description of his apparatus in Dr. Stein's book on "Light" shows that he thoroughly understood the difficulties he had to encounter; and, considering that the advantage of gelatine plates did not exist at that time, it must be admitted that his results were very good indeed; albeit his work bears evidence of material aid at the hands of the *retoucheur*.

Since then many similar experiments have been made in different parts of the world, and Mr. Behnke succeeded twelve years ago in obtaining a photograph of his larynx with no better illumination than the limelight. Among the more recent attempts must be mentioned those of Dr. French, of Boston, whose success has been greater than that of any of his predecessors. Nevertheless all these earlier photographs of the larynx were capable of great improvement, while photography of the soft palate in the act of singing had never been thought of.

Under these circumstances we determined to try whether we could not, at least partly, substitute photographs for the engravings with which we had at first intended to illustrate this book, and we set to work accordingly. Mr.

Bolas, the editor of the *Photographic News*, kindly gave us the benefit of his advice, and introduced us to three gentlemen it is impossible not here to mention, because without their generous help and their inexhaustible resources, we could never have overcome the difficulties which continued to present themselves, and we desire here publicly to acknowledge our deepest obligation to them all.

Mr. H. T. Wood, the accomplished secretary of the Society of Arts, placed at our disposal the laboratory of the Society combining a photographic studio with dynamo-electric machinery, and personally assisted us in many ways. Mr. James Cadett, an inventor and amateur photographer of the highest scientific attainments, devoted many days of his valuable time to our experiments, and he designed the apparatus with which we eventually succeeded. We are further indebted to Mr. J. J. Ackworth, also an amateur photographer, who vied with Mr. Cadett in bringing our undertaking to a successful issue.

We first used two large round flasks filled with a solution of alum to absorb the heat, which we employed as condensers for two powerful electric lights kindly lent and put up by Sir William Siemens. This method of direct illumination we had to abandon as clumsy and unmanageable, and we then used the apparatus of Mr. Cadett's construction consisting of (1) an electric light of about 10,000 candle-power, (2) a water chamber through which a current of water was constantly flowing so as to absorb as much as possible of the heat rays, (3) a condenser consisting of two plano-convex lenses, and (4) a mirror with a plane surface to reflect the light.

This apparatus underwent many slight modifications and alterations as the result of our joint experience and suggestions at our various meetings, but the foregoing is a sufficiently complete account of our means of illumination.

The actual process of obtaining a photograph is shown in our frontispiece. Mr. Behnke has in his right hand the laryngeal mirror, and he sees himself in a small looking-glass attached to the shutter of the camera, so that the image is in an exact line with the sensitive plate. This arrangement, so apparently obvious and trivial, constitutes a most important improvement in the method hitherto employed by others. The operator having focussed the view, jointly agreed by us to be a good one, the sitter is seen to have just given the signal, by dropping the upraised index finger of his left hand, for the shutter to be raised. The lenses used were of the rapid rectilinear kind, and our exposures averaged about quarter of a second. There is no doubt that our results would have been better had the exposures been much shorter; but with the plates at our disposal on those occasions, shorter exposures were impossible.

The frontispiece is made from the original negative and is absolutely untouched. Not even some spots on the teeth and on the back of the throat caused by moisture have been interfered with. The two very bright marks on the spectacles are caused by the reflection of the light upon the edges of the very dark goggles Mr. Behnke, and indeed others of us also, had to wear to protect our eyes from the glare of the powerful illumination. All the photographs of the larynx in the production of various tones which are inserted at page 178, and are there described, were taken the same size as the little picture in the frontispiece. They were then considerably enlarged and marked with letters of reference; after which they were re-photographed to the size of nature.

As to the portraits of the soft palate facing page 215, they were a comparatively easy matter, since they are photographs of the actual condition of things at the back of the throat, which any one could see in the circumstances indicated, instead of being, as is the case with the laryngeal pictures, the photographs of a reflection.

The photographs of the soft palate were, like those of the larynx, enlarged, and lettered for reference, after which they were also reduced to the present natural size.

All the enlargements, as well as the reproduction in collotype (the process employed for the illustrations of this volume), have been made under the immediate superintendence of Mr. Payne Jennings, who is admittedly *facile princeps* in this branch of photographic art.

APPENDIX II.

Copy of Letter from Dr. Wyllie on Approximation of the Pocket Ligaments in Tone Production.

1, Melville Street, Edinburgh,
October 27, 1883.

Dear Sir,—

I am much obliged to you for your letter of the 24th instant, directing my attention to a mistake that has been made in the interpretation by some writers of my views regarding the action of the ventricles of Morgagni, and the ventricular bands, or "false cords."

The account of these views that you give in the proof sent me of your work now in the press is perfectly accurate.

In my 'Observations on the Physiology of the Larynx,' I showed that the ventricles with their ligaments form an important valve, but I said nothing of their relations to voice, with which I believe they have little or no concern.

I remain, dear Sir,

Yours faithfully,
JOHN WYLLIE.

To Lennox Browne, Esq.

INDEX.

A.

Ablutions, influence of, on daily life of voice-user, 244
Aids to voice, by food or stimulant, 254
    ,,   ,, cautions in use of, 283
Air, chemical composition of, 102
  ,, in lungs, complementary, 47
  ,,   ,, residual, 47
  ,,   ,, supplemental, 47
  ,,   ,, tidal, 47
  ,, motive power of voice, 102, 186
Alcohol in relation to voice use, 260
Amusements in relation to voice use, 263
Articulation, importance of, 222
Arytenoid cartilages, 57
Attack, 195
    ,, exercises for, 196
Auto-laryngoscopy, 149, 154, 186
Avery's laryngoscope, 146

B.

Babington's laryngoscope, 146
Baritone voices, 97
Bass   ,,   97, 226
Bennati on removal of enlarged tonsils, 281
Bernays, Dr. Albert, on tea drinking in relation to voice use, 258
Beaumês' laryngoscope, 146
Biot on the voice, 88
Bozzini's laryngoscope, 145
Breathing, abdominal, 49
    ,, artificial hindrances to, 185
    ,, clavicular, collar-bone, or scapular, 49, 180

Breathing, costal or lateral, 49
„ criterion of correct, 184
„ diaphragmatic, 49, 188
„ difference of, between men and women, 49
„ Dr. Paul Niemeyer on, 103
„ injurious influence of wrong methods, 182
„ in relation to voice cultivation, 179
„ lessons for right performance of, 187
„ midriff, 49
„ mouth, 105
„ nasal, 105
Bronchial passages or bronchi, anatomy of, 44
Bronchitis kettles, 282
Buccal cavity or mouth, 79
Buffer cartilages of larynx, 71

C.

Cartilages, arytenoid, position or pyramids, 57
„ costal (Plate IV.), 40, 180
„ cover, epiglottis or lid, 55
„ cricoid or ring, 53
„ cuneiform or "prop," 71, 75
„ „ „ Elsberg on, 76
„ „ „ Madame Seiler on, 76
„ „ „ Witkowski on, 76
„ of larynx, 53
„ pyramid, or position, or arytenoid, 57
„ ring or cricoid, 53
„ of Santorini or "buffer," 71
„ sesamoid, 76
„ shield or thyroid, 53
„ of Wrisberg, 71
Cases illustrative of value of respiratory gymnastics, 132
Catching cold, on, 271
Chest or thorax, anatomy of, 38
„ „ muscles of, 41
Clergyman's sore throat, 274
Clothing, influence of, on daily life of voice-user, 248
Coca-wine as a vocal restorative, 255, 286
Cocoa as a beverage for the voice-user, 258
Coffee „ „ „ „ „ 259
Cold water to throat, 247

Columbat on stuttering, 296
Common head cold, 284
Contralto voices, 95, 226
    ,,   ,, similarity of, to tenors, 95
Corpulence of singers, reasons of, 271
Coryza, 284
Cosmetic powders, injurious influence on health, 247
Curwen on breathing, 106
    ,, his names for the registers, 165
Czermak's advocacy of the laryngoscope, 148
    ,, experiments on closure of soft palate, 82

D.

Defects of speech, 288
Delaunay on variety of voices, &c., 97
Despinez on the voice, 88
Diaphragm, anatomy of, 40
Diet of the voice-user, 252
Diday on the voice, 88
Division of voices, physical causes of, 94
Drinking in relation to voice use, 257
Dutrochet's experiments, 141

E.

Ear, musical; definition and training of, 137, 138
  ,, relations of, with throat in voice production, 135
Echoes, their philosophy, 20
    ,, instances of, in various cathedrals, &c., 21
    ,, Tyndall on, 21
Educational treatment of speech defects, 301
Effervescing drinks, their influence on the voice, 259
Ellis on compound tones, 22
    ,, distinctions between singing and speaking, 35
    ,, pronounciation for singers, 217, 222
    ,, quality of tone, 26
    ,, vibrations of lips, 90
    ,, vowel sounds, 217
Elsberg on nose breathing, 105
    ,, buffer and "prop" cartilages, 71
    ,, vocal nodules, 76
Epiglottis, 55, 156

Epiglottis, cushion of, 73
," in relation to resonance, 78
," uses of, 56
Essential element of the voice is in vocal ligaments, 61
Eustachian tubes (Plate III.), 39
," ," closure of, in relation to voice, 135
Exercise, general, in relation to voice use, 261
Exercises for the lips and mouth, 206
," ," soft palate, 214
," ," tongue, 209
," for attack, 196
," ," attaining "reach," 221
," ," correct breathing, 187
," ," developing and strengthening the registers, 234
," ," flexibility, 223
," ," improving quality, 210
," ," the cure of stuttering, 301
Experiments before the invention of the laryngoscope, 140
," on the dead larynx, how performed, 144, 199
," ," ," ," their value, 145
Expiration, lessons in economy of, 190

F.

False theory of attack, 198
Falsetto, 177, 238
Ferrein on the voice, 88, 140
Flexibility in relation to voice cultivation, 223
," exercise for attainment of, 224
Framework of larynx, 53

G.

Galien on the voice, 88
Garcia, his invention of the laryngoscope, 146
," on shock of the glottis, 198
Gargles, insufficiency of, 247
General exercise in relation to voice use, 261
Glottic chink or space, 65
Glottis, check of, 161
," chink of, 65
," glide of, 161
," its signification, 65
," shock of, 162, 198
," various modes of closing in tone production, 161

Grimm on power of English language, 37
Gruetzner on registers of voice, 170
Gunther on defects of speech, 289
Gymnastics, vocal, as remedy for diseased conditions, 13, 125, 189

H.

Hard palate, the, 80
Head colds, 284
Heinicke on teaching of deaf mutes, 292
Helmholtz, his resonators, 24
    ,, on quality of tone, 26
    ,, ,, qualities of voice, 91
    ,, ,, secondary influences of pitch, 93
    ,, ,, tone of brass instruments, 90
    ,, ,, tuning-forks, 34
    ,, ,, varying quality of tone, 91
Hot condiments, their influence on the voice, 257
  ,, drinks,   ,,   ,,   ,, 257
Hullah on human voice as a musical instrument, 94
  ,, ,, public speaking, 9
Human voice as a musical instrument, 88
  ,, ,, ,, reed ,, 31, 89
  ,, ,, complex in its nature, 93
  ,, ,, flute theory of, 89
  ,, ,, reed ,, 89
  ,, ,, string ,, 88
Hunt on stammering and defects of speech, 289
Hutchinson's table of vital capacity, 121
Hygienic aspect of the motor portion, 102
  ,, ,, ,, resonant portion, 129
  ,, ,, ,, vibrating portion, 126
  ,, ,, ,, vocal apparatus, 99
  ,, clothing for females, 250
  ,, stays, 116

I.

Inhalations of neutral ammonia recommended, 282
  ,, ,, steam to be used cautiously, 282
Inspiration, how accomplished, 47
  ,, lessons in, 187
Interval between eating and voice use, 253
Isenschmid's laryngo-phantom, 154

J.

Jagielski on influence of height on voice, 96

K.

Kempelen's experiments, 140
Klencke on defects of speech, 294

L.

Laryngeal cartilages or framework, 53
„ diseases, 281
„ fatigue, causes of, 130
„ „ how to avoid, 127
„ image, explanation of its reversion, 158
„ „ various appearances of, 170
„ photographs, 173
„ „ the process of obtaining, 304
Laryngo-phantom for teaching, 154
Laryngoscope, description of, 147
„ how to use it, 149
„ invention of, 145
„ teachings of, 156
„ Foulis's auto-, 155
„ Tobold's, 150
Laryngoscopic observations need not imply laryngeal distortion, 152
Laryngoscopy, auto-, 154
„ beginners in, hints for, 149, 151
Larynx, anatomy of, 51, *et seq.*
„ cartilages of, 53
„ description of, as seen with laryngoscope, 156
„ differences of, in children, 83
„ „ „ men and women, 84
„ „ „ Luschka on, 85
„ framework of, 53
„ hygienic aspect of, 126
„ movements of, which can be seen or felt, 86
„ muscles of, acting on vocal ligaments, 62
„ position of, in voice production, 203
„ vestibule of, 73
Laws of sound bearing on the voice, 18
Lehfeldt's experiments, 141

Liskovius's experiments, 141
Liston's laryngoscope, 146
Loss of voice, 281
   ,,   ,, treatment of, 282
Ludwig's names for the laryngeal cartilages, 52
Lungs, anatomy of, 41
   ,, physiology of, 46

M.

Magendie on the voice, 88, 141
Malgaigne ,,   ,, 88, 141
Malt liquors, indulgence in, 260
Mandl on collar bone respiration, 129
   ,, fatigue on the voice, 131
   ,, removal of enlarged tonsils, 280
   ,,   ,, relaxed uvula, 277
   ,, symptoms of ,,   ,, 276
Marshall, Professor, on physiology of voice, 61
Mechanical depression of the tongue, 208
   ,, treatment of speech defects, 299
Merkel on causes for division of voices, 96
   ,, the laryngoscope, 148
   ,, the shape of glottic chink in tone production, 177
Midriff, anatomy of, 40
Mixed voice, or *voce mista*, 237
Mouth or buccal cavity, 79
Mucous membrane of vocal organ, 45
Müller on physiology of pockets of larynx, 75
   ,, the voice as a musical instrument, 142
Muscles of the chest, 41
   ,,   ,, larynx, 62
   ,, of two kinds, 1, which govern shape of vocal chink, 68
                         2,   ,,   ,, pitch of voice, 68
Muscular processes, 58
Musical ear, definition of, 137
   ,,   ,, can be trained, 138
   ,, tone, how to end, 162
Myers, Surgeon-Major, on constriction of the neck, 249

N.

Nasal cavity, how to close, from throat, 81
Nasal resonance, 213

Nasal tone or twang, 27, 211
," how to cure, 214
Nervousness in singing, 285
," relation to stuttering, 298
Niemeyer, Dr. Paul, on process of breathing, 103
Nitrogen, its uses in respired air, 103
Nodal lines, 18
Nodules, vocal, 76
Nose-breathing, its importance in regard to voice, 104, 194
," Elsberg on, 105
," Walsham on, 105
Nose cavities in relation to resonance, 79

O.

Oxygen, its uses in respired air, 103, 104

P.

Palate, the hard, 80
," soft, 80
," ," pillars of, 81
Patent voice remedies, caution against, 286
Pharyngitis (inflamed sore throat), 273
Pharynx or upper throat, anatomy of, 78
," granular inflammation of (clergyman's sore throat), 274
Photographs of larynx, 178
," soft palate, 215
Photography of throat, the process, 304
Physical causes of division of voices, 94
Physiology, vocal, a plea for (*see* Vocal Physiology), 1–17
Pitch of tone, 23
," human voice influenced by windpipe, 92
," ," ," Savart on, 92
," ," ," Wheatstone on, 92
Pleuræ, anatomy of, 43
Pockets of larynx, or ventricles of Morgagni, 70, 157
Pocket ligaments or false cords, 69, 157
Position in public speaking and singing, 240
Posterior vocal nodules, 76
Posture in regard to respiration and voice, 124
Pre-laryngoscopic experiments, 140

Pyramid cartilages, anatomy of, 57
Pyramid muscle, action of, 68

Q.

Quality of voice, importance of, 221
„ „ Deacon on, 222
Quinsy (inflammation of tonsils), 278

R.

Randegger on physical sensations in various registers, 233
Reach of the voice, 221
Reading aloud, Cull on, 11
Reed instruments, 30, 89
Register, definition of, 163
Registers of the voice, in relation to cultivation, 225
„ „ „ "lower thick," 163
„ „ „ "upper thick," 164
„ „ „ "lower thin," 167
„ „ „ "upper thin," 168
„ „ „ "small," 169
„ „ „ falsetto, 174
„ „ „ Gruetzner on, 170
„ „ „ union of, 225
„ „ „ not to be extended, 235
Relations of throat and ear in voice production, 135
Relaxed throat, 272
Residence, influence on daily life of voice-users, 243
Resonance in relation to voice cultivation, 201
„ of tone, its definition, 31
„ „ Tyndall on, 201
„ sympathetic, 32
„ „ Helmholtz on, 34
Resonator of the vocal organ, 77
„ „ „ its hygienic aspect, 127
Resonators of Helmholtz, 24
Respiration chemically considered, 102
„ Curwen on, 106
„ influence of digestion on, 180
„ „ „ stays on, 185
„ „ „ „ Bernard Roth on, 109
, „ „ „ *Knowledge* on, 112

Respiration, influence of stays on, *Lancet* on, 114
„   „   „   „   Mattieu Williams on, 118
„   physiology of, 45, 106
„   importance of right method of, 107
„   lessons for correct, 187–194
Respirator veil, 107
Respirators, 106, 249
Rest of the voice useless without treatment, 275
Ribs, anatomy of, 38
Ring cartilage, anatomy of, 53
Ring-pyramid muscles (back), action of, 67
„   „   (side)   „   68
Ringer, Dr., on tea-drinking as cause of indigestion, 258
Roberts's, Mr. Charles, table of vital statistics, 123
Roth, Mr. Bernard, on tight lacing, 109

S.

Santorini, cartilages of, 71
Savart on the voice, 88, 92, 141
Shield cartilage, anatomy of, 53
„   „   movements of, on ring-, 55
Shield-pyramid muscles, action of, 63
Self-taught art always a fallacy, 4
Senn's laryngoscope, 145
Singing, distinctions from speaking, 35
„   quality of, 222
Smoking in relation to voice use, 263
Snuff-taking   „   „   266
Soft palate, anatomy of, 80
„   education of, 214
„   its importance in vocalisation, 82
„   its mobility, 81
Soprano voices, 95, 227
Sore throat, 272
Sound caused by communication of vibrations in the air to the auditory nerve, 19
„   laws of, bearing on the voice, 19
„   can be reflected like light, 20
„   requires a medium, 19
Spencer on value of physiology, 1
Speaking voice, definition of, 35

Speaking voice, difference from singing, 35
Spirometer and its teachings, 120, 185
Stammering and stuttering, 293
    ,,   statistics of, 289
    ,,   of vocal cords, 298
Stays, injurious influence on respiration and voice, 109
    ,, hygienic, 116
Steam inhalations, cautions concerning, 282
Steed on shock of "upper" glottis, 198
Stone, Dr. W. H., on power of singing voice to combine with significant words, 206, 222
Struthers, Professor, on the pockets of the larynx, 70
Suppers, their influence on life of voice-user, 255

T.

Table of vital statistics, 123
Tea-drinking, its influence on the voice, 257
Teeth washing, &c., 246
Tenor voices, 95, 226
Tight lacing, 109, 185
Thompson, Sir Henry, on cigarette smoking, 264
Thorax or chest, anatomy of, 38
    ,,   ,, muscles of, 41
Throat, relation of, with ear in voice production, 135
Throaty tone, 208
    ,,   ,, how to cure, 210
Tone, force of, 22
  ,,   how produced in bassoon, 31
  ,,   ,,   ,,   clarionet, 31
  ,,   ,,   ,,   flexible reeds, 30
  ,,   ,,   ,,   flute or flue-pipes, 29
  ,,   ,,   ,,   hautboy, 31
  ,,   ,,   ,,   horn, 31
  ,,   ,,   ,,   human voice, 31
  ,,   ,,   ,,   reed instruments, 29
  ,,   ,,   ,,   stiff reeds, 29
  ,,   ,,   ,,   stringed instruments, 29
  ,,   ,,   ,,   trumpet, 31
  ,,   how to end a musical, 162
  ,,   inherent quality of, 28
  ,,   loudness of, 22
  ,,   nasal, 27, 211

Tone, pitch of, 23
,, quality of, 26
,, ,, ,, depends on many causes, 28
,, ,, ,, may be cutting, 27
,, ,, ,, ,, full, 27
,, ,, ,, ,, harsh, 27
,, ,, ,, ,, hollow, 27
,, ,, ,, ,, musical, 27
,, ,, ,, ,, nasal, 27
,, ,, ,, ,, rich, 27
,, ,, ,, ,, rough, 27
,, sensations of, Helmholtz and Ellis on, 26
Tones, compound, 22
,, ,, their analysis, 24
,, prime and partial, 24
,, simple, 21
,, resonance of, 31
Tongue, exercises for bringing under control, 209
,, not necessary to protrude in laryngoscopy, 152
,, not to be mechanically depressed, 208
Tongue-bone, 54
Tonsils, enlargement of, 278
,, ,, ,, symptoms of, 298
,, ,, ,, treatment of, 280
Trachea or windpipe, anatomy of, 44
Tremolo, cause of, 108
,, cure of, 188
Tuning-forks, 34
Türck and the laryngoscope, 148
Turkish bathing, 245
Tyndall on echoes, 21
,, reeds, 30

U.

Uvula, anatomy of, 81
,, elongation or relaxation of, 275
,, ,, ,, ,, symptoms of, 276
,, ,, ,, ,, treatment of, 277

V.

Ventricles of Morgagni or pockets of larynx, 70, 77
Ventricular bands or pocket ligaments, 69
,, ,, NEVER meet in tone production, 75

Vestibule of the larynx, 73
    ,,   ,,   ,, in relation to resonance, 78
Vibrations can be felt, 18
    ,,   ,,   seen, 18
    ,,   Chladni's experiments, 18
    ,,   compound, 21
    ,,   ,,   their analysis, 21
    ,,   may be simple or compound, 21
    ,,   must be communicated to the ear to produce sound, 19
    ,,   rate of, influences pitch, 23
    ,,   require a medium to produce sound, 19
    ,,   simple, 21
Vocal ligaments, vocal bands, cords, or lips, anatomy of, 58
    ,,   ,,   constitute essential element of voice, 61
    ,,   ,,   measurements of, 61
    ,,   ,,   variations of length, &c., in different voices, 95
    ,,   nodules, anterior and posterior vocal, 76
    ,,   organ, anatomy of, 38
    ,,   ,,   resonator of, 77
    ,,   processes, 59
    ,,   tone, 60
    ,,   physiology, analogy with studies in art, 4
    ,,   ,,   ,,   ,, medicine, 5
    ,,   ,,   a plea for, 1
    ,,   ,,   as considered by the Greeks, 9
    ,,   ,,   basis of all right voice production, 8
    ,,   ,,   Haertinger on, 6
    ,,   ,,   how to be learned, 13
    ,,   ,,   Hullah on, 9
    ,,   ,,   ignorance of, cause of failure, 12, 17
    ,,   ,,   in relation to laryngoscopy, 15
    ,,   ,,   Kofler on, 4
    ,,   ,,   Marx on, 5
    ,,   ,,   must be studied as a whole, and not in details, 16
    ,,   ,,   should be taught in universities, 11
    ,,   ,,   why required, 1
Voice cultivation, 179
    ,,   definition of, 35
    ,,   human, as an instrument, 31, 38
    ,,   singing, definition of, 35
    ,,   speaking, ,, ,, 35
    ,,   difference of singing and speaking, 35

Voice, different requirements of singing and speaking, 36
,,   its anatomy, 38
,,   mixed, 236
,,   production, relation of throat and ear in, 135
'Voice, The,' edited by Werner, 288
Voice-user, ailments of a, 268
,,   daily life of a, 243
Voice-box—*See* Larynx, 51.
Vowel sounds, 217
,,   ,,   Ellis on, 217
,,   ,,   how to obtain resonance of, 220
,,   ,,   varying pitch of, 218

W.

Walshe on Dramatic singing, 37, 182, 230
Warden's laryngoscope, 146
Water, cold, to throat, 247
Wax, impacted, in the ears a cause of voice trouble, 136
Werner, Edgar, on defects of speech, 288
Windpipe or trachea, anatomy of, 44
Wine, indulgence in, 260
Wyllie's experiments on physiology of ventricles of Morgagni, 200
,,   ,,   had nothing to do with voice production, 200, 307
Wrisberg, cartilages of, 71

Z.

Zug on defects of speech, 289

www.ingramcontent.com/pod-product-compliance
Lightning Source LLC
Chambersburg PA
CBHW031857220426
43663CB00006B/657

9 7 8 3 3 3 7 8 1 5 1 8 9